SWIMMING UPSTREAM

SWIMMING UPSTREAM

Four Generations of Fishmongering

MICHAEL F. FOLEY

authorHOUSE®

AuthorHouse™
1663 Liberty Drive
Bloomington, IN 47403
www.authorhouse.com
Phone: 833-262-8899

Published by AuthorHouse 09/30/2020

ISBN: 978-1-7283-7141-2 (sc)
ISBN: 978-1-7283-7142-9 (hc)
ISBN: 978-1-7283-7244-0 (e)

Library of Congress Control Number: 2020916590

Print information available on the last page.

Cover photo: Michael Foley and Bill Moloney in front of Foley
Fish Co., corner of Friend and Union Streets.

This book is printed on acid-free paper.

For my wife, Linda Johnson Foley

CONTENTS

PROLOGUE

This is the story of the Foley Fish Company, a small family-run company based in Boston and New Bedford, Massachusetts. Foley Fish has been around for four generations selling fresh, high-quality seafood to restaurants and specialty supermarkets. We are among the four percent of family businesses that have survived into the fourth generation.

Foley Fish was founded by my grandfather, Michael Francis Foley, an Irish immigrant with a sixth-grade education. He came from a farm in Tipperary, Ireland to Boston in 1898 at the age of 16 to work in his brother's fish market, a business about which he knew nothing. His story and the story of subsequent generations of Foleys is one of continual striving to bring to Foley Fish customers only the freshest, most flavorful seafood. We have always had an absolute standard for quality, not a relative one. "Best available" or "good enough" have never been good enough. My wife and business partner Linda Foley, titled this memoir *Swimming Upstream* because producing premium quality fish has always been an uphill battle.

I wrote *Swimming Upstream* to preserve the history of the Foley family and dedicated employees who brought this company to its fourth generation.

Needless to say, I was not present for much of my grandfather's life or my father's early life as I was born in 1941. I have, however, researched written accounts of the times and, and to the extent possible, verified my family's oral history. I have been fortunate to have my Uncle Andrew Foley, historian of the Foley family, for anecdotal information. I have enormous respect for you, the reader, and want to assure you that what has been written is in essence true and reliable. I have taken the literary license to use quotation marks in conversational contexts, not to mislead but rather to bring alive the participants and the times.

CHAPTER 1

THE LETTER

An unexpected knock on the front door. The postman lingered, looking for the tip that usually accompanied a special delivery letter from America. Sensing the importance of the letter, Ellen immediately called Dan in from his farm work. Ellen opened the letter. It was from Roger, their second-oldest son, who had immigrated a few years before to Boston. Roger was requesting that his parents permit his 16-year old brother Michael Foley (MF) to emigrate to Boston to help him run a retail fish market.

Knowing they needed time to deliberate, Dan and Ellen did not immediately disclose the contents of the letter to MF. They always knew that MF, the fifth-oldest male in the family, would eventually emigrate, but not at 16, and certainly not before MF's older brother, Patrick.

Dan, then 73 years of age, counted on MF working the family farm for at least another five years. Roger had stayed until his early twenties and only after fulfilling his family responsibilities on the farm did he emigrate to run a horse stable for the Lodge family on the North Shore of Boston. Losing MF now would present a major hardship for Dan. Dan knew why Roger had passed over MF's two older brothers. MF was much more industrious than either of them, and abler. As Dan often said, "MF was born old, as if he had a past before this."

Ever since Dan's father John Foley lost Horeabbey, their family farm in Rotcoum, Dan had regular nightmares about winter hail damage, the notorious February frosts, and crop-damaging summer droughts which could cut profits below the level necessary to pay taxes. Without MF, Dan feared for the fate of the family farm.

As for Ellen, she believed that five more years on the farm would better prepare MF for the challenges awaiting him when he emigrated. Her immediate worry: was MF ready now? Ellen reflected that MF's entire life had been narrowly confined to their 40-acre farm in Attykitt, Tipperary — excepting school, trips to the pub with his Dad, and Sunday Mass. Sheltered from the outside world all his life, how would MF fare in a big city in America?

A decision had to be made. Ellen knew that Dan was adamantly opposed to letting MF go. After a restless sleep, Ellen sat Dan down and reminded him that they were living the Irish dream of home ownership because her parents had bequeathed their farm to them. Ellen believed that it was their turn as parents to give MF the chance to pursue his opportunity even if timing wasn't optimal. They agreed that the decision would be left to MF.

The next day, Dan and Ellen sat a suspicious MF down at the kitchen table. His parents' grim demeanors suggested a rebuke was forthcoming, perhaps for shoddy work or inattentiveness at Sunday Mass. MF stopped short of a conjecture of divorce, which seemed highly improbable. MF ran out of guesses. As Ellen read Roger's letter aloud to MF, the implications of Roger's request were absorbed, MF said nothing. It was about divorce after all, but it was him doing the divorcing, so to speak.

The Irish emigration clock had always been ticking but Roger's request had accelerated its timing, moving departure ahead significantly. MF had a filial conflict: duty to his parents versus an exciting albeit intimidating opportunity to join his beckoning brother. A sympathetic Dan and Ellen tried to uncomplicate MF's dilemma. They conferred their approval for MF to emigrate now — if that was his wish.

The truth was that MF had been growing antsy on the farm. Work was often redundant and boring, although the rhythms of farm life did give him a sense of security. But he was feeling adventurous, and realized that he desired new opportunities more than a comfortable continuity. He wanted to be on his own. He knew that the risks were not fully knowable but that realization excited him, raising in him a childlike sense of anticipation. Less out of reason than emotion, heart not mind, and attempting to calculate pluses and minuses, his inner voice spoke: "Dob e I geam dom ieacht go Meirice." I have to go to America.

CHAPTER 2

THE FARM AT ATTYKITT

MF was born and grew up on a small, subsistence family farm in Attykitt, a hamlet of no more than 30 families, in Tipperary, in the south of Ireland. Time passed slowly on the farm. It was also measured differently, not by clocks, but by the position of the sun. The typical day started before sunrise when father Dan's gnarled hands tapped MF's shoulders. No chance for extra sleep — "cows don't take a day off," he was reminded. Dressing by kerosene lamps, MF pulled on his oft-mended pants, crammed his feet into his Wellies caked with dried Tipperary mud, and gathered himself to begin his daily chores.

No breakfast until MF had fed the tramping cattle, and the neighing horses, then cleaned their stalls. MF quickly learned horse sense. "I always had to know what was in front of me and when to sidestep." His toughest job was mounding the cut hay onto the tilted wooden trolley to be conveyed hurriedly under the shed roof out of the rain to avoid mold. MF had learned that running a farm was not easy work, especially in the cold months of the never-shy rain, or during the lengthy February frosts. The bane of bad weather was balanced, however, by Tipperary's extraordinarily fertile soil, which gave the family a fighting chance to survive, unlike their neighbors in Western Ireland. (People said that Tipperary's land was so arable you could douse it with beer and urinate on it and plants and produce would still grow.) Darkness did not mark the end of MF's day. After dinner, guided by stars, MF returned to the barn to rub down and blanket the horses. By bedtime, a good tiredness had set in.

In Ireland, the husband was the boss of the outside, the wife the boss of the inside. Ellen, however, who had four sons before having any daughters, needed to press MF, as the youngest, into helping in the house. MF was expected to help his mother with the cleaning, cooking, washing, laundering, bathing, feeding, and serving a family of seven. Their unplugged lifestyle meant working without indoor plumbing, refrigeration, overhead lighting, or washing machines. Their wood-fed stove doubled as cooking surface and heating for the pressing iron. Water came from a well outside. No rinse cycles or clothes dryers. Clothes often took days to dry because of the rain and general dampness. Whether blowing on the lit wood to maintain the fire in the wood stove or hauling water from the well, or bathing the younger siblings, MF was kept busy toiling inside and out.

At meals, social graces and manners were insisted on. Hands washed before meals; grace said before each meal; napkins around neck. No drinking milk before thoroughly chewing and swallowing of food. The clean-plate club brooked no exclusions, and it was emphasized that having good food reliably on the table was a privilege.

The children's religious training fell to Ellen. Dan never interfered, but occasionally, he was overheard to say, "Ellen, don't go overboard on that religious stuff. Scoundrels are to be outsmarted, not beaten off by rosary beads." Like social manners, Catholicism (it was redundant to say Irish Catholic in those times) provided another list of irrefutable do's and don'ts. Life too easy was not good, and Dan felt that his sons were not too good to be bad, so he kept them busy. Ellen emphasized that a reservoir of grace had to be created through good works, and then tapped in time of need. To Ellen, the sacraments, guardian angels, and prayers, unchallengeable as the laws of physics, were indispensable to get to Heaven. Dan's faith was more pragmatic. He would often add that the higher purpose preached was fine and good, but the lower purpose of tasks and chores, done correctly, put food on our plates.

MF's then-ordinary childhood seems to be extraordinary to me in retrospect. It was certainly much simpler than mine three generations later. The Attykitt Foleys were isolated without newspapers, radio, or TV. There were letters and word of mouth. But this isolation had advantages. MF never wished to be someone else, and not knowing much about others' lives, believed his own to be preferable. Mainly, all he knew was work.

Except for the pub and Sundays, there were few respites or distractions. He saw himself neither as disadvantaged nor advantaged, just normal just like everyone else. No one to envy. No superiority, no inferiority complexes. He knew that he mattered. MF's approach to work, and his sturdy sense of self and family would never leave him — this was his heritage and the legacy he left. His focus on work would become second-nature to him. The reassuring "thereness" of the farm was always present in memory, a place where the central truths of life could be found.

CHAPTER 3

NEW INN SCHOOL

MF attended school outside Cashel near Rockwell College, some three miles from Attykitt. The long walk served to condition him in more than just a physical way. He knew every bush and hollow along the way. Clothes pressed, hair trimmed, MF would leave early so not to be rushed. Initially, he was escorted by his older brothers. Later, he relished companionless walks that allowed his preteen imagination to run free. The forests were magical, filled with deer, rabbits, foxes, and wild pigs. No sextant or compass was needed. No signs existed. MF could make the walk blindfolded relying solely on the sounds of the oared cots by the weir in Clonmel, the pealing church bells, the crackling of twigs, the clop of horse hooves, the cooing of pigeons, and the bleating of grazing sheep, a rural chorale. For MF, the walk was a semi-mystical experience, an escape from reality — except for those times when peeing on the side of the road he lost his balance and fell into a well-manured field.

Modern studies have documented the benefits of improved cognition, focus and attentiveness when the brain is calmed. These findings would partially explain how, as his personality cohered, MF emerged as a quiet, secure man. In this, he was somewhat different from his offspring and theirs.

The Gladstone Act of 1881 granted MF and his Irish peers six years of education, unlike his parents who relied exclusively on home learning. At the New Inn Township School MF was taught the basics, giving him the tools for running a farm, but not enough for him and his peers to contend for other occupations. Schooling above sixth grade was a luxury available to only a tiny elite. MF's schooling did afford him playmates beyond his siblings. Acquaintances were formed, but no deep friendships, as each student had to rush home after school to farm chores. No playdates, no sleepovers.

Life on a farm provided a solid prequel to school. Like Dan and Ellen, MF's teachers had unquestioned authority. The curriculum was geared to pragmatics, not intellectual wisdom. Teaching involved drilling multiplication tables learned by rote memorization, for example. MF liked math as it gave him useful skills: counting change, numbering the herd, and later understanding the rudiments of cash accounting and bill paying. No algebra or geometry, as higher math was not deemed necessary to run a farm. The farms were not yet mechanized, so basic physics — gravity, stress, torque, and volume — was not taught.

English class entailed grammar, penmanship, pronunciation, punctuation, spelling, and recitation. MF was able to correct his parents should they incorrectly pronounce a word but he didn't dare. He could wield a pen, and no longer had to mark "X" for his signature. No great literature was studied as teachers would be deemed cruel to encourage higher intellectual pursuits like reading Synge, Yeats, and Shakespeare. Such pursuits were beyond what were needed to run a farm.

Unlike math, which is linear, Irish History proved elliptical, an arc away from reality. For example, it did not address the suppression of the Irish by the British. MF's sanitized history book did not allow him to examine such relevant subjects as the Penal Laws of 1537-1829, which would have provided a deeper understanding of the origins of despair, the pervading sense of worthlessness that dominated the Irish psyche, owing to the draconian confiscation of Irish lands by the British.

Only the basics were taught. No art to fire the imagination with great paintings and sculpture, and no music, as if carrying a tune was enough. These subjects were left to be learned individually. The insular curriculum set by the educational authorities contained no reference to foreign history. If you were curious about the world outside Britain and Ireland, you'd have to borrow books.

There was no class standing, no grades recorded, and so no need for transcripts for the next higher level of education, which was circumscribed anyway. We don't know whether MF was at the top of his class, but, even so, little would be revealed by looking at such a small, rural sample. But I assume MF got his arms around the subjects. Six years of "chalk" would prove to be ample for his future pursuits.

Unbeknownst to MF, a Helen Moloney attended the same school, overlapping for two years, although because Helen was four years younger, MF did not get acquainted with his future wife at the township school. If they had eye contact in a hallway, the moment is unremembered.

Dan knew MF needed experience outside the sheltered confines of the farm and the school. He believed street smarts were a necessary part of his development. Therefore, Dan supplemented schoolwork with special assignments. MF recalls, "Dad assigned me the job of selling our hens' eggs before school started to the largest poultry wholesaler in Clonmel. The wholesalers took the eggs on consignment and paid me after each batch was sold. I became discouraged. Each payday, the wholesaler arbitrarily made deductions citing uneven sizes, market glut or economic downturn. It was a take it or leave it ultimatum. Not knowing that my older brothers had experienced the same shenanigans, I felt that I had failed my family in my first business venture."

What followed was the first of MF's many "woodshed talks" with his Dad. He recalled his Dad stating that "scoundrels populate the business world; they have to be outsmarted." He asked MF how he would change the circumstances and left it up to him to reach the logical conclusion that he had to extend his customer list. He always ended with, "Keep your left-hand high son" (which Ireland's boxing hero John L. Sullivan did not do when he lost his heavyweight championship to Jim Corbett in 1892).

It is evident that his Dad's mentoring was equally as important to his personal growth as his work on the farm, his education at The New Inn School, and his experiences in the streets of Clonmel. Dan had an uncanny knack for business, enabling him to enlarge his "subsistence" farm into a profitable enterprise, growing the farm by the purchase of available foreclosed acres. Sharing his insights with MF would prove to be vital for MF's subsequent success in the American business world. Farm life, basic public education, and family tutoring served him well.

CHAPTER 4

THE PUB

Anonymous – "Irish men are like nobody else in the wide world but themselves; quare creatures that'll laugh or cry, fight with anyone just for nothing else, good or bad, but company."

In 1895, when MF turned 14, he joined his Dad and three older brothers in visiting the local pub, sometimes called the Church of the Holy Waters. Dan felt that attendance at this "pagan" church equaled the effectiveness of Sunday church services in replenishing one's spirits, if not their souls. It was now MF's turn at this rite of passage.

The local pub needed no sign. The front door was propped open with a rock in a futile effort to let the prior night's stale odors escape. Upon entering, one had to navigate the well-traveled, ever-treacherous, mud-filled uneven floors before reaching the scarred tables, caked with ale spills, and the surrounding rickety chairs, symbolic of the men who stumbled out after a night of revelry.

Women were not allowed. Also excluded as a form of reverse snobbery were the "not of my class" Protestant landlords. Once inside, Dan quickly ushered the boys to the least conspicuous back table telling them to keep their mouths shut except when munching on the stale sandwiches washed down by glasses of milk, never anything stronger.

MF was interested in learning what sorts of people were sitting at the tables. Closest to the bar were the heavy "drinkers." They were easy to spot — weary faces and eyes dead, windows to a life that left their spirits broken due to decreasingly bearable versions of their pasts and futures. Despite their slurred utterances, one could still glean, as MF did, that there was a position common to them all: they took no personal responsibility for life's defeats. They believed they were the defenseless prey of British landlords, the victorious hunters. There was no mud fresh on their boots; they had given up, no longer able to decant their setbacks. Heaven on earth was liquid oblivion and the hope that after drinking you could forget that the day made you sorry to be alive. Cruelly, even the magic of drink had weakened for them, no longer anesthetizing their pain.

The next group, the "yammerers" took center stage in the middle of the pub. They specialized in talking the most, saying the least, and at times not talking to anyone, just talking out loud, as MF recalled. Descendants of the leprechaun school of folklore, this group blathered away without any sense of the silliness of their inane notions. Conversations with them were often futile, often monologues, seldom dialogues. Their stories always ended with, "It was the truth so help me God." They talked indefatigably without pausing for consideration by and for others. To them all the Irish wrongs would be righted with a sprinkling of fairy dust. MF, reticent by nature, would later state his dislike for their flighty conversations and insincerity, a feeling that stuck with him throughout his life.

The "angries" (sometimes called *Caisearghan*—Gaelic for dandelion) referred to sour persons who dwelt on the existing unfair systems of governance in Ireland. Clan ties were the only inheritance they honored. They couldn't forget the Penal Laws of the century before that barred Irish Catholics from owning property, attending schools, and voting. Emboldened by their ales, full of a false bravado reflecting a deficient confidence, these well-fortified cynics would trumpet their heroic ability to single-handedly outfight any ten Brits. They held that a good fight would somehow burnish relations with their long dead compatriots, and paraded their atavistic anger as if it would kill their enemies.

The remaining patrons, Dan's set of friends, for whom the pub was a place where the jibing and joshing never ended, was the most welcoming group. For them, the pub was a place to get together, not to get even. Laughter enabled them to preserve the comical aspects of life. The Foley boys were the only ones who left without drinks on the breath. These "early rising" boys left before the "late night" men who, with thickened voices would often utter, "Oh God make me good. But not just yet." The ructions, as the Irish called them, the uproar, the insults, the disturbances were over until another night.

On the way home, MF, troubled by the drinkers' hopelessness and the angries' resentments, summoned up courage to ask his Dad, "Why were some of the people so mad at their Protestant neighbors; was it because they were not Catholic?" Dan, ever the mentor, would only reply, "No, it is deeper than that." Upon reaching home, Dan had one final reminder, "We never bring tales from the pub home," a rule that stayed with MF his entire life. He was a tightlipped man.

Later Dan listened to MF's take on that evening: "Plenty of laughter, but foul language and signs of despair such as I have never seen in the Foley home." Hesitant to impose a judgment that might belittle MF's findings, Dan would only say that MF might withhold final judgments until he had gained more life experience. Years later MF would make the same suggestion to his youngest child: my Uncle Andrew. In time, MF realized that the pub provided necessary therapy. The bending of ears and elbows, the drinking and smoking that did their health no good at all, fortified their spirits, released anger and angst, and left them feeling fit as a fiddle. In the privacy of their bedroom, Dan told Ellen that MF seemed much older than his age, as if he was born old, born with another past, and that his awfully small, narrow world on the farm had been enlarged by this faintly felt past. His childhood was ending.

CHAPTER 5

DEPARTURE

Having made up his mind, MF announced his intention to answer Roger's call to America. As promised, Ellen and Dan bestowed their blessings. They were proud he had figured it out on his own, free from negotiation and outside influence. In the days that followed, MF fought off nervousness and reservations.

Never would he forget the farm or his family. While confident that he had made the right choice, MF was less sure that he would ever feel the same completeness again. He knew he'd miss his parents, and the chats and squabbles with his brothers and sisters. No longer would he mark his height on the attic beam. No longer would he be able to climb the oak tree that his grandparents planted honoring his birth. MF was sure he would remember his 16 years living on the farm: 16 autumns highlighted by a mellow sunshine in early Fall; 16 winters mending and repairing worn-out boots and harnesses while unsuccessfully trying to stay warm in the chilling winds; 16 springs plowing ridges and furrows for seed plantings, slowed by wheels clogged in mud; 16 years of summer harvesting, the sacking and storage of barley in their barn; 16 years of worrying about the rainy season, "a fifth season" that had a mind of its own when to occur, which was often. All this was just under his skin. MF would miss his "private zoo" — the neighs, the moos, the coos, the pesky insects, and the scratching mice, but not cleaning out the barn, or latrine duty.

Although his parents had given their blessings, they could do little to hide their sorrows and concerns. Alone, MF would be a target for con artists, pickpockets, and swindlers. He'd heard the woeful tales of how Irish emigrants sailing aboard aptly named "coffin ships," with overcrowded quarters, inadequate medical supplies, poor sanitation, and deadly outbreaks of typhus and cholera, suffered and died. Dan and Ellen had cause for worry.

MF's packing was simple as all his belongings fit into one bag and were sufficiently worn out not to catch the eye of a thief. MF brought his Wellies, his church shoes, a knitted woolen sweater, a hand-me-down wool coat, three frayed woolen shirts, two pair of underwear (one worn and one for washing), soap, towel, toothbrush and paste. Ellen made sure MF included a rosary and a sepia picture of the family. MF left behind his unused razor, the piece of sod his brothers had jokingly stuffed into his bag, and his worn thin farm gloves, no longer needed.

On the eve of MF's departure, great efforts were made by all to be in control of their teary emotions, which proved unsuccessful. Sobbing during daytime gave way to wailings and loud laments, typical of an "Irish Wake" at nightfall. The family knew that the old times would never be again. MF's only relief was his bedroom, already cluttered by sisters Alexandria's and Lily's dolls marking their soon-to-be residence. But sleep was impossible. Ellen and Dan had spared him from feeling disloyal, yet guilt lingered as he knew that he was breaking a bond by prematurely removing himself. No one had been disapproving, but that was not the same as approval. At breakfast, MF had no appetite; it was the first time he didn't eat what was put in front of him. Ellen and Dan did not complain. Immediately ahead was the difficulty of saying their final goodbyes.

Dad announced, "It's time to go." One by one, MF's remaining siblings, with emotions as fragile as tea cups, took their turn to wrap their arms tightly around MF, showing him how much he mattered. Holding the longest was Ellen, who was losing another son. "Not one moment will you be out of my thoughts," she whispered in MF's ear just moments before leaving the house in which he had spent his first 16 years. Barely able to conceal his feelings, MF retreated quickly so as to not be seen choking back tears, departing thankful that his leave-taking was mercifully short as he was always uncomfortable with displays of emotion. I can't imagine what he felt. I'll always wonder. Was he fearful? Did he have second thoughts?

MF's ship, the Bothnia, was scheduled to depart Queenstown (now called Cobh) on September 12, 1896. The 70 miles to Queenstown was too far for a horse. Dan purchased two tickets, one for the train ride from Limerick Junction to Queenstown, a 25-mile trip, and one for his trip to Boston. Last week nothing had changed, a week later everything had.

Few words were exchanged; everything that had to be said had been said in their woodshed talks. Dan had no more advice for he had never made the journey that MF was about to make. They would have to trust their memories as to voices, laughs, and smiles. Memories would, perforce, begin to retreat.

At Limerick, Dan gave MF his tickets. Other than reminding his son to keep his jacket always on to protect the money sewed into his inside pocket, Dan was incapable of words. They parted with a nod. Unexpressed feelings and unspoken words would become a Foley trait. We don't know what, if anything, they regretted not saying.

"Tickets, please."

CHAPTER 6

SAILING

The view of Ireland disappeared from the stern of the Bothnia. The distance ahead was enormous, nothing but days on end of empty sea. Finally, alone for the first time in his life, MF realized he didn't know much about America, not to mention the fish business. Seeing it on a map had only told him that it was far away, and, while, Roger's letter trumpeted some successes, Dan had warned him, "Irish pride has a way of leaving out the failures." How he would behave was weighing on his mind.

MF was not alone in the cramped, unventilated, below deck quarters. Many other immigrants were aboard. Many were farmers from the poorer western communities of Ireland, peasant villages. Living close to the margin of subsistence, they too needed America to work for them. They, too, had gone as far as they could in Ireland. They were leaving the shadow that hovered over many Irish lives, seeking a chance to grow and thrive. Boston beckoned.

What MF and his fellow passengers could not know was that the odds of success were stacked against them. In his book on immigrants, *The Other Bostonians: Poverty and Progress in the American Metropolis, 1880-1970*, Stephan Thernstrom demonstrated that the prevailing folklore of "starting at the bottom and moving to the top" was a myth. Only one in seven Boston immigrants moved up to a job on the other side of manual labor; only one in twenty moved up to the professional/major proprietor stratum; hence, 95% of Boston immigrants never attained "white collar" occupations. As an unskilled manual worker, MF was fully aware that he was starting low, but, fortunately, he was ignorant of the steepness of the climb.

Which is not to say he was confident. Not entirely. He was aware that he could fail because ambition and drive were not enough. But where drive was concerned, he knew he would not be beat. He had faith in himself. Working fourteen hours a day, seven days a week on the Foley farm meant that he could endure the tough patches, take his hits, and push forward. He had, he believed, the necessary grit. Although, at 16, in a new country with only an older brother who knew his name, and unable to tell a carp from a cod, would he be able to compete in the rough and tumble Boston fish business against more experienced workers twice his age?

So much was unknown. His current status of no status was an important marker from which to measure his progress. He did know that what his parents had freely given him would have to be earned all over again. But he had a sinecure (however humble); he had his health, his religion, his history, and he'd come of his own free will. It was his choice and his chance. He was a plant taken out of soil and transported to a new land. Would he grow?

CHAPTER 7

ARRIVAL IN BOSTON

After 20 days at sea, the Bothnia moored in Boston, Massachusetts. As MF stepped off the ship, his life possessions on his shoulder, the sights before him made Tipperary feel very distant. Another world appeared, both disorienting and foreign. The tall buildings ringing the Boston skyscape made him feel frighteningly small. His prior benchmark for height, the tallest oaks in the farm, was now obsolete. The incessant thuds of machinery were intermittently punctuated by the neighing of horses and the bellowing of cows. The flickering gas lamps and the billows of smoke ascending from the nearby factory stacks pushed MF into a never-imagined modernity. The strange new smell of petroleum fumes emitted from factories replaced the manure odor of the farm. It was a huge remove from Attykitt. He might have felt as insignificant as a pebble in the nearby Atlantic.

Standing on the wharf, MF found that his search for Roger was more difficult than he'd anticipated due to the fact that the greeters were all bundled up to ward off the fall chill. It had been four years since MF had seen Roger, now 24. Fortunately, Roger easily recognized MF, still childlike with his distinctive red cheeks. A hug and a few welcoming words from Roger eased MF's anxiety. Roger had never been the warm, cuddling sort, not possessing a mouth eager to smile. Today was different. His customary serious demeanor softened into an approving grin. MF and Roger had never been close, separated by eight years and two brothers, Jim and Patrick.

Roger, who was bossy, prided himself as a judge of people. He knew how to size them up. Roger knew that MF's emigration, earlier than his, was gutsy. He was aware that brothers Jim and Patrick could be trusted, but he opted for the younger MF because of his demonstrated capacity for work, and his ambition. Jim and Patrick were content on the farm, and liked the known. They did not want more than they had. Not so for MF. How right Roger was remained to be seen.

Riding in Roger's horse-drawn fish cart, MF was agog at the maze of torturously narrow, paved streets connecting the center of Boston to the south end of the city where they were headed. Roger forewarned MF that unlike the endless paths of Ireland, Boston's tangled streets often dead-ended without warning. After two miles, the street names (another first for MF) gave way to alphabetical designations like "C" and "D" streets, which later would signal "Southie," the place he would be living.

A colony of wooden, three-story tenements lined the streets, connected everywhere by laundry lines. MF was surprised by how the clustered tenements were so tightly crammed that no grass could grow between them. There were no fields to lie down in. No gardens to plant vegetables or places to start a garden. Children sat on fire escapes and front stoops because there were no playgrounds.

While Irish families took in emigrant relatives as a matter of course, MF felt awkard as he was moving into an already cramped apartment, not to mention that he would be paying rent: his labor would be payment for room and board. He was given a couch in their parlor to sleep on. There was no privacy and the thin, uninsulated walls did little to block out neighbors' voices. Only one shared bathroom existed per floor. MF could not dawdle as the gurgling pipes always signaled when it was time to move on. Doors were always locked. Local newspapers such as the *Boston Globe*, *Boston Herald*, and the *Boston Evening Transcript* reported occasional shootings in Southie. Health risks abounded, stemming from unsanitary conditions; there were no garbage pickups.

Bess, Roger's wife, acted as the gatekeeper for the apartment, never allowing cheaper "swill milk"— milk from cows that were fed on whiskey and beer, often mixed with ammonia to cut the smell — to enter their home. For this new fish venture to work, all three would have to stay healthy. Doctor's house calls cost $4.00, four times the daily wages of an unskilled worker. Apothecary shops sold cheap, but lethal remedies to the unsuspecting. Mothers of colicky babies could buy inexpensive *Radway's Renovating Resolvent*, which contained arsenic, cyanide and ether; many babies would fall asleep never to wake up again. Bess and Roger would never buy this antidote as they never had children of their own. Bess prided herself on keeping a clean and inviting house, even smartening it with little touches like shades and curtains.

In the year before MF's arrival, Boston's population grew 24% from 363,839 to 448,477 in 1890. This surge resulted in excess labor supply which kept wages extremely low. Fortunately, living costs were low so one could live on almost nothing then. Competition for the better jobs would confront MF as foreigners, mostly Irish, would grow to account for almost 45% of the males 21 and over by 1910. MF was not alone, as after 1895, there were more Bostonians with Irish-born parents than with American-born parents.

MF was not overwhelmed, nor helpless, just unknowing, which was good because the distance traveled from Ireland would be dwarfed by the distance yet to be traveled. Tomorrow he would start his first day in the fish business, secure that he had a home to return to every night, but insecure inasmuch as he had no guarantee of success. He had a clear sense of himself, not uncertain of his purpose, perhaps unusual for someone his age.

Michael Foley and Roger Foley in front of
Roger's Eliot Street Fish Market

CHAPTER 8

A NEW BEGINNING

The day after MF arrived, Bess tapped him on his shoulder at 3:30 a.m. MF didn't need to be woken, as he had been awake for hours anticipating his initial day, the first of 24,090 days he would spend in the fish business.

Street signs barely aided by the flickering gas streetlights, made navigating the three miles from Southie (lower Boston) to the Back Bay (a part of upper Boston), a hazardous adventure. A labyrinth of sudden left and hard right turns abruptly stopping in dead ends challenged even the most brilliant cartographers. Roger and MF arrived with the sun at the R.J. Foley Co. retail storefront at 213 Eliot Street. The store's location would have been ideal 50 years later (where the Wang Center formerly stood), but in 1896, it lacked the foot traffic necessary for a successful retail operation. Roger could not afford the steeper rents charged for a "stall" in Faneuil Hall, a half mile north. Established in 1742 as a town hall, Faneuil Hall was later repurposed to be the city's central market for fish, produce, meat, and poultry. Roger was denied the "one stop shopping" advantage that his competitors at Faneuil Hall enjoyed.

If there was a less green color than green, it would aptly define MF's status as a beginner. No one knew less about fish than MF. In fact, he'd never caught a salmon on the nearby River Suir in Carrick. He did not know haddock from cod or oysters from littlenecks. MF had no handrails — no fish primers, nor training manuals. Wisely, Roger initially assigned MF to low-end tasks: sweeping the sidewalk and the store floor, washing the retail fish case and fish storage tubs, cleaning the pushcarts and setting up display trays. Most physically challenging, MF chopped blocks of ice into pieces for cooling the fish. He was the apprentice, and no one was beneath him.

Roger introduced MF to his new farm, the North Atlantic, a nutrient-rich fishing ground akin to the rich fertile soil he had tilled at Attykitt. He traveled daily to the four wharves stretching into the bay on a two mile stretch of seashore, not far from Roger's store. The draggers and trawler fleets landed at T-Wharf, India Wharf, Rose Wharf, and Atlantic Avenue Wharf.

MF's first challenge was learning the ins and outs of fish-buying. Roger, skilled with horses, was no help as he was also a novice at the game. It would be a steep learning curve for anyone, but quite daunting for a 16-year old, landlocked immigrant with a sixth-grade education. Roger had not yet built a relationship with anyone, and the process of selecting quality fish, MF quickly saw, was chaotic. No formal fish auction existed. Without an orderly, structured buying process, MF had to teach himself. What made it more difficult was that the seagulls were not the only thieves on the wharves. He soon learned that these transactions would require all his wits.

Early on, MF would give Roger cause to wonder if he had chosen the right brother. For starters, MF would fail to notice the seller's foot on the scale. Not infrequently, mean-spirited competitors would steal fish from MF's pushcart when, in the winter, he would step away to warm his hands over the oil can fires. Scoundrels would send MF to "phantom" boats allegedly located at another wharf. Even older Irish, mostly resentful old timers who had not achieved their version of the American Dream, would gruffly tell MF "take it or leave it," rather than negotiate. Information on how long boats had been out fishing — critical to getting fresh catch — was rarely shared with MF. And sometimes those who did share this information proved to be less than honest. MF began, slowly, to develop his BS detector.

Although the family farm had taught MF the value of hard work, the insular, sheltered nature of the Foley farm precluded opportunities to develop enough street smarts, notwithstanding his experiences with selling eggs. MF was struggling, his reticence not allowing him to show how much he didn't know — his reserve was his armor. He was thrust into the ring and, on many days, he needed to take a standing eight count to clear his head and steady his wobbly legs.

One route MF could take was to buy fish from "lumpers" who, as on-shore employees of the boats, unloaded the fish from the boats' holds (called pens). Skippers often paid lumpers in fish, all of which were naturally the top of the catch. MF declined, knowing he was starting at the back of the line, and that cutting ahead of the boats' non-lumper customers would serve to alienate everyone.

Another source of fish were the day boats — hand-lined dories, sixteen-foot, two-man, oared rowboats that fished in the inshore shoal areas (within five miles of the shoreline). MF greatly respected these fishermen's work ethic. Their arduous routine called for laying out lines of 500 baited hooks in rough seas, retrieving the lines, every two hours, often in the fog, one-man rowing and the other hauling, around the clock without sleep. But day boat fish were the freshest and thus the best quality.

Unfortunately, the majority of the day boat fleet sold their catch to local buyers located at distant Cape Cod towns, or at Gloucester or Martha's Vineyard. The cost of transporting fish from these locations to Boston would be prohibitive. Another problem was that day boats caught species that did not sell well in Boston–scup, bluefish, and herring. The same drawbacks applied to the pound net fishery, which used stationary gear in shallow waters.

Ultimately, MF devised a "premium payment" system whereby Roger Foley Co. would pay a price of one-tenth of a penny above that day's asking price per pound of fish bought, which on a typically priced whole fish of one penny per pound, translated to a ten percent premium. In return, MF was allowed to hand pick his fish. This partnership depended on immediate cash payments and, more importantly, that MF not become an impediment to the operations of the sellers. Fortunately, MF had won the admiration of sufficient skippers, because, like his father, he had a way of not offending people. He kept his head down and his mouth shut. He knew his place.

The right to pre-inspect the fish before buying did not guarantee success. But it gave MF an edge. Fish were unloaded alternately from starboard and port "pens" (to maintain ballast), resulting in the commingling of the fish caught on different days. Fish caught on the first day of a five-day trip were four days old when landed. To obtain the freshest product, MF wanted fish caught only on the final two days of the trip. This arrangement gave him, finally, a chance to succeed.

Roger and MF knew that R.J. Foley Co. was a marginal entity that needed to differentiate itself from major competitors. They had the choice of being the low-end or high-end fish buyer. Years later he explained why he and Roger went high: "If our competitors were all quality nuts, R.J. Foley Co. might have been forced to become the best junk fish merchants, selling on discount prices. Fortunately, our competitors were not that fussy, so Roger and I were able to go high end and distinguish R.J. Foley Co. as "the quality fish purveyor in Boston." Importantly, MF was saying that this policy decision was driven not dogmatically but pragmatically.

But there was little wiggle room. There were no second chances. Every fish had to be a ten out of ten, which meant that he had to learn firsthand the tests by which to grade fish, namely the touch test (fish in rigor mortis state); the sight test (red gills, bright gut cavity after evisceration); and the nose test (no fishy odor whatsoever).

Tricky too, was determining just the right size of the fish order. It was almost impossible to accurately predict daily sales, as Roger's business had not produced predictable daily purchase patterns. Foot traffic varied, sometimes wildly. Overbuying led to holdover fish that often lost freshness. Under-buying created shortages that would irk customers, sending them to competitors who were less concerned with quality.

MF was fortunate to return home nightly to Bess's positive attitude, a welcome counterbalance to the usually stoic Roger. Always upbeat, Bess would greet them daily with reassurances of future success. She never complained about their foul-smelling fish clothes. MF would jokingly say, "Bess could have chilled the clothes, cut 'em up and sold them as bait." Little touches like curtains replacing shades softened the sparse appearance of the apartment, creating a cozy and welcoming home. The home and her delicious meals warmed the cockles of their hearts, replenishing their energy for the next day's battles.

But as Roger counted each day's takings, tallying cash inflows against outflows, it was clear that the store was not making money despite improvements in buying. Cash reserves were dwindling. A new sales strategy was needed, or Roger would have to close his store before their first anniversary. Fortunately, MF had a plan. And it was not to return to Ireland.

CHAPTER 9

THE BRAHMIN SOLUTION

MF did not come this far to lose, and going back to the farm was out of the question. But all was not bleak. There was an abundance of fish. Expenses were cut to the bone. Mistakes were addressed. Other remedial actions were taken, but one serious problem remained: not enough customers. Roger had originally relied on the Irish connection to work. It had not. Although the Irish were fast becoming the largest ethnic group in Boston, the majority of these uneducated immigrants were saddled with low-paying manual jobs that required them to subsist mainly on vegetables and potatoes, not fish. Daily, MF walked to work alongside a milkman who told him that his job was to deliver milk, eggs, and butter directly to homes in downtown Boston.

"Why not home delivery of fish?" asked MF. No other fish purveyor in Boston had considered it, primarily because of the high labor costs attached to home delivery. Some fish purveyors, especially those well-located in Faneuil Hall, succeeded by having their customers come to them. Roger was not succeeding; his location was obscure, remote. His back was to the wall. Home delivery was less a choice than an imperative for survival.

Roger initiated the program, focusing on sales to Brahmin families representing the wealthiest two percent of Boston. Trying to kickstart the "Brahmin" strategy, Roger contacted the Lodge family, who had employed him as a horse trainer, and requested a testimonial for R.J. Foley Fish Co. The Lodges declined, citing that it would be improper to do so since they could not attest to Roger's attributes as a fishmonger.

Without the Lodges' help, Roger focused his efforts on two wealthy neighborhoods, Beacon Street and Commonwealth Avenue, both of which were distant enough from Faneuil Hall to make the home delivery program attractive. Roger assigned MF the task of generating sales. On Sundays, he would prospect on streets filled with red brick brownstones gated by cast iron railings, highlighted by lacquered address signs, with brass knobs and numerals on the front door. These fine homes belonged to the rich. People knew one another, those they did not know they regarded with suspicion. Over the side or back door on many of these homes was a sign: "Tradesmen Only Entrance."

Roger played the Irish card, hoping that the head domestic, who determined purveyor selections, was Irish Catholic. However, while the idea of selling to a Brahmin household was clever, it had a major drawback. The Protestant Brahmins were intolerant of Catholics, and if the head domestic could be convinced to choose an Irish purveyor, he or she could easily be overruled. Thomas Nast, the preeminent cartoonist for *Harper's Weekly* from 1859 through the1880's, caricatured Irish-Americans as orangutans jumping out of trees, menaces to society. Ads in the *Boston Herald* and *Boston Transcript* stated, "NO BLACKS OR IRISH NEED APPLY." Brahmin children were prohibited from playing with Irish kids. NOC was the acronym said in whispered tones: "not of my class." Covenants in mortgages often prohibited sale or rent to Irish. The Brahmins did not see Irish as worthy rivals, not at the turn of the century. The Brahmins, like their British forefathers who suppressed the Irish in Ireland, wanted the Irish immigrants to keep their distance.

MF was unbothered by their prejudice. It was what it was, and was not unexpected. MF knew the places of each ethnicity. The Irish were at the bottom, while the Brahmins were at the top of Boston society's hierarchy. MF admired the Brahmins' success. They had impressively advanced to controlling positions in law, education, medicine, and banking. MF wanted to emulate their success and become a somebody in the fish business. He often told me, "I did not want to copy stupid people." Their formula had worked — perseverance, prudence, self-control, savvy, and frugality. He felt they could have handled success with more finesse than was exhibited in their prejudicial signage. The Brahmins, not owning any fish companies, couldn't hurt R.J. Foley Fish Co., but they could help it by becoming customers.

An unbidden MF started with visits to get appointments. Properly entering the "tradesman" door, a well-scrubbed MF, symbolically with hat in hand, planned to show his manners by not sitting down until he was asked, and by deferentially pulling out a chair for his hostess. This strategy was not needed. Upon hearing his name and brogue, many doors were slammed in his face. A dismal start.

A resilient MF continued his calling program. In June, MF eked out a few appointments. At these follow-up meetings MF would explain his unique retail seafood program, the centerpiece of which was daily pre-ordering and delivery of quality fish to their doorstep, saving them the daily trek for fish to Faneuil Hall, all at no extra cost. Queried about his promise of quality fish, MF, in an amplified brogue, proudly stated that only R.J. Foley Fish was allowed to handpick its fish. Unfortunately, each call ended with a polite "I'll get back to you." No one did.

The blunt truth: MF was not connecting. He had not made sense of his audience; perhaps spending too much time worrying about his performance, and not enough about the prospect's concerns. As it turned out, MF's youth was a negative. His prospects could not believe that a teenager just off the boat from Ireland could compete successfully against more seasoned, older, wiser fishmongers that were his competitors. A lack of confidence trumped the promised convenience.

Roger and MF, maybe because of Bess's votive candle requesting God's intercession, came to realize that a key ingredient had been omitted from the sales pitch. Roger and MF hadn't given the customers the right of seeing the merchandise before buying. So, they scrapped the pre-order requirement. Customers would now be given the right of selection or rejection at their back door.

MF returned to each prospect that had given him an audience. His amended plan yielded one prospect on a trial basis. But in a short time, others followed. Roger realized he had no alternative if he wanted to stay in business. He approved the new plan.

CHAPTER 10

THE SPLIT

When he started, MF did not anticipate that Roger would be a difficult boss. On the family farm, MF had thought they were similar. In retrospect, it may be that these now-unfolding personality differences — MF's natural charm and warm reticence in contrast to Roger's strained charm and cold reticence — were always there, but unnoticed because management decisions on the farm had been left to their father, and never questioned. The boys' independence was inhibited in that they felt disobedient or disloyal if they voiced disagreements too often or too loudly. Roger and MF had been like sheep — fenced in, their characters not fully formed.

But in Boston, MF noticed that Roger, under stress, had changed. He was no longer the person who always got along. Roger had become more reserved, aloof, and judgmental. He refrained from giving MF deserved pats on his back. Never once did Roger give MF credit for the creation and successful implementation of the home delivery program, which saved the company. Never would Roger reassure MF when he stumbled. Far be it for him to utter reassuring statements such as, "You learn from your mistakes, you'll get there."

At home, Roger was churlish. One time MF brought home sea scallops for dinner as he knew Bess loved them. Roger was incensed, and scolded MF: "You have no right to bring home fish without my permission." Even after MF had told him that a scalloper had given them free of charge, Roger did not budge. MF was embarrassed for Bess. She was the essence of goodness, and yet, frictions such as these were becoming a pattern, making living together increasingly uncomfortable for MF.

Further alienating MF, Roger changed his first name to the anglicized Rodger in the hope of broadening his company's appeal to the WASP clientele. It almost seemed that the brothers were from two different families. MF could only imagine how their parents would react to the name change. Years later, David Lyken, a behavioral psychologist, discovered what MF was learning via experience: "Siblings are like people who receive telephone numbers with the same digits arranged in different sequences."

After three years, MF decided he had enough. MF told Roger he was leaving. Roger had always known MF wouldn't be working for him permanently, but he didn't think he would leave this soon. He exploded in anger, and accused MF of betraying his trust. In truth, his anger stemmed from the fact that he knew how important MF was to his company's success. MF volunteered not to compete against Roger. It was a huge concession. MF had been the face of the R. J. Foley Fish Co. and many customers would follow him to his next seafood venture. Roger, however, was not placated. He threatened never to speak to MF again, and he didn't.

Later, when they bumped into each other on the fish pier, Roger would never acknowledge him. Roger was not able to replace MF, confirming MF's importance. A few years after their split, Roger was forced to close his company and return to Ireland. Whatever they were to each other before was now lost forever.

MF had no place to stay. He was back to where he was when he stepped off the Bothnia, three years earlier. He was alone and broke. He would need to accumulate capital to start his own business. He wondered how he would pull this off. But first he needed a good paying job — a first for him.

CHAPTER 11

A NEW BOSS

MF knew that he was not ready to start his own fish company. His first venture had failed, although he had gained invaluable experience. But he needed more experience in business practice —he was still swimming upstream. Fortunately, he was no longer a peripheral figure in the fish business. The competition had let him know that they'd be interested in him should he ever leave Roger. One of them, a merchant named Katz who had made his money in other non-fish ventures, needed help with his retail fish operation, which was operating on the thin line between survival and failure. Katz possessed a sharp eye for up-and-comers and found MF to be a compelling candidate, despite his age, only nineteen, and limited experience. He was especially impressed by the home delivery program MF had created. If MF could win over the bigoted Brahmins, MF should be able to succeed for him — even with his finicky Jewish customers. Mr. Katz offered MF a management position, generous pay, plus a bonus depending on profits.

Before accepting the job, MF disclosed the potential sticking point of his non-compete pledge to Roger. Katz's retail store, however, was located in Dock Square, a good distance from the Back Bay so he wouldn't be competing for Roger's customers. But in spite of being impressed with MF's program, Mr. Katz believed it was too expensive to run successfully. He had other ideas for MF.

MF began working in a capacity in which he had no prior experience — managing people. He was to be the boss of people 30 years older than him who had more years in the fish business than he had on earth.

Immediately, he realized that to succeed he must emulate his father's management style. Out-toil the toilers. Show, not shout. But there was a big difference between the farm and the retail fish market. His father had unquestioning obedience. MF would have to earn that status.

His biggest challenge was to learn how and when to say "no." MF was not a shouter, he was a nudger. Early on, the harshest words MF would utter were, "You can work and talk at the same time." He'd heard the same countless times on the farm. Because it was usually easier to do something himself instead of asking, or ordering, another person, he would too often take this path.

A few months into the job, MF learned that this path was not always the best course. He faced a small crisis, after requesting a worker to stay late in order to pick up some mackerel, which was coming off the boat in the early evening. The man refused, saying he had put in a long day and was going home at the regular time. MF replied, "If you choose to go home, don't bother coming back to work tomorrow." The worker never returned. He and others learned that when MF tightened his gaze and cleared his throat, you better listen up. The question of whether MF was going to be a babysitter or a boss was answered.

Other challenges awaited him. Fish sales were a problem. MF's predecessor was deal-oriented rather than quality-minded. Like many, he confused price with value, thinking that the cheaper fish meant more value for the customer. MF took over buying, resuming the buying connections that had worked well for him at Roger's company. The inconsistent quality problem disappeared.

Not so easy was a crucial customer issue, one faced by all seafood retailers. Do you sell what you want the consumer to buy, or sell what the consumer wants to buy? The prior regime had inconvenienced the customers, not themselves. Special customer requests were dismissed with lame stories of bad weather, or that quality or quantity was not just right. MF knew that they would put up with such excuses for only so long, and then go to a purveyor who was more accommodating. His salespeople's attitudes had to be altered. The new mindset was simple: customers paid their wages and their satisfaction was job number one. Going forward, special requests were not only fulfilled, but also welcomed. MF led the retail unit until he could groom a replacement. His personality made him a natural salesman. He was a pleaser, always polite, likeable, and a charmer who made every woman feel like a queen. In time, buying fish at Katz market became pleasurable. The bottom line grew. MF's changes led to stability and protected the workers from layoffs, thus providing for the security of their families. In time, MF scarcely had to raise his voice.

As business improved, MF identified men to take on various of his duties. With a bit of free time now available, he began to carefully scout locations for his own future enterprise — he'd learned the hard way how a bad location could be deadly. Like his Dad, who knew every patch on his farm, MF would spend hours walking the former cow paths of downtown Boston to find the ideal location. Regular foot traffic was a sine qua non.

MF's planning was based on an analysis of the travel of the "suits"— the moneyed crowd working downtown as successful stockbrokers, commercial bankers, lawyers, doctors, and businessmen. He scouted the city's train stations to determine from which the majority passed through daily to their homes in the suburbs. The South Station served Quincy and Braintree, while the North Station served Winthrop, Nahant, and Beverly, and the Back Bay Station served Brookline and beyond. MF soon discovered that North Station had the heaviest foot traffic. Next, he studied maps and walked the streets to ferret out which were most often walked to North Station. The most traveled streets were Friend and Union Streets, across from the famous Union Oyster House where at the end of the day, a drink could be had. Fortunately, this area was across town from Roger's store on Eliot Street in the Back Bay. It was a street-smart decision in more than one sense.

CHAPTER 12

MARRIAGE

Standing: sons William, Andy, John, and daughter Helen Moloney
Seated: Johanna and Michael (The Boss)
Moloney and daughter Margaret

Helen Augusta Moloney, the oldest of seven children, was twenty-three
years old on the day in early 1907 that her parents, Johanna née Hennessey
and Michael Moloney, welcomed Ellen and Dan Foley to their farm at
Knockgraffon in Cahir, Tipperary to discuss her possible marriage to MF.
Both the Moloneys and Hennesseys were powerful families, well-known
and respected throughout Tipperary County. Through farm acquisitions,
Knockgraffon had grown to be a "large" farm defined in those days
as over 250 acres. The Moloneys excelled at breeding prize-winning

thoroughbred horses and Hereford cows, which were sold directly to wealthy buyers in England.

"Hannah," as she insisted on being called, was a compelling role model for Helen. She was a maverick who did not conform to the sexist stereotype that deemed women to be unsuitable for manual labor. Up at 4:00 a.m., Hannah often would be seen defiantly smoking a clay pipe while leading the harvest workers. Hannah taught Helen how to sheath stalks of threshed grain. She was raised as a co-equal to her four brothers. Often Hannah would be heard pushing her sons to keep up the pace that Helen set. In her early teen years, daughter Helen was put in charge of the hen and milk houses, reporting directly to Hannah. On Ireland's farms men customarily dined before the women, but not at Knockgraffon. Helen inherited her mother's tornado-like drive, which gave her an inner assurance and confidence that would define her. Her father, Michael, was also known as "the Boss," owing to his stern, mirthless visage. Totally consumed by his breeding business, Michael left the child-raising to Hannah.

Helen had known of MF from their years at The New School, the National Elementary School in Cashel, but not well as MF was three grades ahead of her. And although the Moloney and Foley families attended the same local Catholic Church, Helen and MF's daily farm chores precluded any time for socialization. Matchmaking was the way marriages came about in Ireland. No marriage would take place without parental consent. The children would not be consulted until both sets of parents had agreed to the match.

The Moloneys knew MF to be a well-raised, polite, hard-working teenager who, word had it, was doing very well for himself in Boston. Helen was no doubt pleased that MF was not the oldest Foley boy as he would have remained in Ireland and she'd be a farmer's wife. At the matchmaking discussion over tea at Knockgraffon, seven miles from the Foley farm at Attykitt, the two families agreed to confer their consent should Helen and MF desire to marry.

It had been ten years since Helen and MF had seen each other, so the young couple had some thinking to do. The Foleys gave a recent photo of MF to Helen. The picture revealed a young man of average height with a serious demeanor wearing spectacles with very fine rims. Staring into the sunlight, MF's eyes were squinty, like a wise owl. The Boss acknowledged that MF did not look like a cart horse, rather more like a thoroughbred. But he cautioned Helen that Irish families only communicated a son's success, never any failures. She would have to make up her own mind.

An Irish girl without a dowry ("spre" in Gaelic) often had to emigrate and be employed as a domestic until she'd saved enough for her dowry. Helen, the daughter of a well-off family, would have a dowry without working. Unchaperoned, she immigrated to Boston and took an apartment at 176 Hillside Street, Dorchester, Massachusetts in the upscale Irish neighborhood of Mission Hills.

The courtship began. A lot was at stake as divorce was not an option for Irish Catholics. Marriage was not a fait accompli; both sets of parents concurred that, while arranged, the marriage would not be forced. They would make up their own minds after taking each other's measure.

MF was quite taken by the grown-up Helen. His first impression was of a lady of noteworthy presence, not spoiled, not coquettish, full of life and energy. She certainly had a mind of her own. She was sturdy. Talkative, but not in an off-putting way. MF was glad she carried the conversations. She was handsome, not beautiful, but this was not an issue, for beauty, as the Irish adage goes, never boiled a pot. Helen was clearly a lady of taste, well-grounded, and eminently respectable. MF wanted to rise in the business world and she would be a good helpmate.

Michael Foley (MF)

MF was a tough read for Helen. He was not one to talk about himself, as if it was impolite. A young man with old-world manners, he was unfailingly polite, striving to make Helen feel respected and quite special, courting her dressed smartly in a starched white shirt with a high collar. There was no hint of disingenuousness as MF's face and his words were always compatible. The MF Helen had seen in the photos in Ireland showed the same man she now saw in front of her. He was unexpectedly suave, not in a slick manner, rather genuinely smooth and charming, which she learned later, belied an inner drive and determination. He possessed a maturity that said he had never been young.

MF kept things to himself, especially when it came to his business. When he did speak, it was in short sentences. Helen would know when MF had something important to say as MF would narrow his eyes, tense his lips, clear his throat — not only to purge the phlegm, but also to collect his thoughts — and then say something worthy of consideration. The fish business would not be discussed at home. MF's reticence notwithstanding, Helen realized MF was a go-getter, as well as a man of great promise.

Another subject not discussed, or discussable, was sex. MF assumed that, as one of seven Moloneys, and as a worker on a farm that bred horses and cows, Helen was fully informed. He knew Helen was of irreproachable morals. Both knew that any children would be raised as Catholics. There was much to consider, little to discuss.

MF also knew that he and Helen accepted the customary arrangement: the mother was in charge of the home; the father ran the outside business. MF placed incalculable value on the continuation of this tradition, each responsibility requiring separate, full-time management. Helen was also committing to a dowry of unspecified size that the Moloneys would give to MF after they were married. The size of a dowry in those days was three pounds per acre of land owned. At 200 acres, the anticipated dowry would be 600 pounds. It could be higher, inasmuch as the Moloneys did not have to set aside funds except for their only daughter. The oral history of the Foley family erroneously suggested that the dowry enabled MF to start his own fish company. Not so. MF had saved substantially more than the prospective dowry, and had established the M.F. Foley Fish Co. in 1906, two years before they were married. The dowry, therefore, was not a consideration for MF, either for marriage or for business.

Togetherness brought about by mutuality of background, of religion, and farm life was a good starting point. In the year-long courtship they both realized that the other aimed high, not out of insecurity but from ambition. Not only were they go-getters, but they were confident that they could rely on each other. The final decision to marry would depend on an emotional connection. Neither would compromise for the sake of convenience, or parental approval. Both were too honest and too respectful of each other to ignore an absence of mutual attraction. Fortunately, they liked each other. One kiss presumably led to more. Intimate unknowns would stay that way — shrouded forever.

On October 6, 1908, Helen Moloney and Michael Foley were married at the National Cathedral Church of Boston, perhaps in one of the side chapels, as it was a small wedding with only William Moloney (the third oldest boy after Andy and John Moloney) present to give away the bride.

Neither could predict the shape of things in the future. Growing up they had seen and interpreted their parochial world through their parent's eyes and words. Moving forward they would navigate a less certain, less safe, fast-changing world. To survive — in fact, to succeed — they would depend on the rooted sense that, together, they could prosper better as a couple than individually.

CHAPTER 13

THE START OF THE M.F. FOLEY FISH COMPANY

MF had a recurring dream that haunted him, stoking his anxiety. It went like this: he returned to the Foley farm — Attykitt. He couldn't get in. All the windows were locked. The house was empty. Footprints had been washed away. No signs of human life remained, only darkness.

Yet undeterred by this dream of failure, MF set out to establish his own company. Over the five years after departing Roger's company, MF had lived frugally and saved enough for start-up capital. He wanted to be debt free — good choice as the Brahmins still controlled the Boston banks. No unproven Irish immigrant — especially one who did not know how to construct pro-forma financial statements — would be eligible for a loan.

MF subleased a room in the back of a flat iron building located on the corner of Friend and Union Streets, two blocks west of Faneuil Hall. Boston's fall from a position of supremacy as a critical port city in the early 1900s had recently resulted in a decline in business at the Faneuil Hall marketplace. Its once grandiose buildings had fallen into disrepair, becoming unattractive and unsafe for shoppers. Harvard owned the flat iron building, but his landlord was Railway Express, who leased it from the University. The building's original owner was Charles Adams, grandson of President John Quincy Adams, and the former American Ambassador to England, who had bequeathed the building to Harvard. The room was cramped, and barely accommodated a retail counter, fish storage compartments, and a cot where MF would often sleep to safeguard the facility.

He'd done his math. MF estimated his breakeven sales volume to be 1500 pounds of whole fish sold per week, after which he could pay himself. Not at an insurmountable rate, he hoped. But at first, his sales were too small to bring in enough income to cover his costs. Ironically, MF's "non-compete agreement" with Roger spared him some unnecessary labor expenses. He considered selling from a wagon, but from his farm days, MF knew that the initial costs of a wagon, a horse, and oats, with livery bills, blacksmith bills, and driver costs. These costs were prohibitive to making more than a subsistence income. He needed a strong economy, and a busy store.

But MF was lucky to be starting a fish company in Boston in 1906. Demographics were on his side. Boston's population had surged 31% from 362,839 in 1880 to 475,465 by 1910. Fertility rates of immigrant families remained high resulting in growing numbers of mouths to feed. Boston had a strengthening economy.

MF's targeted customer base was the "suits" that traveled by train from Boston to their homes in Winthrop, Nahant, and Beverly, the first ring of populated suburbs north of Boston. MF's building offered a geographical convenience as the storefront was located midway between the downtown financial and business districts and North Station, the only major depot for trains travelling to the North Shore communities.

Railway Express initially rejected MF's untested company as a tenant because they were not sure MF would survive in business given all the fish competitors in nearby Faneuil Hall. This was a huge setback, but MF persisted. MF devised a business plan that he hoped would allay the fears of Railway Express. Foley Fish would be the cleanest retail fish market in Boston, and markedly better than the other fishmongers at Faneuil Hall. Foley's would institute a unique procedure which entailed hosing down work area and sidewalks every hour, hoping to impress and entice potential customers — especially the "suits" who didn't want any fish scales on their wingtips. Further, MF would scatter cedar sawdust on the floors twice a day to absorb any liquids and emit a fresh smell. Foley Fish would raise the bar — no other fish company could match this commitment to sanitation and customer comfort. MF petitioned Railway

Express and the firm eventually changed its mind and permitted MF to sub-lease on a trial basis.

In his research, MF noticed that his competitors, seeking to catch the eyes of passersby, piled their fish too high, often three-tiered. The "pile high" display system did draw customers in, but on slower days, the fish on top depressed those on the bottom, creating offensive odors and liquid dripping on the floor. MF's assessment: "Pile it high, see it die." In contrast, Foley Fish Company's display system featured fish iced and displayed on single-layered metal pans from which the juices had been cleaned away. Not only would Foley customers see the fish, but the display would pass the "nose" test.

MF knew he could never succeed if he could not provide a "no leak" fish package for the train ride home. Conventional wrapping entailed using porous newspapers. Foley Fish were wrapped with one absorbent sheet around the fish (not newspaper), followed by a second sheet of waxed paper – all sealed by tape. No smells, no leaks, no unnecessary laundry bills. MF figured that the extra paper costs were significantly less than losing a customer. More cents to get no scents made sense to MF.

MF knew that, ultimately, he had to win over the suits' wives who, without Irish domestics, needed a simple way to cook fish. Instead of the lengthy, cumbersome method of baking whole fish (with bones), MF would custom cut boneless fillets that could be sautéed or baked in less time than vegetables.

MF quickly learned that having a good cutter could be the difference between profit and loss. Cutting fillets from a whole fish created a new cost, the "off the knife" cost. The key determinant of that cost was the cutter's yield. MF understood the concept of yield from his days on the farm when he flailed the barley ears to get to the useable hay. He knew yield was what you ended up with compared with what you started. He applied this yield concept to his retail fish business.

Having learned division at the National School, MF could compute fish yield by dividing the weight of the whole fish (denominator) into the weight of the cut fillets (numerator). With the yield computed, the "off the knife" cost of the fillets was determined by dividing the yield into the original cost of the whole fish.

Assuming the whole fish cost to be ten cents a pound and the cutter's yield to be 40%, the cost "off the knife" of the fillets, would be 25 cents ($.10 divided by $.40). To set the retail price, MF would add his profit markup — say five cents per pound to his "off the knife" cost to arrive at a retail price of 30 cents per pound for fillets. If a less effective cutter yielded only 33%, his "off the knife" cost would rise to $.35, a significant eight cents higher than the more effective cutter. This extra cost would exceed his profit markup of five cents per pound by three cents – a loss leader.

MF could not learn to be a good cutter, however hard he tried. Good cutters were born with the skill, and able to deftly cut along the bone, making the necessary slight adjustments for the irregular vertebrae — all without leaving any edible flesh on the bone. The best cutters were from either Sicily or the Azores, off Portugal, and learned their trade at an early age in local tuna factories. When it came to hiring cutters, MF would not poach from his competitors. Fortunately, he found a Sicilian immigrant who was working on a fishing boat who had just married and wanted to avoid long fishing trips.

MF started the MF Foley Fish Company in 1906. Would he be able to realize the American Dream and silence the fearful dreams of failure that haunted him? He had done good research, hired good workers, had a gimlet eye for detail, was not slavish in following customary methods, and had sufficient cash to make adjustments as needed. He had made decisions above his weight and beyond his years, and given himself a chance to succeed. Had he been here in an earlier life as his father suspected?

CHAPTER 14

STARTING UP

MF knew that the first years of operation would be difficult. Worse, he knew that he might fail. He had formulated a sound plan, but as his father often said, "You don't always get what you merit." Sales to prized "suits" were steady, but the store was not yet meeting breakeven projections. The Friend Street entrance was not inviting, especially in the morning with vagabonds and drunks from nearby Scollay Square sleeping on the sidewalks. MF had to "favor" the local cops with "take home" fish to correct this problem. Compounding his problems, most of the Irish living in South Boston and Dorchester found the trek to Foley Fish too distant. The Irish boost that he'd hoped for was feeble. To compensate, MF took no pay.

The slow start complicated buying. No two days of sales were alike, creating "undersold" situations on one day, and "oversold" situations on another. Lacking refrigeration, the "holdover" fish had to be thrown out. Heavy customer traffic created "out of stock" situations, which were painful. Charting a discernible customer buying pattern would take time. On top of these supply and demand problems was the weather. Fog, high winds, and storms kept fishing vessels either in port, or delayed at sea awaiting suitable weather. Radar was still decades away, and navigation along the rocky Eastern coastlines was perilous. (Every schoolchild in New England knew Longfellow's famous poem, "The Wreck of the Hesperus.") Customers expected quality fish every day irrespective of weather. Becoming a reliable purveyor of quality fish was critical if Foley Fish Co was to survive.

MF's game plan was also hindered by the lack of experienced personnel. Other than his cutter, he was a one-man show and finding good help was difficult. As head fish buyer, MF needed to be at T-Wharf to correct the underbuying problem, but he couldn't be away from his store after the 8:00 a.m. opening. His full-time presence at the sales counter was mandatory, but this made going to the piers two or three times a day to purchase fresh fish impossible. His cramped retail space made things worse. One block away at Faneuil Hall ten competitors with many years in the fish business were in operation, which meant that MF, the newcomer, had only one chance to impress new customers. When he did finally hire a helper, he was unskilled and was only good at minor tasks such as hosing down the sidewalk, removing smudges from the glass case, and scrubbing the scale and counter to a spotless state. Everything else fell on MF's shoulders. He knew that a sale was more than a fish changing hands. He had to build lasting relationships and his presence and personal touch, therefore, were as important as the quality of his fish. He would show each fish to every customer, citing the signs of just-caught freshness —no smell and no discoloration. He then gave cooking advice and finally wrapped the fish, not in used newspaper but in no-drip paper. When a customer returned, MF would welcome him by his first name and ask how the family liked his fish. His helper could not be given this job. It soon became apparent that if he had to a full-time presence in the store, he would need to have a full-time fish buyer.

He needed a seasoned veteran he could trust. He checked his contacts at the wharves. Unfortunately, no experienced buyer was willing to leave a steady job to go to work at a new untested fish company run by a 25–year-old immigrant. But, word of mouth reached Frank Souza, then 20 years old. He knew the odds were against him. One of Souza's credentials was that he was the son and grandson of Portuguese fishermen who had married fishermen's daughters. His fish education had started early, in his mother's womb, one might say, and was continued during long stints on his family's boats. He knew fish.

Souza had leathery skin from his time at sea, and penetrating eyes, accompanied by a slight smile, a genuine, not sly, smile. When asked a question he answered in monosyllables, which impressed MF, who was similarly reserved. MF saw a young quietly confident man, comfortable in his own skin, without any chips on his shoulder. When MF inquired as to his qualifications, Souza used many of the same words that MF did in his interview with Mr. Katz five years earlier, when he was the same age as Souza. He spoke of family, work, respect, and appreciation of the opportunities that the fishing industry offered. Calling MF "sir" despite their closeness in age, was a good sign. Souza stated his body of work, explained how he started at the bottom then took on every job on a fishing boat except navigation. MF knew that Souza would be accepted by the fishermen as one of them. He would not try to cheat them by misrepresenting top grade fish as mediocre in order to knock down prices. But he was tough enough to stand up to fishermen trying to take advantage of his ties to the fishing community, expecting him to overpay for mediocre fish.

Recalling his days being tricked by the egg wholesaler in Clonmel, MF inquired, "What do you know that I don't about tricks played by fishermen?" Souza cited Sunday dinner conversations when his father discussed how some fishermen mixed older fish with newer fish when offloading, and as MF had witnessed, the trick of stepping on scales to add weight. Souza's father once fired a cousin who tried these scams. Enough said.

One thing MF suspected was that Souza had only eaten the freshest of fish, as his family would bring home "snack" fish given to the crew as a bonus. Viscerally, he knew the quality standard that MF insisted upon for Foley customers.

MF sensed a natural fit. Going with his gut, he hired Frank Souza at $10 per week wage, money which came out of MF's savings. MF was betting the ranch on this 20-year old immigrant. And Souza was betting his future on MF. It stood to reason that they were a perfect fit.

CHAPTER 15

THE EARLY YEARS OF
M.F. FOLEY FISH

MF decided he would not micro-manage Frank Souza, who he realized had a good eye for fish and a deft touch with people. He told him to design his own buying strategy, letting him stick with his experience and instincts. It proved to be a good decision.

Souza kept away from buying fish off the large steamers. He favored the "Italian Fleet." Like Souza's ancestry, the Sicilians were born boatmen. This fleet was composed exclusively of little motored dories – 16 to 40 feet in length, which fished the inshore waters from Boston to Plymouth. Their "long-lining" fishing method involved a heavy line called the "ground" line, often 50 fathoms long, to which lighter lines called "skates" were fastened. The skates were paid out of tubs (usually four tubs) from the dories with baited hooks attached every three to four feet.

The fleet's daily catches were offloaded at T-Wharf, famous as the site of the Boston Tea Party. Souza trundled the Foley fish cart down the short two blocks east by way of South Market Street sometimes three times a day. It soon became known what Souza was after and knew well: quality. The Italian fleet, maybe thinking he was Italian, or maybe because Souza bought exclusively from them, did not charge a buyers' premium (which the steamers did). That Souza was not a loudmouth helped. The upshot was that Foley Fish now had more consistent quality than the larger fish retailers of Faneuil Hall. These operators bought mainly from the large boats that were out at sea for three to four days, which meant that their first day's catch was always three days older than Foley's fish.

MF needed to find more customers. He knew that low-income earners were mainly buying inexpensive fish. He would not be able to attract them with the pricier cod, haddock and flounder. Souza's connection with the Italian fleet provided the solution. This fleet caught a good amount of inexpensive, inshore, fresh herring. MF could profitably sell a dozen herring for five cents, enough to feed a family of six. Consequently, herring soon became a staple at Foley Fish. The Portuguese kid rescued his Irish boss with his Italian connections. Sales jumped. Profits followed, buoyed by the influx of Italian immigrants settling in the nearby North End section of Boston.

The local Boston cops — supposed Irish allies — began ticketing MF for parking his fish cart on side streets. He knew from Ireland that a workable system was based on favor, not laws. Therefore, he paid a protection tax — an accommodation made in the name of survival. MF was learning that he needed to know a lot more about how things were done in Boston. He wanted a more worldly perspective than his parochial upbringing had given him. He did not want to be unprepared when the "pols" came with their hands out. Some of these gents were like the "blatherers" he had met at the Irish bar growing up; they spoke much but said little.

To deal with this problem, he needed trustworthy, smart people with whom he could discuss his problems, and he soon established friendships with three of his customers. These were improbable alliances, given their respective ages, occupations, ethnicities, and educational differences. Boston lawyer Joseph O'Connell, Benjamin Swig, a successful Jewish businessman, and Mr. Morse, a well-connected WASP who was a leader in the thriving leather industry, became MF's advisors, advising him on banking, politics, and legal issues. MF called them his "Kitchen Cabinet." They would meet monthly at the store over sips of Irish whiskey. All four shared a deep distrust of James Michael Curley, the four-time mayor of Boston, who would later spend two terms in jail for fraud. A skilled manipulator, Curley had beaten John F. Fitzgerald, the incumbent Mayor (and father to Rose Kennedy), by threatening to release damaging information about "Honey Fitz" and his purported affair with a 20-year-old cigarette girl named Toodles. The scandal precipitated Honey Fitz's withdrawal from the upcoming mayoral election. No one needed to be advised to keep their distance from Mayor Curley.

In 1914, the New England Fish Exchange, the self-appointed overseer of the fishery, relocated from T-Wharf to the Boston Fish Pier, off Atlantic Avenue. Major fish wholesalers and processors moved their facilities to locations on both sides of the pier to facilitate unloading from the fleet of deep-draft fishing schooners. Minor fish retailers located off the pier, including Foley Fish, were compelled to pay a fee when buying at this pier. MF knew that the Italian fleet would be forced to move to the Boston Fish pier, and he did not want to pay the resulting upcharge. He huddled, therefore, with his brain trust to decide if he should join a group of dissident dealers who wanted to sue the New England Fish Exchange on anti-trust grounds. Joseph O'Connell believed that MF and his group had a winnable case.

In 1918, the trial of the "Brain Trust," as it was called by the local newspapers, was heard before Judges Bingham, Aldrich, and Johnson. The issue turned on whether the New England Fish Exchange could expel processors if they bought fish, as Souza did, outside the Exchange. Judge Aldrich probed whether the conduct of the Exchange amounted to regulation or control. The court held that the Exchange was guilty of restraint of trade under the Sherman and Clayton Antitrust Acts. This important ruling allowed M.F. Foley Fish, a non-member, not only to buy fish on the Exchange, but also, on the same favorable terms as the Exchange members paid.

As for the supply side, fish landings were prodigious. The *Boston Globe* market reports for a representative week in September 1906 revealed the landing weights by boats as follows: Priscilla (15,000 lbs.), Yankee (18,000 lbs.), Kernwood (12,000 lbs.), Emily Cooney and William Morse (439,000 lbs.), and 75 smaller boats delivering up to 10,000 pounds each. In sum, a typical week's landings in this period exceeded 1,250,000 pounds of haddock, cod, hake, flounder, and pollock. This hefty supply translated to extremely low prices. Auction prices averaged: haddock: 1 to 2 cents per pound, large cod: 4-5 cents, large hake: 5 cents, small hake: 1-3 cents, and pollock: 2-3 cents. Retail fresh prices for the two biggest sellers: small cod, 4-5 cents per pound, and haddock 4-5 cents. These prices contrasted favorably with sirloin steak, retailing at 25 cents per pound, and chicken at 15 cents per pound.

More costly "specialty" fish such as salmon, halibut, and swordfish would be offered to the "suits." Lacking the tanks, MF decided against offering live lobsters. "Fancy" fish such as mackerel, bluefish, and shad would require an order in advance as these species travelled over the road from Cape Cod, Newport, and Point Judith, Rhode Island. Whole fish were sold as is, with the offer to gut and clean them at no extra cost.

With Frank Souza buying "bullets" (in the fish industry, the fish that met the highest quality standards) the local economy booming, and fish landings at their peak, the M.F. Foley Fish Co. started to take off, with customers often standing in line waiting to be served. Soon, MF outgrew his back-room storefront. He needed more space, or he might lose business in the cold winter months. And so, not wanting to give up his location, MF became the sole lessee of the entire seven-story flat iron building, replacing Railway Express, his landlord. He was now paying rent to Harvard College. As the sole tenant, MF asked for and received permission from Harvard to construct two large windows on both side streets, windows similar to those seen at Boston department stores such as Filene's and Jordan Marsh, thereby creating "window shopping" that gave passersby a full view of Foley's cutting and retail operations. He hoped the views enticed customers. MF was only 31, but was already successfully operating a major retail business in a seven-story building in the heart of Boston.

CHAPTER 16

MOVE TO SUBURBS

MF and Helen were proud to be from Ireland, but did not want to be defined by it. They did not seek close-knit ties with fellow Irish immigrants who settled in the Irish enclaves of South Boston and Dorchester. MF often said, "I did not come here to meet more Irish. I came here to become an American." They were proud of other Irish immigrants for striving against great odds to reach a better life in Boston. MF and Helen felt it was dishonest to pretend to a false humility, considering the company's financial success, nor would they accept what others had designated to be their proper place.

After living in an apartment in the Mission Hills district of Dorchester from 1908 to 1910, the Foleys moved to a house at 77 Lake Street in Brookline. The move was prompted by the imminent arrival of their first child, Helen Foley, born April 6, 1910. It was a two-story home with three bedrooms, and within walking distance of the trolleys that took MF to work. The house was located in a pleasant middle-class neighborhood, which happened to be the same neighborhood that the newly married Rose and Joseph Kennedy would choose for their starter home at 83 Beals Street. The purchase of a home was an uncommon and significant achievement for people of their age, especially first-generation immigrants.

Helen had been exposed to wealth growing up. The Moloney farm was substantial for the time, though smaller than the adjoining estates owned by the aristocratic British landlords. Hannah and Michael Moloney socialized with their neighbors, who invited them to their hunting clubs. Riding with the hounds in brilliant crimson coats, starched white pants, and high-polished black boots provided Helen a glimpse of an appealing lifestyle. She certainly aspired for more than her parents' success; else she would have remained in Tipperary marrying a first-born male who would inherit the family's farm.

The Foley family would subsequently outgrow their home on Lake Street, due to the additions of my father, Francis Foley (FF), born October 1913, my aunt Virginia (Ginny), born 1916, and my Uncle Andrew, born 1921. Mother sought not only a substantially larger home, but also one which would be located in a more prominent section of Brookline. MF was unwilling to purchase a new home until he could afford to fully pay for it in cash. Fortunately for Mother, Foley Fish was making good money, allowing her to commence her search for the "rightful" place for her and her enlarged family.

Mother confined her search to areas near Beacon Street in Brookline Village. There, they would be surrounded by like-minded neighbors who were well-off, not by birth, but self-made, similar to MF. Ethnic diversity was preferred over the closed caste system of Boston's Brahmin population that lived on the Boston end of Beacon Street and dominated the downtown social scene. A first-generation immigrant, especially an Irish Catholic owner of a fish company, would not be comfortable living among the power elite, nor would their exclusionary attitude be acceptable.

Of utmost importance to Helen and MF were the schools. In reach of Brookline were the acclaimed Runkle, Newton Sacred Heart, Winsor, and Dexter Schools. At any of these schools the Foley children could receive an education vastly superior to that of their parents, one that would put them on a more equal footing with Brahmin families competing for acceptance at the best colleges.

Mr. Morse, one of the members of MF's Kitchen Cabinet, had formerly owned a seven-bedroom Victorian (built in 1893) on 56 Windsor Road, in an upscale neighborhood within walking distance of a trolley stop. Mr. Morse had sold his home to Emma Pierce of the well-regarded S.S. Pierce Company, a distinguished food emporium for the wealthy. When Morse learned that she was putting the house on the market, he passed this information on to MF, who bought 56 Windsor for $18,000 cash. Mother's august vision became a reality. With the deed came a standing that announced to the outside world that the Foleys had arrived.

CHAPTER 17

HOUSE OF WINDSOR

In 1921 Mother arrived at 56 Windsor Road, Brookline, her ultimate home. The semicircular portico supported by Grecian columns promised a magnificent interior. Its contents would embody how she wanted to be viewed. MF had done what he had to do at Foley Fish, accumulating enough money to afford this home. At 56 Windsor, his only duty was to allow Mother to decorate the home as she saw best. MF never sought the spotlight, leaving Mother to have center stage all to herself.

Mother's mind was for their home décor to reflect refinement. Furnishings were not to dazzle, nor be falsely grand. Mother contracted with a professional photographer to photograph the rooms. These photos would be used in planning meetings with antique dealers and interior designers. Input would be received from them, but she would make all the final decisions. What was fashionable at the time would be less important than what would be acceptable over time. She didn't want anyone to be whispering that her style was proof that she was not there yet. Nothing could be too obvious. Everything would have to reflect taste, not ostentation.

Upon entering the home, one's attention would be drawn to the prominently visible framed blessing of 56 Windsor by Pope Pius XII. Off to the right beneath the stairs was a slant-ceilinged cloakroom containing a telephone and a dinner gong. The spacious living room would eventually be made more inviting by floor-to-ceiling French windows, embroidered pillows adorning silk brocade sofas, and lacquered inlaid antique tables strategically interspersed amongst decorative chairs, and anchored by richly colored Oriental rugs. Adjacent to this room was a solarium highlighted by tapestries and some museum quality antiques too exquisite to sit on or use. The living room opened dramatically to the dining room. The centerpiece was a mahogany dining table personally selected and transported from England by Mother. It was large enough to seat 16. The crystal chandelier would highlight the stemware, sterling silver, Imari china, and Minton oyster plates (often containing delicately brined oysters shucked minutes before). Mother served the finest, freshest food, always plainly prepared, a contrast to the elegant serveware and the opulent furnishings. Across from the living room was a piano room. A Steinway ebony grand dominated, standing guard over photographs of the Foley children. Piano lessons were mandatory for all four.

On the second floor, there were four bedrooms, two for the Foley girls, Helen and Ginny, and the master for Mother (or Nanny, as her grandchildren called her) and MF. The remaining bedroom could be used for guests. The boys were on the third floor.

The master bedroom, MF's sanctuary, was a good place to shut up alone for reflection. Here, away from the four children, he could unburden himself by studying work problems without interruption, and sleep peacefully, allowing his unconscious to bring answers by the next morning. An embellished crucifix protected each bed. A phial of holy water, imported from Lourdes, offered spiritual renewal. Like his father, MF would say, "Mother is the pious one," disclaiming reliance on the supernatural.

Mother's sanctuary was the cramped den, adjacent to the master bedroom, cozily cluttered with old newspapers such as *The Catholic Pilot, The Boston Transcript* and *The Boston Herald*. After dinner, Nanny would turn on her Philco radio (no gramophones or Victrola), and say the rosary with Cardinal O'Connell and later, Cardinal Cushing. Bits of bric-a-brac, personal treasures, family pictures (mostly of Irish ancestors), keepsakes, and savings account books were stuffed into an armoire, including her jewelry that was stashed in a "food" bag for safekeeping. No second-place trophies could be found here.

The well-hidden back stairs ascended to the third floor which held four bedrooms where the boys Frank and Andrew, and later, the live-in help would reside. For the boys, it was the only place they were allowed to play. It was a stage for spirited exchanges and yielded unending memories for the Foley boys.

The extravagance of 56, in contrast to MF's modest farmhouse must have made it hard for the children to imagine their father's upbringing. The trappings of elegance would have been unimaginable for MF in his youth. His unease with his well-appointed home diminished over time, and he began to evince admiration for what Mother had created.

Where parenting was concerned, MF agreed to a hands-off policy. His concession was not made begrudgingly, as this policy fit comfortably with his personality and nurturement philosophy – he shied away from confrontation.

Despite their differences, or perhaps because of them, Mother and MF were quite a formidable team. MF was fortunate to have a take-charge, competent, devoted, and durable wife. Mother was fortunate to have a successful husband who could underwrite her desired standard of living. MF was the CEO of the Foley Fish Co. and Mother was CEO of 56 Windsor. Both remained uncritical of the other. A reserved MF was not distant, but generally protective of his thoughts and emotions. Each was indispensable to the other's success in their separate spheres. They were quietly confident that not only was the other's sphere of activity in good working order, but also that they had each other's back when either's world did not. They were devoted to each other, and their "yin and yang" created a harmony.

Living room at 56 Windsor, early 1920's

CHAPTER 18

ANOTHER LETTER

A letter from Helen's brother, Bill Moloney, curiously addressed only to MF, arrived asking MF for a job. Neither MF nor Bill knew each other well. They were brothers-in-law, but had only met at the wedding, and then when they brought baby Helen back to Ireland on the Baltic in 1912. This did not inhibit Bill, however, from requesting a job at the M.F. Foley Fish Company.

Born in 1893, Bill was two years younger than MF and nine years younger than his sister Helen, the eldest Moloney. Like MF, Bill was the fourth oldest in his family, and therefore was not in line to inherit the Moloney farm. Yet, the request was a surprise because Bill had just graduated from Rockwell College in Cashel, Tipperary. In fact, he was the first Moloney, or Foley, to ever go to, let alone complete, college. It was thought he would choose a career in finance in a big city like Dublin or Cork. Bill knew, of course, that MF and Foley Fish were doing exceptionally well — ownership of a large, handsome home in a prestigious Boston suburb was proof. Bill was shrewdly reaching out to MF for a job opportunity and a new career in Boston.

In his letter, Bill acknowledged that he had no seafood experience, while deftly implying that the same could be said of MF at his start. He, wisely, made no mention of a management position, prudently stating that he would, like MF, expect to learn the fish business starting at the bottom, with no favors expected, nor a timetable imposed. He offered to pay his own way to Boston.

Bill Moloney was not a Foley. MF was impressed that Bill was willing to join Foley Fish without any guarantees other than the opportunity to prove himself, demonstrating drive and commitment — both of which would be essential requirements. Yet, MF recalled that his own hasty decision to work for his brother Roger did not end well. This request, however, was very different. MF was not seeking to hire Bill. MF was the owner whose approval was sought. Bill was the rookie. Any split later on would be Bill leaving, not MF. Still, there was a nagging question: was bringing Bill Moloney into the Foley family business a wise idea?

MF's decision to hire Frank Souza earlier, his first major hire, had come only after MF had ample time to check out Souza's background and on-the-job performance. No hunches. No family entanglements. The idea of hiring Bill troubled him so much so that he decided to seek counsel from his Kitchen Cabinet. MF's advisors knew that, in time, MF would need to develop an operations manager, as MF and Frank Souza weren't enough to run MF's expanding enterprise. Furthermore, they said, Foley Fish would need a financial expert. Since Bill Moloney majored in finance in college, he could fulfill that need, maybe, at first, not full-time. The Kitchen Cabinet unanimously supported the hiring of Bill, provided that there were no strings attached.

MF met with Mother before making his final decision. She had stayed out of the decision, pledging that she would not interfere in the business relationship between MF and her brother Bill. But she realized that unforeseen events could severely test her concurrence with the hire.

MF hired Bill without the two men taking the time to explore one another's expectations. This omission had doomed MF and Roger's business relationship. MF was making the same mistake.

CHAPTER 19

WORLD WAR I

By 1915, M. F. Foley Fish had grown for nine consecutive years. Boston's annual immigrant growth continued at a brisk 20 percent. The burgeoning population boded well for continued growth. Fish prices remained low largely because the catch rate outpaced the birth rate, enabling supply to continue to exceed demand. Family incomes began to climb as the offspring of prior generations of immigrants had better paying jobs than their parents. Living at home with their parents, the offspring usually pooled their wages, resulting in the average family's income rising significantly in Boston. This expanded family food budgets.

Since Foley Fish had been successful without Bill Moloney, MF saw no need to rush his apprenticeship, which was not to Bill's liking. But in the early going, Bill found MF to be an ideal boss. MF didn't supervise him too closely, letting work experience be Bill's teacher. Bill was put to work in the retail, reporting to Frank Souza. Mistakes were expected and MF was tolerant. Bill sought to accelerate his training program, but he quickly found out that his desire for greater responsibility met with aloofness on MF's part. Bill began to learn about MF's concise method of interaction. MF would first narrow his eyes to telegraph the importance of what he was about to say; then continue, "You are not ready yet," to be followed by an indirect glance and a withdrawal of focus, ending in MF looking away in the distance as a way of conveying that the meeting was over. Despite Bill's overconfidence, bordering on hubris, MF was warming to Bill. They shared more than similar backgrounds. Each was determined to succeed and both had developed a strong work ethic toiling on the farm. MF became increasingly more confident that Bill would work out. But there was no special hurry in sharing his feelings with headstrong Bill.

Bill made a striking appearance. He was handsome, and, like his sister, possessed a compelling sense of self. There was fastidiousness in his appearance that reflected a keen attention to detail. Nothing was out of place. He was tall (over six feet) with jet-black hair parted in the middle, and he gave off an independent air. He wore severe wire-rimmed glasses over the bridge of an aquiline nose and protruding ears, all of which magnified a set of piercing eyes remotely controlled by a hidden on-off switch to brighten his visage with charm when the audience required. What MF initially missed was that this switch controlled a "split personality" that embodied two personas – the pleasing, outgoing side and a darker, plotting side. Overall, he gave off an air of intellectual intensity. MF had concerns that Bill's self-assurance would be off-putting to others. His flinty visage and inflexibility made him intimidating. Like MF, Bill did not tolerate blatherers, nor suffer fools.

Optimism about future success at Foley Fish Co. changed when war broke out in Europe. The assassination of Archduke Ferdinand, heir to the Austro-Hungarian Empire, led to Austria declaring war against Serbia on July 28, 1914. This created a ripple effect, and in eight consecutive days Austria, Germany, Russia, France and Belgium were at war. The United States was conspicuous in its absence. President Woodrow Wilson pledged American neutrality, and kept the United Sates out of the war until 1917. Globally, it was a terrifying time as international trade stopped and European banks cashed in American stocks for gold. In Boston, there was a silent distancing as if the war was unthreatening with little impact to the local populace. Most in Boston and throughout the United States felt that the war would be over quickly.

Although Ireland had a turbulent history, MF himself had never encountered war. He had no frame of reference. It made no sense to him. The war was so foreign to MF that he often misidentified bombers by calling them "bumpers." He had no idea what it was like to live in a city being bombed. And there was no room in his emotional self to delve further. Foley Fish occupied all of him.

By 1915, Germany's submarines had sunk many unarmed American ships, ultimately forcing President Wilson and Congress to end America's neutrality and to declare war on Germany. Needing recruits to fight in the war, Congress discontinued the small volunteer army and replaced it with the Selective Service Act, which required married men up to the age of 31 to enlist. There was an exception, however, for married income-earners whose dependents relied exclusively on their income. Despite being 33 years old and a sole-earner, MF's Kitchen Cabinet recommended that he apply for the dependent exemption. MF applied and was granted a dependency exemption. Support of his dependents in his absence was not assured. There were no rich relatives in the U.S.

The U.S. government began soliciting food purveyors to contract for shipments to be shipped to the troops in Britain and France. MF saw his opportunity to get involved. He hired Tom Fay, who specialized in government food contracts. Fay proved to be an incredible salesman for Foley Fish, winning a disproportionately high percentage of government food contracts for shipments to regional U.S. military bases such as Fort Devens (Massachusetts), and Fort Dix (New Jersey). When other fish dealers, jealous of MF's success, complained that he was overpaying Tom, his response was, "When you get a great salesperson like Tom Fay, it is impossible to pay him too much."

During America's involvement in WWI, food prices had gone up by 84% due to rationing. The cost of living in 1919 was double what it had been in 1914, when the war began. Incomes fell. Worse, a highly contagious influenza epidemic broke out in the U.S. in the fall of 1918, brought on by soldiers returning home from the war. Six hundred and sixty-five thousand Americans died of influenza, more than six times the number of U.S. soldiers who died in combat. Understandably, people became very careful where and how often they shopped. Not being located in the crowded Faneuil Hall helped, but there was no immunity from the economic downturn. Foley Fish's retail sales dropped for the first time since opening in 1906.

On January 2, 1918, M.F. Foley Fish Co. was incorporated in the Commonwealth of Massachusetts. Three hundred shares were issued — two hundred-ninety-eight shares to MF, one share to Helen Foley Sr., and one share to James A. Foley, MF's brother, as he was the only brother left without a prospect of ownership of the family farm. MF was appointed President and Treasurer and Helen as the Clerk. Directors were the three shareholders, and MF's annual salary was set at $24,000. In the same year, the company bought the entire building at Friend and Union Streets from the Adams Trust, held by Harvard College. The purchase necessitated a mortgage loan from the Merchants National Bank of Boston.

Foley's accounting office had been poorly run by a bookkeeper who was clearly under-qualified to manage the increased filings with the State, as well as the new borrowing relationship with the Merchants Bank. MF fired him. In retaliation, the fired bookkeeper threatened to tell the government that MF was underreporting income, which he was not. Instead of paying a ransom, MF sued the bookkeeper for libel. At the end of the non-jury libel case, the judge ruled in favor of MF and said, "I've listened to Mr. Michael Foley during his entire trial. You would say, as I do now, after meeting him, that this man would never cheat me, you or the government."

MF hired Rena V. Oberson as the new head of the accounting department. Ms. Oberson proved indispensable. A stern, imperious lady, Ms. Oberson refused to take orders from anyone but MF. With MF's support, Ms. Oberson ran a tight ship not allowing suppliers or employees to bend payment terms. No lame excuses would be tolerated. She was also a reliable sounding board, recommending to MF that he not put his wife on the payroll as many other private companies had. She believed it would set a bad precedent for other family members who might come to expect the same special treatment.

MF was developing a keen eye for talented people and key personnel.

CHAPTER 20

BUSINESS STRATEGY SHIFT

Retail fish sales grew again after WWI ended. Yet, MF was concerned because the immigrant migration into Boston was slowing, while the exodus of middle-class families to the suburbs was increasing. The commuter customers he had acquired through his "suits" strategy had captured some of the suburban emigres, but not enough to make him confident of sustainably high future retail sales. On top of this, the end of the war brought the company's military wholesale business to a sudden halt. Always looking ahead, MF began planning for a new source of business.

MF knew that he could establish satellite retail Foley Fish outlets in the affluent suburbs, but declined because the added rents, labor, and trucking costs would preclude satisfactory profits. Alternatively, he realized that he could start a wholesale business that could complement his retail business.

Just as MF's home delivery fish program had been inspired by the milkman who walked with him to work every morning from Southie, MF got an idea when he noticed trainloads of meat brought in by Railway Express trains from the Chicago Stockyards to Faneuil Hall's meat purveyors. Why, he asked himself, couldn't Railway Express haul his products to Chicago? Couldn't he send Foley fish to landlocked cities in the Midwest?

The train system was the linchpin of MF's new wholesale program. Hartford, CT, Allentown, PA, and Philadelphia, PA, as well as Chicago, had regular freight service, and shipping goods from Boston was becoming routine. The trains operated by The Railway Express Agency, he realized, could transport fresh fish overnight to cities in New England and the Middle Atlantic States and, ultimately, the Midwest. MF would be going against his risk-averse conservatism with this new venture, but he would be expanding while his competitors stood still. His entrepreneurial instincts were just as strong as when he made the decision to leave the farm for America. Without a doubt, his decision to open new markets beyond Boston would become a major factor in the future success of the M.F. Foley Fish Co. If he could make it happen.

Wholesaling was a totally different ballgame than retail. Success at retail did not guarantee success in wholesale, especially since few knew of Foley Fish's quality reputation outside Boston. Due diligence was required. MF's questions were numerous and myriad. How reliable were Railway Express trains? Would Foley Fish sell to regional wholesalers who would represent Foley Fish, or would Foley Fish compete against these wholesalers by going direct to their customers? Who would be the Foley sales personnel? What calling territories and prospects would be targeted? What credit terms would Foley require?

MF did not immediately have answers, but he quickly concluded that his first priority must be hiring a wholesale manager — he couldn't run both retail and wholesale operations. No other Boston fish purveyor was operating a wholesale business beyond Boston. To bring on an experienced wholesale person, MF might have to hire a "beef" guy, who undoubtedly knew very little about fish. The other alternative was to promote from within Foley's. As he had demonstrated with the hiring of Frank Souza, MF was not afraid to put an untested guy into a leadership position.

Tom Fay was nearing retirement. He had done well with the military contracts, but this proposed business start-up would require an energy level that he didn't possess. Bill Moloney was another possibility. Although he'd never had to meet a payroll deadline, and had never managed a production group, he'd earned MF's respect for his hard work and his intelligence. He possessed the savvy and toughness required in this new management position. Bill was a quick study, ambitious, and unafraid of a new venture, and these qualities convinced MF to make him Foley's first boss of wholesale. He would report directly to MF.

MF and Bill quickly learned that processing fish for wholesale would be more difficult than first thought, and necessitate a major shift. A new conveyor system would be needed to process the large orders expected from wholesalers. No such assembly line currently existed. More cutters would be needed. Until then, a "jury-rigged" system would be established that would have each cutter cutting fish into tubs, then hand-carrying to a packer's table — a cumbersome and inefficient system.

Neither MF nor Bill could draw on their personal farm experiences to make sense of this production challenge. Both had processed barley with hand-held scythes and bundled it by hand into a shelf for storage in the barn. Mechanical threshers and shearers weren't in use until after they had emigrated. In short, they knew nothing about mass production.

The challenges would be many. MF lessened the pressure on Bill by telling him that he expected months to pass before seeing any profits. What concerned MF the most was the threat to quality. His only fear was not a slow start for wholesale, but a compromise in quality in the name of efficiency. That could be doubly damaging. He knew that it might jeopardize his fledgling wholesale operation by devaluing Foley's reputation in their new markets, but also adversely impact their retail operations at home in Boston, which was, still, the "bank" underwriting and subsidizing this new venture.

The stakes were high.

CHAPTER 21

WHOLESALE DECISION

Should Foley Fish sell directly to a regional wholesale operation? "Of course you should, they will be against you, otherwise," many told MF. "They are the major players, not you. They own the accounts; their customers probably have been personal friends for years." Why then would MF consider selling directly to the customers of such a wholesaler? He did not know of a single meat or poultry purveyor who had chosen this direct method, and selling to an experienced regional firm was much easier, of course: the one shipment, one phone call, one bill of lading, and one collection. Conversely, if Foley Fish, bypassed the regional wholesaler and sold directly to restaurants, the company would be required to make multiple shipments, multiple phone calls, multiple bills of lading, and multiple collections from smaller enterprises. These small restaurants would not be as financially stable and reliable as a big wholesaler. Finally, Foley Fish would have to hire more salesmen to prospect and manage new accounts.

MF sought Bill Moloney's advice. Bill would need a new salesforce to prospect in the targeted territories. Shipping to one large account would avoid the prohibitive shipping costs of "small" orders to the single restaurants. Doing business with both large and small customers would be complicated by one critical deficiency — Foley Fish had no production line.

Similarly, Miss Oberson, operating a one-person accounting department, strongly preferred "one receivable, one payer, over many." She noted that the physical proximity of a wholesaler to customers would make it easier to assess their credit worthiness than it would be for her to do it long distance.

Like Bill, MF knew it would take time and money to hire new cutters, new production handlers, and new sales personnel. He was also concerned that this new group be fully trained in the proper handling of Foley Fish, otherwise, the wholesale concept would not work.

As owner, MF had another objective that his managers overlooked — profitability. Unlike the "cutter/processing mark-up" at retail, MF foresaw that Foley Fish could earn and thereby justify another markup, a "distributor's mark-up" which the wholesaler would charge for the same work, namely, order processing, shipment tracking, and delivery. Why shouldn't Foley Fish charge this distributor mark-up which, when added to Foley's processing mark-up, would make Foley Fish more money than they were making with their retail operations.

MF made the landmark decision. M. F. Foley Fish Co. would become the first food purveyor to bypass regional wholesalers by selling directly to customers. It might seem a decision bordering on heresy, and not consonant with the nature of shy, non-confrontational MF. But it demonstrated that he was a buck-snuffing entrepreneur who would not sidestep a battle if he thought it was worth winning and winnable.

Bill needed salesmen well-schooled in the workings of the fish industry. Not mere order takers because, initially, there would be no orders to take. Foley salesmen would have to find and educate prospects on the different quality fish: the highest for fish caught on the last day of the usual four-day trip, the lowest, the first day. They would need to describe Frank Souza's on-site hand picking the top of the catch while refusing the bottom of the catch, which might be sold to Allentown's Wholesale in Boston. Comparative tests between Foley's fish and, say, Allentown Wholesale fish would need to be conducted. Foley's contention of unequalled and consistent high quality not necessitating returns would take a while. Customer dissatisfaction with Allentown Wholesaler fish might lead to some trying Foley fish, but that could take too long.

Pressure was on Souza as Foley's head buyer. The quality bar would have to be raised even higher than it was. Shelf life of fish defined in hours for Foley's retail customers would be defined in days for Foley's restaurant accounts because of the time needed for transportation. Bill Moloney and

Frank Souza would have to prove that Foley fish on its third day at the restaurant was better than the wholesaler's fish on its first day at that same restaurant. Trust had to be built, confidence earned. Proof of the pudding was the fish. Foley's couldn't match the wholesalers' service advantages afforded by their close proximity to the customers, but the wholesalers couldn't match the consistent quality of Foley's product.

While Bill had a gem of a salesman in Tom Fay, he knew he needed to hire another top salesman. Bill knew of a charismatic young man who could, in time be perfectly suited for the sales job — Michael Moloney, his younger brother. Michael was the youngest of the Moloney siblings. In 1922, he was 18 years old, 11 years younger than his brother Bill. The elder Moloney admired Britain. Michael did not. Michael was impressed with the 1918 Irish revolution against Britain. He joined the Irish rebels participating in the post-1918 Civil War in Ireland. Mike left Ireland as a fugitive with a price on his head. Family lore had Michael, on the run from British troops, landing in the U.S. with a revolver in his bag. The garrulous Michael was hired as a Foley Fish salesman with the expectation that he'd never have to use his gun to win over a prospect.

MF and Bill planned to offer seasonal fish, exclusively from Cape Cod that would appeal to high-end resorts and upscale restaurants. Seasonal fish were migrating fish whose movements could be predicted based on seasonal water temperatures. Arriving in early spring would be salmon; in the late spring, mackerel; in summer the striped bass; while winter flounder would come inshore as Cape Cod waters began to cool in late fall and early winter. No other port could produce more varieties of fish than Boston. Shellfish from Cape Cod could become signature items on menus. Railroad connections between Cape Cod and Boston would enable overnight delivery to Foley Fish in Boston. Inland competing wholesalers were too far away from the resource to match Foley's availability, reliability and just-caught or harvested freshness.

Souza initiated buying relationships with shell-fishermen, and "hook and line" fishermen in Cape Cod, located in the ports of Chatham, Wellfleet, Yarmouth, and Provincetown. He soon learned that both caught more fish than local retail markets could sell. His timing was good. The advent of tourism and commercial development on Cape Cod, which would later threaten the Cape's ecology, had not occurred.

The advantages of a growing "offshore" fishery, combined with the nascent "inshore" connections could, MF optimistically concluded, translate into a sourcing advantage offsetting the disadvantages of shipping distances and non-daily deliveries. More fish purchased per order would also reduce the delivery cost on a per pound basis. All in all, the positives of selling direct outweighed the negatives. But now, how was MF going to pull it off? No one else thought he could or should.

CHAPTER 22

NEW PRODUCTION ASSEMBLY LINE

The challenge of orchestrating the Foley Fish wholesale production line was and is not unlike the challenges faced by an orchestra conductor: both involve the timely coordination of many moveable parts. There is an interdependence inherent to a fish-cutting assembly line that necessitates fish be processed in a coordinated, logical flow, moving constantly in an uninterrupted, dependable pace. The pace and flow are determined by the deft decisions of the production manager. Henry Ford had done it for cars in 1913, and MF would accomplish it for fish in 1919.

MF appointed Bill manager of the yet-to-be conceived assembly line – a new train on new rails with a high risk of derailing before it began. Until the bugs were worked out, Foley's train would sometimes be late due to the unanticipated, unforeseeable interruptions and delays that are inherent to the fish business.

Bill wisely started backwards, first examining the requirements of the shipping department, then those of the fish-packing department, then the cutters' needs, and then those of the line personnel. Next was Souza. His orders had to be sorted and aggregated by species and sizes. Finally, the path led back to the sales staff that took orders — the starting point. MF and Bill walked again and again through the steps, following the road fish should travel. It was full of left turns, right turns, exits, and lots of "u turns," until they got it right.

A hypothetical workday could require the following: 20 orders for shipment that evening to 20 restaurants in Allentown, Pennsylvania, due the next business day. Bill would sift through all 20 orders to distill a production sheet as follows: One hundred pounds of cod fillets equivalent to 250 pounds of "whole" cod, 200 pounds of haddock fillets, which converts to 500 pounds of "whole" haddock; 500 pounds of salmon fillets, equal to 1,000 pounds of whole salmon.

One Foley cutter should be able to cut all 1,750 pounds of whole fish in the time allotted, provided all three white fish were in the plant ready to be cut. This was not a given as the fickle ocean and erratic Boston weather often did not cooperate. Bill would have to interrupt the scheduled cutting sequence to work in any "late arriving" fish.

Lacking a conveyor belt, the fillets would have to be carried to the packing station, further slowing down the production. The packers would then pack the fillets into ten-pound tins, weigh each tin, label the species, and finally tally the "exact" weight, if less than or above the standard ten pounds. The completed fillet tins would be stacked by species in a separate holding bin. Armed with a customer "pick list," the Foley shippers would then fill each customer's order in a well-iced wooden barrel. MF bought his barrels from a cooperage started by Patrick Joseph Kennedy, grandfather of Joseph Kennedy Sr. and great grandfather of JFK. The shipper would mark the sales slip with the final weights for the bill of lading. It was a cumbersome process that would be made more complicated by added orders of shellfish, swordfish, and tuna, and "specialty" species. Should the shellfish delivery be delayed past the first pick-up time specified by the American Express trucking department, Foley Fish would have to notify the customers of this shortage – news that would make neither the customer, nor Bill Moloney, nor MF happy.

Confronted with these onerous sales and production challenges, MF could have understandably scraped the entire nascent wholesale operation, but he didn't. He had learned on the farm that nothing is easy. MF clung to the idea that Foley's would win with quality fish, and the conviction that once a prospect tried Foley's, he would want another shipment. But MF knew that the Foley retail operation would have to carry its sister wholesale operation longer than he had initially anticipated. Unfortunately, retail sales were slowing due, largely because the diphtheria outbreaks after WWI caused people to stay indoors.

In an effort to boost retail sales, MF moved Foley's retail operation to the front of his recently acquired building. He had concluded that his location was under-promoted, and that he needed heightened visibility and a more commanding presence in Boston. He thought improving his signage would help. He contracted for an elaborate masthead reading: Foley's-Boston's "Real" Fish House. He hoped that the adjective would convey integrity and reliability to customers.

This new porcelain sign would cover the entire front of this architecturally notable flat iron building. It stood just above the enlarged "show" windows, which also aided in capturing the attention of passersby. Later, MF would add a lighted marquis that highlighted recipes and "fish in season" specials.

MF's Kitchen Cabinet continued to be helpful. Mr. Morse, who had years of experience with assembly lines at his Boston leather plants, offered to set up a meeting with the leading manufacturer of customized production lines.

Theodore Roosevelt had just instituted rigid federal food inspection programs for meat plants (the fish industry was and would continue to stay unregulated for many years) following the outcry stemming from the 1906 novel, *The Jungle*. Upton Sinclair's exposé graphically depicts the deplorable working conditions in Chicago meat-packing district. Joseph O'Connell knew that these regulations would be inevitably extended to the fish industry, so he gave MF a copy of the regulations, despite knowing that the wretched practices cited by Sinclair were unthinkable at Foley Fish. MF adopted every recommendation possible to reinforce Foley Fish's commitment to the highest sanitary standards in the fish industry.

CHAPTER 23

BILL MOLONEY'S NEW CHALLENGES

Flatiron building, corner of Friend and Union Streets

Bill Moloney chafed at being in the shadow of retail, but loved the excitement of designing the new wholesale operation. He knew that wholesale was a burdensome stepchild, but he saw an opportunity to stand out if he could overcome its start-up difficulties. Accustomed to success, Bill did not want to be viewed as underperforming. But he struggled with employee management. He was firm and inflexible. His smile could abruptly turn into a menacing look, and he was not a person to cross. His disapproval was once described as being, "like a knife cutting across your skin."

He was smart enough to know that he couldn't be dictatorial as he was in unchartered waters. He had to suppress his ego and overconfidence. To his credit, Bill demoted himself to become a production guy on the floor, not an easy move for a "lettered" man. He and two other blue-collar production guys became equals on the Foley Fish wholesale production team. The team was comprised of Charlie Richardson, Davy Friedman, and Bill. Together, they would figure things out, just like he and his brothers had done on the Moloney farm. As might be expected from their trial-and-error approach, things were initially messy and inefficient. But in time they adopted good ideas, such as cross-training, wherein each person could alternate between the roles of cutter, packer, and shipper. A cutter could, after cutting fish, fill in as the second shipper. As the shipper swapped jobs with the packer, they became more sensitive and respectful of each other's jobs. For example, the shipper helped by feeding fish to the cutter at the beginning of each workday, and other times when he was free. Fortunately, sales orders were moderate to start with, thereby allowing time to devise solutions to chronic problems. One such solution was setting the customer ordering protocol, which called for orders to be submitted one day ahead of shipment. This enabled Frank Souza to buy-to-order, rather than guessing what would be needed. Another remedy was to "out of stock" situations. When they occurred, sales personnel suggested product substitutions such as hake for haddock or pollock for cod. From customer complaints, they learned that both cutter and packer should cull out "borderline" fish. Earlier, they might have said, "It'll get by" or "It looked good when it left Foley's." There was an imperative that the fish be of such high quality that they wouldn't be compromised by any of the intermediate steps between Foley's plant and the restaurant.

These three men lived and breathed the work challenges. Bill's personality adjustments worked well, and his two colleagues were not afraid to speak up. They enjoyed the collaboration. It was a good lesson for Bill in his first year as wholesale manager.

Bill could focus on production issues because he could rely on his brother Mike to handle sales. Mike Moloney was a born salesman. From birth he was personable, polite, and loved people (except the British). He had a genuine interest in each person's life. He would learn, and more importantly, never forget, the customer's children's birthdays, anniversaries, the school grades and sports played by children, all of which helped him to neutralize the wholesaler's customer familiarity. And he was never hesitant to accentuate the brogue when speaking to a Callahan or Murphy. While he had blarney coursing through his veins, he was a very smart salesperson. Sensing a resistance to the freight charge, Mike would meet the objection by pointing out that after 100 pounds, there was no freight charge. If a customer called who was ailing, he'd send him cod liver oil, an Irish remedy for all that ailed you. Prudently, he would never badmouth local distributors who remained important to the customer for non-fish products. Mike had focus; he specialized full time in one product: fish. He always used a positive approach. "Foley's job is to put more customers in your restaurants," he repeated. Once he found out a restaurant's best seller — say meat loaf — he would say "Foley Fish will do honor to your meat loaf." He conveyed the notion that he had a personal stake in the restaurant's success. He was also smart enough not to make a dumb inaccurate promise, such as: "I'll personally make sure you get our best fish." This promise might lead to the idea that Foley Fish had several quality levels, contradicting the company's assertion that it had only one grade of fish — the best.

Mike was given calling responsibility in Connecticut, Eastern Pennsylvania, and western Massachusetts, targeting schools, hospitals, and well-established Country Clubs like Saucon Valley in Bethlehem, Pennsylvania. Cafeterias, luncheonettes, and tea rooms thrived serving simple, home-style cooking. Horn & Hardart, Bickford's, and Schrafft's did not have fish on their menus, so cafeterias were not initially targeted by Foley Fish.

Furthering the wholesale effort, Bill Moloney, when he could, would call on the prestigious country clubs in Boston. Bill became friends with Francis Ouimet, the teenage caddie who astounded the golfing world by winning the US Open at The Country Club. Ouimet introduced Bill to the club's buyer. Bill's status as the number two man at Foley's gained him access to colleges (Harvard, Smith, Holy Cross, and Boston College) especially the latter two, considering his Irish Catholic heritage.

During this time, MF and his family would stay at resorts such as Woodstock Inn (VT), Greenbrier and Pinehurst in the South, the Vinoy Park Hotel (Delray Beach, FL) and the Breakers (Palm Beach, FL), which eventually led to creating accounts with all of them. MF, while traveling in 1920 with his family on the Cunard "Winefredia," for a two-month trip to Ireland, befriended its skipper, Captain Doyle, and often dined at his table. This relationship led to years of business from Cunard. Not bad for a kid who a few years earlier rode in steerage from Ireland on the Bothnia.

CHAPTER 24

ROARING 20S

MF quietly observed the roaring twenties. While others indulged in frivolous living acting as if they had achieved what MF had accomplished, he stayed clear-eyed. MF couldn't forget that you could not take daily meals for granted. He maintained the same lengthy work schedule that he had begun when starting work at the R. J. Foley Fish Company. Six a.m. Monday through Saturday, his busiest retail day, closing at eleven p.m. when his crew would begin their "weekend" by walking to nearby Scollay Square to drink up their week's wages. Prudently, MF would mail a portion of their week's wages to their home to ensure that their families could eat.

MF did not regard himself or his work as exceptional. Many other immigrants had succeeded. There was no special reason for jubilation or irresponsible living. He was well-off, but he did not assume that he had it made. His father had taught him to be distrustful of those preaching that the good times would remain permanently.

Some envious observers, noticing MF's success, could not believe that he could make that much money solely from his fish business. Others questioned how the Foleys could afford a new house, a summer vacation in fashionable Nahant, and trips to Ireland. Ever envious, they spread a rumor that MF was a bootlegger. The Volstead Act of 1919 prohibited the sale, transport, delivery and possession of liquor. The rumor mongers alleged that MF was trafficking whiskey with the fish he bought from Nova Scotia.

MF was not a bootlegger. However, he was not ready to forego Irish Whiskey. He found a bootlegger who would deliver monthly to 56 Windsor in a customized, window-blackened hatchback coupe that could handle barrels of whiskey. The bootlegger would siphon off the whiskey into gallon cans and carry them up the back staircase to MF's third-floor attic. When questioned years later, MF admitted that he was guilty of possession of liquor, but was not a bootlegger. "I didn't need extra money," he said, but if I did, I would never dishonor my family's name."

The abundant supply of fish became even more plentiful after World War I when steam engines were supplanted by diesel engines in the fishing fleet. This technological advancement expanded the reachable sphere of the Atlantic Ocean without adding fishing days to a trip. The first trawlers introduced in 1906 had grown to over 300 vessels by 1930, allowing fishermen to catch and sell more fish. Consequently, local fish prices remained at pre-1906 levels, substantially lower than alternative meat prices.

By 1920 Irish immigrants had economically advanced. Thirty-five percent were now in white collar positions. The Irish middle class had emerged, and many of them moved to the suburbs of West Roxbury, Jamaica Plain, and Roslindale. By then, MF's "suits" strategy had prospered as more "suits" were moving from Boston to its suburbs. Whether through positive word of mouth, new retail Foley signage, the absence of supermarkets, or Mother's Novenas, Foley Fish's share of this enlarged market grew.

A new "sacrifice" generation from southern and eastern Europe had now emigrated to Boston. Over 40,000 immigrants from Eastern Europe arrived – mostly Jews, MF's future neighbors in Brookline. The Irish worked with their hands, the Jews with their heads. The Jewish rate of upward mobility was double that of other ethnic and religious groups at this time. They represented the last major wave of immigrants to Boston after federal anti-immigrant laws limited the number of immigrants coming into the US. In the first decade of the twentieth century, 339,000 Irish emigrated to the U.S., whereas by the late 1920s, Irish immigrants had not used up their annual national quota of 28,567 immigrants. MF could not expect Foley's retail operations to experience new growth from then on, except by increasing market share.

During the better part of the twenties, the stock market roared ahead. From 1921 to 1924 the Dow Jones Industrial Average (DJIA) doubled from 92 to over 200 signaling a historic bull market which lasted to late 1929. Many people, trying to get rich quickly, carelessly bought stock on margin. The nine-year stock market run that saw the DJIA increase tenfold came to an abrupt end on "Black Tuesday," October 24, 1929. Stock prices plummeted without warning, losing over $30 billion in two days. Panic set in. Some banks collapsed under the weight of uncollectible margin loans, and because of a run on deposits by traumatized depositors. Gross National Product fell 30% and consumer spending declined 19% from 1929-1933. Business bankruptcies mushroomed. Unemployment rose quickly to over ten percent, eventually peaking at 25 percent by 1933.

MF's father Dan had taught him to be always prepared for the worst, but this stock market crash and ensuing Depression were worse than any imaginable worst scenario. The market collapse was a shock. It was incomprehensible to MF. He never understood the securities world of puts and calls, options, going long, going short, so he avoided all investing except for his shares of the M.F. Foley Fish Co. that he privately held. He had decided to trust only himself and the fish business he knew. Previously, MF had secured strong financial backing from the Hibernia Bank, but he now went to the larger New England Merchants Bank and said to Allan Sturgis, "I want to know where I stand. And I don't care what you say, I need proof." Mr. Sturgis responded with a large standby line of credit proving that the Depression bankers loaned to dependable, successful businessmen, no matter that they came off the boat.

The oral history of Irish Potato Famine of 1845-49 was instructive to those who suffered during the Depression. MF's family had experienced a similar despair when his paternal grandparents went homeless after being evicted from their foreclosed farm. But that crushing disappointment was two generations ago. Now, every day MF saw the humiliated newly poor, their heads bent, standing in breadlines, hat in hand begging for food. Former breadwinners came to Foley Fish looking for any low-paying menial job. Appliances, jewelry, furniture were peddled. Wives were forced to seek employment when there were no other viable options. Their dignity was taken. MF loaned to many friends, even knowing repayments were unlikely. These were sights that he thought he had left behind.

The Depression not only affected the wealthy, it also impoverished many of the middle class who slid backwards from white collar to blue collar jobs, from office worker to street cleaner. From July 1931 to December 1932, unemployment in Boston was 29.72%. Boston-based textile companies were either closing or moving to the South. The once prominent leather industry began to fade from existence. These were ominous signs for Foley Fish, which lost more than 25% of its retail customer base. Uncertainty spread. Employees feared receiving pink slips. Newspapers shouted negatives. Too many people began to live on almost nothing. Could Foley's ride out these dark times? MF believed he could because people needed to eat – especially affordable seafood meals. The already bargain retail fish prices could go lower as competitors lost business. Many competitors would go out of business. MF knew that he was fortunate to have started Foley Fish 23 years earlier. He had built up a solid book of business. The company had no debt, other than the standby line of credit. Like others, MF did not know how long the Depression would last, but remained confident that Foley Fish would still be standing when it was over.

Foley's wholesale business was more vulnerable. There were only 48,000 taxpayers in the U.S. out of 132 million who now earned more than $2,500 per year. The Depression would lower these numbers. There would be less excess income available for the more affluent to spend on vacation at resorts and/or luxury liners. MF hoped that the retail operations could continue to subsidize the wholesale operation. He plowed back profits each year into the company, which could be tapped if necessary.

While he knew that the good times of the Roaring Twenties were not endless, MF was less certain about when the Depression would end. The declining purchasing power of Americans could go on for a long time. MF agreed with his Kitchen Cabinet that the economy was not self-correcting. He knew it was folly to expect that business would turn around quickly. President Hoover's corrective strategy of higher taxes and less government spending proved him to be "thick as stone." Ireland had not rebounded from the Potato Famine and the British government that espoused the same economic corrections as Hoover.

People were searching anew for "somewhere over the rainbow where troubles melt like lemon drops." Dreaming such dreams wasn't MF's way. MF knew that the qualities that this Depression's resolution required were the "courage" of the Cowardly Lion, the "heart" of the Tin Man, and the "brain" of the Scarecrow.

CHAPTER 25

THE HUNGRY 1930S

The failure of the American economic system seemed indisputable after the market crash in 1929. The "free enterprise" system became a dead concept. Some people no longer felt that they were or should be the agents of their own destinies. A safety net was needed. How wide reaching a net was the issue of the times.

"Laissez-faire" doctrines opposing government interference in economic affairs beyond the minimum necessary fell out of favor. FDR determined that his government had to assume final responsibility for the well-being of individuals. At the outset MF, unsurprisingly, given his family's experience with the oppressive British government in Ireland, was mistrustful. A "do-nothing" government was preferred to the "do-no-good" government MF had seen firsthand with the corrupt Mayor Curley acting as a Santa Claus in Boston. Now, President Roosevelt was replacing him as the new Santa Claus. Excepting the Volstead Act of 1933 repeal of prohibition, MF did not agree with most of the New Deal legislation relating to minimum wage, Social Security, and collective bargaining for unions. MF thought FDR's priority ought to be focused on "pre-retirement" earnings. He did applaud Roosevelt's Work Progress Program that allowed the unemployed to learn a trade and earn a living constructing dams, bridges, and roads. In 1935, the Wagner Act entitling labor unions to be organized was enacted. MF felt the government had overreached. He was not about to abdicate his management responsibilities to any third party.

MF grew up under father Dan's paternalistic management on the farm. Dan had unchallenged authority. The boys never questioned his rules. His system worked. MF copied Dan's paternalistic approach treating each Foley Fish employee as a member of the corporate family. There had been no labor issues, no grievances cited to justify the need for a union. MF ran his company differently. There was no child labor, no unsanitary work conditions, no layoffs, no wage disputes, or cheap expendable labor exploited. MF paid above-average wages. The profits of Foley Fish determined wages, not union demands. The Foley workers trusted MF to run a strong company that would give them job security. The formation of a union that told MF what to pay his men, what hours they would work, what he could or couldn't do, was unacceptable. His workers made no demands for a union.

The Kitchen Cabinet forewarned MF of the inevitability of unions. MF's early exposure to unions, however, was unfavorable. The four-week Fishermen's Strike of 1917 had been disruptive. The Boston Policemen's strike in 1919 when union gangs of thugs took over the city and broke windows at Foley's did nothing to change his opinion. Any discussion of a union at M.F. Foley Fish was answered with a "rhetorical" question by MF, "What would happen if the union representing fish processors settled for a lower wage level than existed already at Foley Fish?"

MF focused his undivided attention on strengthening his retail and wholesale fish operations. A deep, long lasting, economic slump was projected for at least ten years. Consumers at restaurants and at retail fish stores would be consuming less, maybe much less. MF did not need a new script, but he could not stand still. Running in place was not an acceptable alternative. He could not wait for a miraculous recovery orchestrated by FDR.

During this period, MF had withdrawn from the retail setting, spending more time with Bill Moloney in wholesale. He had confidence in the very knowledgeable, witty, and affable Frank Milley running the retail operation. Frank's quick wit was evidenced when updating MF on any customer's death. When MF asked the deceased's age, Frank responded, "Your age." But in the mid-1930s MF became more visible again on the retail floor. He reached out personally to each customer conveying that he knew their heartache and their sense of despair because he grew up on a subsistence family farm in Ireland, and that Foley Fish, his company and employees, were committed to making fish even more affordable for their families. MF established fish-of-the-week specials on his outdoor marquee sign, highlighting new, low-priced, high-quality underutilized species, such as tautaug fillets at 15 cents per pound and whole butterfish at 10 cents a pound. He promoted in-store specials where anyone who bought two pounds of fish would receive ten free clams. Later, MF would advertise specials in three major dailies: *Boston Evening Transcript*, *Boston Herald* and *Boston Globe*.

MF was also more proactive in his wholesale business. He wanted Bill and Mike Moloney to better understand their customer/prospect base so they could become more effective salesmen. He hired Charles R. Flanders, former chef at Murray's Roman Gardens (NYC), Carlton Terrace (Cleveland), Clark's Hotel (Boston), and the Eitel Restaurants (Chicago). Charles began writing a book of easy-to-read culinary essays covering 33 East Coast species. Each species description included a brief history of how caught, where caught, and in what season of the year on one page and recipes on the facing page. Flanders's first pamphlet was copyrighted by the M.F. Foley Co. in 1930.

At MF's request, Flanders also compiled a pamphlet describing seafood's nutritional values as reflected in the research of the times. These write-ups were intended to help restaurants plan menus, and allow their wait staff to become more knowledgeable and, in turn, more helpful to their customers. In 1936, Flanders produced a more elegant and informational version of his earlier efforts. Foley Fish also provided "daily explanation cards" for each dining table, plus highlight strips to emphasize specials. The new book's appendix included a seasonal schedule of all the species, health information, quantities needed to be ordered for 50 servings, a shellfish count chart, and scallop and lobster sizing. What would be called "The Foley Blue Book" became an instant hit. The Blue Book was a great door opener, and Foley's salesmen gave a complimentary copy to the restaurants they visited. The book was years ahead of its time. Rave reviews circulated establishing instant credibility for Foley's, not only as a fish processor, but as a worthy consultant.

Foley price bulletin, week of June 8-13, 1936

Pamphlets by Charles Flanders for M.F. Foley Company, 1930

CHAPTER 26

NEAR DEATH

It was 1932. MF's life was in jeopardy. He was close to dying. His appendix had ruptured causing acute peritonitis, which was not then treatable because sulfur drugs and penicillin were not yet available. The doctors told the family that there was little that could be done medically. It was up to the Lord. His doctor at the Faulkner Hospital gave him a one-in-five chance of recovery. At the height of the crisis, his doctor summoned the family to MF's bedside fearing that he would not make it through the night. A priest from St. Aidan's Church administered the sacrament of Extreme Unction and the last rites to the extremely frail MF.

Bill Moloney approached Mother (his sister Ellie, as she was called in Ireland) and "reassured" her that she should not worry about the survival of the Foley Fish Co. She could transfer ownership to him and he would take over the running of the company. Bill's helping hand was actually a hand on a dagger. Like a fox waiting to spring on his prey, Bill was deviously trying to hijack the company from the "dying" MF. Mother saw her brother Bill's attempted coup as a thinly veiled blackmailing threat that he might leave the company should she refuse to sell MF's controlling interest to him. A stunned, contemptuous Mother adamantly refused.

Two days later, MF miraculously recovered. The doctor said, "God, MF, and me had carried the day." Foley family lore at its most hyperbolic asserted that MF's amazing recovery was prompted by Bill's attempted usurpation. MF, however, showed a blind spot for Bill Moloney's dark side. He had no suspicion of Bill's dark motives. He did not see that Bill's feigned friendship camouflaged unbounded ambition and vanity. MF had over-trusted him, but his deceitfulness was well hidden, unseen behind his charm.

During MF's various absences and vacations, he'd left Bill in charge without incident. What MF missed was Bill's considerable will to control, which drove him to his total ownership maneuver. What Bill missed was that his indomitable will to control had created a resistance in his own sister.

MF was predisposed to sidestep conflict, perhaps instructed by the Irish maxim, "No sense lifting a scalding pan, wait and let the water cool." MF was not vindictive, and did not fire Bill. MF's oddly calm and controlled response in this charged moment was less an act of kindness, however, than one of pragmatism. In MF's eyes, Bill had learned that there would never be a Bill Moloney Fish Co. replacing the M.F. Foley Fish Co. He did not wish to penalize Foley Fish by firing an overreaching manager who otherwise had done a terrific job.

Mother played a key role in this family drama. She was a stabilizing force; she and her husband were akin to a ball-and-socket joint that righted the Foley's in a time of crisis. She proved her mettle.

The Foley Blue Book, 1936

CHAPTER 27

UPBRINGING

MF and Mother lived separate lives. MF was totally consumed with the running of Foley Fish. The parenting of their four children, Helen (b.1910), Frank (b. 1913), Virginia (b.1916), and Andy (b.1922) fell to Mother. Her indisputable authority (she never had to say "because I said so") as the matriarch of 56 Windsor derived not only from their marriage pact, but more so from her dominant personality, which was traceable to her autocratic father (the "Boss"), and her corn-pipe smoking, "frontier" mother, Hannah. She commanded attention by her habit of making lightning determinations of right or wrong, black or white, which resisted all explanation. Mother designed, managed, and regulated her children's' lives. Not infrequently, but always out of public view, she displayed a short temper in the face of an unsanctioned act by one of her children. When Mother needed help, MF would pay for experts. Twenty-five-year-old Catherine from Ireland was hired as a live-in cook, while seventeen-year old Bridget from Northern Ireland became the housekeeper. Catherine and Bridget freed Mother up to career-plan her children's lives.

She carefully determined such matters as the acceptability and preferability of friends, play dates, clothing, and schools. Mother insisted on the finest schooling, which led to the two boys attending Runkle School in Brookline, a private elementary school, and the girls attending Sacred Heart Academy. Mother did not coax, rather she compelled, with an eye to success. Mediocrity was unacceptable. Achievement was a matter of habit formation attained by repeated efforts. Failure, or mediocre performance, meant that her children were not trying hard enough. Sons

Francis and Andrew were expected to attend a top college, marry the correct wife, a well-bred, college-educated, Catholic lady, and succeed in their chosen vocations. Daughters Helen and Virginia were expected to attend college, have coming-out parties, wear proper wardrobes, and marry successful Catholic men. The common denominator for all children was that each would carry themselves with dignity that reflected well on the Foley name.

Socially, Mother was the gatekeeper, which was a bit tricky as MF was not "clubbable," never having joined a social organization in Boston. They entertained, of course, inviting certain neighbors and business friends (Bill Moloney and his wife, however, ceased to be invited to 56 Windsor after MF's health scare). Compensating for MF's social reticence, Mother was a superb hostess — she came, of course, from a more socially aware family. She possessed an impressive bearing, one, perhaps, with which she was born. It sent a clear message of having arrived in polite society. An accomplished conversationalist, she took a strong interest in others' stories and lives. Years later, a friend, Diarmuid O'Connell, would recall Helen Foley as "a regal lady, the epitome of grace, lovable and interested in me." By contrast, MF had a glazed and distant demeanor that kept people at a distance. At home, he needed an undisturbed kind of existence. Their small circle of trusted friends included Brendan O'Reardon, the Irish Consul; Captain Doyle of the Cunard lines; William Flanagan, a prominent haberdasher; and Joseph O'Connell of the Kitchen Cabinet, with whom MF felt comfortable.

Sundays were reserved for morning Mass at St. Aidan's Church in the Coolidge Corner area of Brookline, and for Mother's lighting of blue votive candles (for every child and relative back in Ireland, a ceremony that could last as long as Mass). Church was followed by the family dinner, the only meal to include all the children, who on all other days, ate in the breakfast nook off the kitchen. More often than not, MF was not home for family dinners, due to working late. Mother's rules for washing hands, elbows off the table, and cloth napkins on the lap were important, but her chief goal at family gatherings was to insure there was no airing of unpleasant emotional problems in his presence. The children could not, would not, act out. When they had personal problems, they were expected to pretend they didn't exist, but they could save them for a private conversation with Mother. MF was always served first. Finishing first, MF could escape to the privacy of his bedroom, sparing him from the kids' chatter and permitting him time for contemplating the upcoming week at Foley Fish. After Sunday dinner, Mother and Virginia would often sneak away to visit Michael Moloney to exchange news from Ireland.

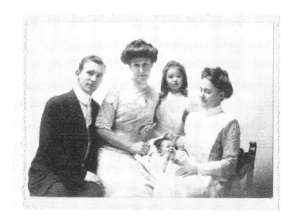

MF, Helen, young Helen, baby Francis, and baby's nurse, 1913

The Foley children wanted for nothing material. Despite Mother's over-management, family warmth pervaded the home. Each child felt loved even when it was conditional. There was a sense of harmony in the home starting with MF and Mother; discord between them was very rare.

The four children were as different as unrelated people from separate families. Helen held similar aspirations to her mother. She sought to go beyond her birth and breeding, seeking social acceptance beyond even what her family had already achieved.

Frank was the law-and-order nice guy. Unlike his older, sometimes resistant, oppositional sister Helen, Frank was a pleaser. Ginny, as Virginia was called, was smiley, full of gaiety always making her parents and those in her presence happy. Andy, 12 years younger than Helen, was a free spirit, not at all under his mother's thumb. Starting his first day in the fifth grade, Andy decided not to go back to his former school, so instead, on his own, walked into Runkle School and enrolled as a student there, which he became.

My father, Frank Foley (FF), never questioned his mother's dictates. Her certainty made his life simpler by removing ambiguities. He did as he was told. In contrast to his older sister Helen, he was a welcome relief for Mother. FF always wanted to succeed in a manner acceptable to his mother and father. He never wanted to be found deficient. But he was not a saint as he did have to go to confession, suggesting not everything was revealed to his parents. Always a self-starter, FF did not need words of encouragement. He inherited his mother's trust in the ritualized, dogmatic Catholic religion. His was an unquestioning faith. The Catholic Church had a deep influence that shaped his approach to life. Commandments were handrails that fit his desire to see the world as black and white, right or wrong, no gray matter. FF's religion allowed him to be anchored and unconflicted by the complexities of life.

MF might appear unthoughtful when measured in terms of today's parenting. He was of a generation that gave neither ribbons for participation, nor trophies for victories. MF did not play children's games (he never had on the farm), or carry his young children on his shoulders. He did not teach them how to ice skate (he himself didn't know how). He could have taught them how to swim or ride a bike, but he didn't. MF's love was from a distance — not rare in those days. He was a kind man who would take out his pocket watch for his young children to hear the tick tocks. It was difficult for this unemotional man to express his love in a conventional or prescribed way. Intimacy seemed beyond his capacity.

He wanted to give his children all the advantages he had to give, without imposing any of the disadvantages. His quiet style was a product of his upbringing. He had created a protective shield best summarized by the Irish mantra, "Talk, but reveal little." MF kept his own counsel. He did not preach to his children. He cared about their feelings, but never to the point of coddling them. MF believed that each child must experience life on his or her own, unhindered by parental interference. MF never would boast, "In my day, etc." Nor would MF tell them what to do. MF felt that setbacks made you potentially stronger, provided you solve them by yourself. He believed that if he interceded, he would deprive his children of learning and, therefore, not only not improve, but also not find out about themselves. He knew that you can't summon your strengths until you first discover these strengths.

MF's reticence had to be frustrating for his children; this kind, generous man concealed his inner self from those who adored him.

Because of this distance, MF became a compelling person to all of us. His silences created an aura. My Uncle Andy recalls, "When I was ten years old, Daddy would walk me to the local grocery store for an ice cream cone after dinner. Just walking with him, I can't tell you how happy I was. It may be the best memory I ever had of him."

His incomprehensibility would draw you in trying to figure him out, but frustratingly, you could never get close enough to discover much. You knew 56 Windsor would not have happened without him. He sought for the Foley children the advantages he never had himself. He wanted each to have a good start in life, and that would be enough because everything else would remain a mystery. MF did not reveal himself lest it give power to others over him. But he did not want power over them, rather he hoped that they would be empowered by his silences. This altruism reinforced the compelling impact he had on his children. His detachment was a form of armor, but was also an offset to his wife's controlling instincts.

Foley children: Francis (Frank), Andrew,
Helen, Virginia (Ginny), c. 1924

Another pivotal decision arose, this time not because of a health threat. MF was approached by an attorney named Santry, who was on the Board of the Brookline Trust, and whose wife Suzanne knew Mother from their fund-raising work (along with Rose Kennedy) at St. Aidan's Church. Santry wanted to propose the Foleys for membership in The Country Club (TCC), the oldest such club in the U.S. He had discussed his idea with a number of his fellow members, all of whom agreed on the need for socially acceptable new money in the current dark financial times. It would also demonstrate TCC's democratic inclusion of an Irish family. They hoped that the older members could tolerate a few Irish in their club, but knew that their sponsorship would not guarantee membership.

Mother was ecstatic. She knew herself well — even more, she knew what she wanted. She knew that in refined social circles she was regarded as a parvenu, an upstart with newly acquired wealth and not yet accepted by the upper class of Boston. MF, on the other hand, was well satisfied with his position. He respected TCC's members for their accomplishments in the business world. He was concerned, however, about the members' children who may have had a life spoiled by wealth. Some of them might believe that because they had been born on third base, they had hit a home run. As MF thought more, he became worried that some of these well-to-do, overindulged children could become the new role models for his four children. MF did not need to read F. Scott Fitzgerald's *The Great Gatsby*, where he wrote, "Let me tell you about the very rich. They are different from you and me. They possess and enjoy early and it does something to them, makes them soft where we are hard."

MF and Mother's partnership was tested as they disagreed. Mother was insistent to join, MF resistant. MF sent son Andrew and daughter Ginny as emissaries to dissuade her, all to no avail. MF finally said no to Mother, a first. For the reserved MF, whose children were accustomed to his wordless expectations, this unprecedented decision reverberated, especially when they learned his rationale for not joining TCC. Not so with his wife. It was a rare period of discord. MF wrote a gracious letter to his nominee expressing what an honor it was to have been considered for membership, but that the demands of running his fish business precluded his ability to enjoy the many benefits that TCC offered.

CHAPTER 28

FRANK FOLEY – DECISION

FF was an easy child. He was self-directed, needing few words of encouragement. Too serious to be a comic book guy, but regular enough to read the daily sports section of the *Boston Herald* to follow the Boston Red Sox and the Boston Braves — focusing on Sibi Sisti, Mother's favorite ballplayer (because of his name). Ginger Ale was his preferred soft drink, way better than the cod liver oil forced on him by his mother. Their family doctor, Doctor O'Toole, the man with the rattling needles, did not bother FF, who grew up never taking Novocain. After Mother finished listening to gravelly voiced Cardinal Cushing say the rosary over the radio, FF would be allowed to turn the knobs of the Philco radio until he found the station for the mystery show, *Inner Sanctum*. Free of household chores, he organized a newspaper delivery team venture, a venture that paid him better than MF's wholesaling in Clonmel.

FF attended the Runkle School, a prestigious primary school in Brookline that fed graduates to prominent secondary schools like Boston Latin and Milton Academy. After school, he played sports – football, hockey, and baseball — at the nearby Dean Playground. After graduating Runkle, FF went to Boston College High School, an esteemed local Catholic day school run by the Jesuits. It was good match as he appreciated the Jesuit's sense of order and hard work. His most academic challenge was Greek I, which he stubbornly chose because it was the toughest course there. FF graduated in the top ten percent of his class in 1932. Being a feeder school to Boston College, also run by the Jesuits, the Jesuits expected FF to attend B.C. He did not, but instead applied to

Harvard College and was accepted despite (or because of) B.C. High refusing to give him a written recommendation. Mother and MF did not bow to the Jesuits' pressure, even after they had been warned that Foley Fish Co. would lose the fish accounts at the Seminary and at Boston College (which happened). A hundred years earlier, FF would not have been accepted by Harvard, as acceptance then was determined primarily on the dignity of the family and its social standing rather than just on academic performance. As unlettered first-generation immigrants, MF and Mother were justifiably proud of his admittance to Harvard. Mother, always socially-conscious, was elated.

In recognition of FF's acceptance to Harvard, Mother gave Frank permission to separately travel to Clonmel, where he worked in the summer on the Moloney and Foley farms. During my trip to Clonmel with FF, 45 years later, he reminisced about this particular trip, calling it his best summer ever. "This time, I was treated as an adult. I was one of them. They involved me in their manual labor: milking cows, chasing chickens, cleaning water troughs and rotating flocks of sheep on various grazing grounds. Hard work and long hours. I loved the friendships formed. Not that it was all work. I would often tell my cousins how lucky they were to have cows that shit and peed on their land so that plants could grow without their help. On weekends we would go to County horse fairs. We'd bet on the horses, never winning. As mementos, I saved the coins that we swapped. The older cousins took me to the pubs never letting me pay for anything. Quite a gift as I drank a lot of beer that summer. On my last night my cousins serenaded, dedicating their songs to me, calling me a fellow Irishman."

"Years later, I reflected on these visits," spoke an unusually expansive FF. "I didn't realize at the time what a unique gift my parents had given me allowing me to walk around in my father's shoes when he was on the same farm, some 42 years earlier. My father's upbringing at Attykitt was not the 'immigrant handicap' that the Maureen O'Hara movies showed, rather his start gave him an advantage that I didn't have in my early years at 56 Windsor, where no chores or responsibilities for the family were imposed. I recognized that my father — whom I had idealized, had a flaw in parenting us. He was too undemanding of us. His financial success was softening him and us. I recalled my sisters Helen and Ginny often going to the Foley Fish plant to hit our father up for spending money. My Dad's upbringing on his farm was more appealing to me than my own at 56 Windsor."

Mother (3rd from left) at daughter Ginny's wedding. MF
(far left) in his preferred position on the sidelines

FF was reputed to be the first graduate of B.C. High to attend Harvard. He was the only freshman in the class of 1936 to come from a Catholic secondary school. A vast majority of his classmates graduated from such noteworthy prep schools as Andover, Exeter, Milton Academy, Browne and Nichols, St. Paul's, Middlesex, Nobles and Greenough, Groton, St. Paul's, St. Mark's and Boston Latin (collectively called "St. Grottlesex"). FF easily made friends with the preppies as he was raised in the same Yankee value system (manners, self-reliance, scruples) as they were (excepting anti-Catholicism and bigotry against the Irish). He did steer clear of the snooty types. His roommates at Winthrop House were all from blue-collar working-class families — an Italian (Maiullo), a Jew (Rosen), and a West Coast kid (Larry Crampton) who went on, under the tutelage of the legendary Henry Lamar, to be the undefeated intercollegiate boxing champion at the 125-pound weight category. Harvard's social clubs were still closed to FF — the collegiate version of Irish need not apply. Like MF, he was unbothered by this exclusion. He went on to become President of the only national fraternity on campus — Sigma Alpha

Epsilon — never to be confused with the Porcellian or the Owl Club. His Harvard was different from that of the Cabots, Lowells, Saltonstalls, and David Rockefeller, a classmate. His roommates were not on any debutante's invitation list.

FF never made a pretense of erudition. He was a plugger – studious, but not the scholar like his younger brother Andy. Majoring in Economics, he passed all his courses receiving "gentlemen's B's" and an occasional A (not in Greek). He played football on Richard Harlow's varsity and junior varsity teams, and was lead defenseman on Winthrop House's hockey team.

Mother presumed that FF would join Foley's after Harvard. But it was not inevitable to FF or MF. A tightlipped MF had not provided any assurances about a career path at Foley's. MF had characteristically avoided being seen as influencing FF's decision. He knew that his own decision to come into the fish industry as an immigrant would be clearly different for his son as a Harvard graduate who, unlike him, had many career choices. FF's Uncle Bill was not at all encouraging, telling him, "This is a cutthroat business, full of scoundrels who will eat you — a rich man's son — alive. How stupid could you be to consider this place after Harvard College? The only job worth having here is owner. Your father is only 54 years old; he will never retire." FF hated Bill for his attempted coup — another reason not to come to Foley Fish.

FF's closest college buddies had no job waiting for them. John Adzigian, an all-Ivy halfback, wanted to be a high school teacher and athletic director; Joe Maiullo needed to go to law school before he could have a position back home at a Detroit law firm; Joseph Martin and Jerry O'Connor were headed to the Harvard Business School for careers in corporate business. His roommate Larry Crampton was investigating a job at Aramco in Saudi Arabia. David Rockefeller and FF were two of the few grads who had a family firm they could join, albeit very different ones. FF did not want to waste MF's money in graduate school education. He could have gone directly into a training program at a local bank like New England Merchant Bank managing his parents' money, but he wanted to succeed on his own (later he enrolled in night courses in finance and corporate law at a local college).

His parents had generously given him a three-month, all-expenses paid, trip to Europe as a graduation present. FF would have enough time later to map out a career plan, so he concentrated on enjoying the parties during graduation week.

Unplanned was wrecking MF's prized Cadillac (all his life, FF regarded red lights as suggestions). The crash, his third in four years was the third strike, a wake-up call telling him that he was a spoiled kid going in the wrong direction. "This is not who I am or who I want to be," he told himself.

FF started work at Foley Fish the Monday after his graduation in 1936. Returning the generous gift of a ticket for Europe, FF said, "I'm the least street-smart person ever to go into a business that requires street smarts above all else. I'm behind — way behind — so I better get started immediately." Recognizing that he knew too little would stay with him his entire career.

FF, the Harvard grad, would start in the same place as MF, his sixth-grade educated father, did 25 years earlier, in the fish cellar. He knew that MF was better prepared for this future than he was.

Was he crazy? No just different, perhaps unique.

CHAPTER 29

THE ROOKIE

Frank Foley (FF), early 1930s

When FF started at Foley Fish, the company did not have a formal training program. There were no mentors, you simply learned by doing, a process of osmosis in "fishology." Showing no favoritism, MF assigned his son to work in production under the "tutoring" of Uncle Bill Moloney.

Still harboring hopes of being MF's successor, Bill resented, no, he hated his nephew, not wanting his potential rival to come into the family business. A personal vendetta against FF began on day one. Bill went out of his way to make FF's life miserable. A suffocating critic, Bill would be heard loudly proclaiming after FF had miscalculated a freezer inventory, "You'd think that a "Haarvard" boy could add and subtract." MF would not intervene.

Washing "gurry" barrels stuck with clinging fish, working overtime without extra compensation, shoveling four tons of ice daily, then carrying bushel baskets to the shipping section 40 feet away, FF was the new recruit in Bill's boot camp.

Bill's vendetta would eventually backfire as the undeterred FF soon earned the respect of his fellow employees. He poured his whole self into Foley Fish. He kept his head down, his mouth shut, and worked harder than anyone else, but never showed them up. Despite living at 56 Windsor, FF never went over Bill's head to complain to MF.

FF was wired differently than most men of his age and accomplishments. His statement about being the least street-smart guy in the fish business, while self-motivating, was how he really felt. No job, however menial and redundant, would be unworthy of his fullest efforts.

Fortunately, in time, as Bill became more preoccupied with building wholesale sales, FF began a three-year training program of sorts, rotating through all the major processing departments, unloading fish, icing and storing fish in the basement's cooler, packing fillet orders, and sorting and packaging shellfish. His internship began under Frankie Lynch, a cigar chomping, foul-mouthed curmudgeon who was responsible for unloading the "Portagee" Souza's fish. "I don't know why they assigned you to me. I operate the basement elevator. It's not complicated, you tug the rope down or up depending on the direction you are going. Then you move the fish to the cooler where that "deaf son of a bitch," Huey O'Brien, takes over. The cops in the back alley are pains in the ass, always with their hands out. I tell them to find a real job. The local bookie doesn't give me any tips, saying I'm a grouch — imagine that?" Frankie told FF that he was too nice a kid for the fish business and that if he stayed, he better learn how to swear. The Foley tradition of yelling "Mahoney" (to silence swearing) when ladies and nuns came on the processing floor was in honor of Frankie.

Next FF moved to duty under Bob, the self-appointed "Great Abbott" at the order desk. "Why are you here? You're the owner's son, aren't you? You did graduate from Harvard, didn't you? Are you nuts? Try other things — travel, get laid, sleep late — Foley Fish will still be here when you return." Besides the parental guidance, FF treasured Bob Abbott's lesson in how to remove the eyeballs from dead fish to be used as ammo to be thrown at the other workers' heads. FF demurred.

FF was set on getting a graduate degree in life not available at Harvard. He was then assigned to Vito Cherissimino, the lead cutter, and later the union steward, as everyone else was too smart to take this unrewarding job. The Irish group would brag how they had given it to the "big-headed Italian" (which he wasn't). Vito was easy to pick out of a crowd at Foley's. He wore his pants up to his nipples and chomped on a deadly smelling stogie that at five cents was four cents too much. Years later, Vito met with FF to complain about the hiring of Jimmy Golden, a black man. FF said, "If I had asked your fellow workers about your appointment here, you wouldn't have been hired." Vito never brought up the complaint again.

Joe Pitts, the head of the packing area, was always immaculately groomed as if he was coming in for a photo shoot. Joe talked more about hair than fish. It was too late as FF was totally bald by 30, but Joe would persist: "Massage your head three times a day from the neck up to get the blood circulating; it'll grow back."

Jimmy Barker did not need Joe's advice; he had a full head of hair. Running shellfish was his "sideline," as he loved boxing. He took FF to the Boston Arena to see Kid Gavilan throw his famous bolo punch (uppercut), and World Featherweight Champion, Willie Pep. FF already knew a lot about shellfish from his summers harvesting littlenecks with his toes in Nahant, so they spent most of the time discussing upcoming fights to attend.

Next was Russ Rohrbacher, who was the only one his age. He had been promoted early to foreman. Being a diabetic, Russ listened — not always easy for a Kraut — to his doctor's advice as to insulin and no booze, turning into "Atlas" on the floor. Russ dispensed advice to everyone, including FF — "Don't cross Bill Moloney" (too late); "If you lose out, you can always bet on the dogs at Wonderland, I have a foolproof betting system." But FF never had any spare cash; he left his uncashed decks in his bureau drawer at 56 Windsor.

FF loved working with Frank Souza. Souza was like MF, in that he rarely talked. It was as if he suffered from lockjaw. Chewing on the same cigar the entire day to get his money's worth, Souza would answer FF's questions with mumbled two-word answers in Portuguese. Souza was cautious and wary of alienating Bill Moloney, so he didn't get too close to FF. As the cautious Portuguese outsider, a reserved Souza was wary, and like boxing great John L. Sullivan, always held his left hand protectively high. He was not eager to teach FF everything he knew about fish buying, lest he lose his job to him.

During this period, FF worked alongside the other Irish, Portuguese, and Italian workers. He looked up to them, valuing their work ethic. He also began to formulate the management strategies he would use down the road. He justified the lengthy apprentice timetable as perhaps his last chance to learn the business from the bottom up. Finally, after moving out of Bill's sphere, he discovered that at times it was a fun place as well as a work place.

But FF did not like all he was seeing. He felt that too many Foley workers and managers were not sweating the important small stuff. When working in the shipping department, he saw that the delivery of orders was not all that well coordinated with the time and place of delivery: early morning city deliveries, early afternoon Cape Cod Express deliveries, and late afternoon Railway Express pickups for the Minuteman, a refrigerated cargo carrier that left the North Station promptly for next morning deliveries to Chicago. Often, he observed, outgoing shipments were not ready in time, and so the product was a day older than it should have been when arriving at its destination. In the shellfish department, he saw "littleneck" orders filled with "cherrystones." In packing, mismarking of fillet cans as to species occurred too frequently. The freezer sheet didn't differentiate one-pound cans of crab flakes (an inexpensive filler) from one-pound cans of crabmeat (an entrée), causing incorrect shipments. In short, the system was loose and creaky.

The work crew was a hard-living group. No members of the Temperance League here. Some too frequently returned from their 15-minute afternoon break with booze on their breath. In the sales office, salesmen were allowed to drop prices to induce sales. At Christmas time, some fish packages were "missent" to a chef's home.

FF said nothing. "Who asked for your opinion?" would have been the response if he had. It frustrated him that MF never once sought his input. FF wondered if his father was even aware of these problems, and thought he might be too removed from the action, confining himself upstairs to retail and his first-floor office away from the action. MF was not managing his company. He was allowing Bill Moloney to be commander-in-chief without oversight. Foley Fish was not the company it once was. People under MF were playing fast and loose.

No one else was losing any sleep over the problems, except FF. No one was focusing on the details. Neglect was setting in. Like a crucible that requires added heat to stir up the solution, FF was getting more hot and more bothered; he knew that eventually he'd have to speak his mind. Confronting MF with his findings would be daunting, but he determined that he was the only one who could.

CHAPTER 30

CONFRONTATION

Telling his father that Foley Fish was faltering would have been unthinkable for FF a few years earlier. He had never confronted MF on any issue, and now, as a rookie, he was about to criticize the way he ran his company. There was no right time, but FF knew it was the right thing to do.

FF presented an analysis documenting the absence of quality control throughout the store. Not mincing words, "Foley Fish is going in the wrong direction. To not acknowledge these problems is to risk Foley Fish slipping into a second-rate fish company," he wrote. Seeing that MF, while concerned, was reacting to his disclosures in his usual steady, quiet, and unresponsive manner, FF boldly asserted that MF was too removed from the action, and was compounding management problems by making Bill his unchecked commander-in-chief. There was too little oversight. Both MF and Bill were hell bent on sales growth, while ignoring the harmful effects on an overworked, undermanaged production team. MF, always one to employ the silence that made him a good listener, said little except that he would review FF's findings and respond later.

MF realized that Bill Moloney had gone out of his way to make life miserable for FF. MF had not interceded as he felt that his son needed toughening, plus it would accelerate his gaining respect from his co-workers. MF did momentarily think that FF might be finding fault merely to justify himself, but realized that would be out of character. MF's reaction to FF's critique was that many of the problems cited were readily correctible. Not venial sins, however, were the price discounting and the chef's favors. They would be halted. Ms. Oberson would scrutinize all invoices to enforce compliance.

FF was still young, only 23 years old. When MF was that age, he had already accumulated more years of experience in the fish business. Another concern was that FF had never seen the company's financials. Foley's was still quite profitable, although it was experiencing a deceleration in its sales growth rate. The substantial influx of immigrants in the first two decades of this century had ended. Supermarket chains and "Ma and Pa" neighborhood stores were appearing. The Great Atlantic and Pacific Tea Co. (A&P) had established a wholesale fish operation on the Boston Pier. As a forerunner to Walmart's modern discount format, A&P embarked on an aggressive fish discounting strategy to win customers. Frank Milley was doing a great job as manager of Foley's retail operation, but the demographics were not encouraging. To compensate for retail's declining sales, Foley's wholesale operations had to step up to fill the void. 1937 saw a deep recession; GNP fell 30% due to the over-contracting of monetary and fiscal policies. High income earners, targeted by resorts, were hit by a marginal tax rate increase to 75% from 59%. This was the context for MF to consider FF's analysis.

Bill Moloney was a gifted marketer. He had recently implemented a new marketing program. He negotiated with Hertz to paint an eye-catching mural panel on the sides of Foley Fish leased trucks. The mural pictured an iconic Gloucester fishing Captain in his yellow oil slick steering the fishing boat while battling the elements of the turbulent seas to bring fish to you, the Foley customer. It was designed to suggest a John Wayne type man of action that the customer could unconditionally trust and respect. Foley's Boston's Real Fish House appearing in old-fashioned type face appeared over the mural, and made a simple but powerful connection between fishermen and Foley Fish – an unbeatable combination. The bold, strong green colors of the truck were a daring feature, as it was the time when affluent people, frightened by the Lindberg baby kidnaping and blackmail, bought black cars to avoid drawing attention. The "road" advertisement was a first in Boston. Bostonians and New Englanders would now see Foley Fish at such prestigious stops as the Ritz, Mass General, Harvard College, and the famous Locke-Ober restaurant.

MF couldn't risk alienating Bill or Mike Moloney, as both were invaluable salesmen delivering an impressive number of new wholesale customers like the Lake Placid Club in NY State, The Mt. Washington Hotel at Bretton Woods, The Balsams at Dixville Notch, The Pinehurst Resort, and The Country Club in Brookline. Bill Moloney had started at Foley's the year FF was born. The experience gap was too wide to overlook. FF had never run any operation other than his newspaper route, and didn't know as much as he thought he knew. Last year on a shrimp-buying trip to Florida, FF overbought (double what was needed) and was now learning how to sell off the extra shrimp. More valuable lessons had to be experienced. He wasn't ready for a management position.

MF told his son, "You think you know better than everyone around here, but you need more experience before you will." MF wasn't opposed to FF's eventual promotion to executive management, but not yet. He told FF he intended to put him in sales, working with the Moloneys, for the next few years. A dissatisfied FF quit. A stunned MF was unhappy. Bill Moloney was of course, ecstatic.

CHAPTER 31

MOTHER INTERVENES

FF left the meeting with his father unsatisfied, feeling that his comments were not taken seriously and, perhaps, that he was taken lightly. Quitting was FF's version of a hunger strike, or a game of chicken: "Who would blink first, MF or FF?" He hoped it would lead to MF re-evaluating the situation. It was a makeshift strategy to shatter his father's complacency. FF felt compelled to make a stand, not so much for himself as for the company's future. He believed that the problems he uncovered could, if not corrected, take on a life of their own. His measurement stick was not his idealized vision of what the company could become, but what it had once been. His argument was not about transforming Foley Fish Co. from good to great; it was about preventing it from going from good to mediocre.

FF took a job on the night shift at American Express loading cargo onto freight trains. Obviously, this was an interim step. Earlier, he had taken night courses in business law thinking he would someday need the knowledge at Foley Fish. Now he might have to consider other career options. Mother broke the stalemate.

Unbeknownst to MF, FF met with his mother at her request. He summarized his reasons for quitting, careful not to frame the dispute solely as a personality clash between him and her brother Bill. Knowing that MF could be angered by her interference, he cautioned her not to take sides. But, like a moth drawn to light, Mother stepped into the dispute, incapable of standing on the sidelines.

When she confronted her husband, he replied, "I can't afford to lose

Bill Moloney, so unless Frank backs off, he will be out. Frank is not ready yet. He is not indispensable. He is still too inexperienced. Frank was born when Bill started at Foley Fish, giving Bill 27 years of experience compared to Frank's three. Frank is too impatient. He has overstated the production problems, perhaps, as a way to push Bill aside. His quitting is a temper tantrum."

Her rejoinder went something like this: "Yes, Frank is inexperienced, but so were you at his age. Did you forget that you quit your brother's firm over similar issues? I know our son. He would not manufacture his criticism for self-promotion. Who are you going to believe? Frank or my brother Bill, who brutally betrayed you? If you became deathly sick again, who can I turn to? I will never sell Foley Fish to Bill. Frank is the only one. Do you want to risk losing him? I understand why you want to keep both men, but you must find a way to not lose Frank." Mother had violated her non-interference pledge, but her action prompted MF to meet with his son.

MF spoke, "I know about the bruising relationship between you and Bill. I also know more about what's going on the production floor than you realize. I don't dispute your findings. I've climbed similar hills as you are now navigating, so let me give you my thoughts based on my personal experience. By quitting, you are giving up a unique opportunity. If you work somewhere else, you may never become an owner. The new place will have similar problems. Are you going to quit again when you encounter a Bill Moloney-type in charge of operations?"

MF promised, "I will tighten my grip over the floor operations, but you need to get into sales. I want you to work side by side with Mike Moloney. In time, we will sit down again to discuss your promotion to executive management, provided you continue to prove yourself as deserving."

Bill Moloney and Frank Foley were two men from two different centuries. FF was the 19th century guy — a micro thinker concretely thinking in terms of simplicity, order, rules, and details. Bill was the 20th century guy — a macro thinker — promotional, corporate, and worldly. FF had no artifice; Bill was loaded with it. FF possessed a small ego. He was self-effacing and much more self-critical than Bill, who had an oversized ego.

Yet beyond those dissimilarities, there was one shared fatal similarity. Both defined power the same way — not by having a lot of people below them, but by never having anyone above them. Neither could ever work for the other. MF knew this. One would have to lose, the other win. But for now, MF hoped to postpone that inevitability.

Years later I asked my Dad, "What would you have done if you didn't return to Foley Fish?" He replied, "I was confident that I could become a successful manager of a business enterprise, so I would have pursued other business opportunities."

CHAPTER 32

FF RETURNS

FF's ultimatum was akin to a novitiate walking into the Vatican and saying wholesale changes were needed or else the Catholic Church would not survive, a sacrilege. His risk-taking reflected the street smarts he mistakenly said that he lacked. Although he had backed himself against a wall without a fallback position, he had read MF perfectly. For both men, the price of FF staying was less than the cost of his leaving.

FF enjoyed his rotation through sales, learning from Uncle Mike, a consummately skilled salesman. While Mike's sales style was not his, FF respected Mike's personality-driven approach. It was one that created a close bond with customers, who not only liked him but trusted him. They relied on his menu suggestions. They became loyal Foley customers. FF's months in sales were a relief from the tensions experienced while working with Mike's brother, Bill.

MF then assigned FF to the new position of production management quality control, reporting directly to MF. Bill was shifted to sales full time, still reporting directly to MF. Bill was incensed by the downgrading. He had misread MF's silences as tacit approval. He was now experiencing MF's hidden Celtic hardness and tribal loyalty. In a conciliatory gesture, MF appointed Bill as a Director at the Company, replacing his brother Jim Foley. But no shares were given to Bill. Bill, however, was paid extremely well, allowing him to afford a substantial home in the posh suburb of Wellesley, a company car, and a country club membership. No other fish company could match Bill's pay package, but MF could not predict whether his generous salary would convince Bill to stay. He was confident that his son would.

FF's instincts told him to address shortcomings immediately. He was not starting from scratch. He'd followed his nose throughout the Foley plant sniffing out problems for the past three years. He knew, however, that he would get his head handed to him if he was too abrupt. He was now in charge of men twice his age, some of whom had been his instructors. Bill Moloney, of course, was hoping he'd fail.

While changes couldn't be delayed, fixing deeply imbedded production problems would take time. Foley Fish was growing fast, and the prevailing management style was loose and lax. FF needed to establish systems that would not only control production, but also synchronize it with sales and purchasing operations, as they were interdependent.

His first move was to establish an "anchor desk," where he would sit. It became his command central. All sales slips would come to him before going to production. Every slip would be time stamped and then forwarded according to three different time segments: 6-8 a.m. Boston local deliveries; 8-12 a.m. New England deliveries; and 1-5 p.m. train deliveries. Processing would have its priorities set by shipping schedules, a clear improvement over the old method, which had distributed sales' sheets in random, timeless bunches. An inordinate number of mistakes were occurring late in the afternoon, based on a just-get-it-done attitude, rather than a done correctly attitude. To tamp down the late afternoon order surges, FF reinstated the requirement that all orders, especially the overnight shipping ones, had to be received one day before the shipment day. He became the circuit breaker stopping the overloading of the processing line.

Production snags had also been caused by insufficient product inventory, which prevented orders being filled expeditiously. FF compiled data on sales by day, by species, and by geographical destinations to better enable Souza to purchase fish in a timelier manner.

Perhaps more important was what he didn't do. He could have taken the easy way out by stockpiling quantities of fish. He refused. Quality control of a perishable product was dependent on not taking short cuts. Daily price sheets became the job of the anchor desk, not the sales department. No pricing exceptions were allowed.

In May 1940, Germany invaded Holland and Belgium, followed by the invasion of Russia in June 1941. On December 7, 1941, Japan bombed Pearl Harbor and World War II began for the United States. FF was called up for the draft. MF had never anticipated losing his son to war. Fortunately for Foley's, FF had inherited his father's poor eyesight, and flunked the eye test. He was granted a deferment. We now know why FF played center on the Harvard football team, and not pass-catching end.

The United States experienced its biggest production boom in history because of the war. Its annual investment in industrial production increased from 5% of GNP in 1940 to 67% in 1943, primarily because of spending on national defense. American mobilization transferred ten million people out of the civilian labor force into war zones by the end of 1941. Ration books were issued for sugar, coffee, butter, cheese, gasoline and meat. Fortunately, fish purchases were kept unlimited.

Patterns of living were abruptly changed. Gas rationing curtailed car use. Prices of all staples rose due to shortages caused by the war. With wages fixed by executive order, family budgets were squeezed. Women left home to work in factories to substitute for the men shipped overseas to fight. Homemakers had less time to cook. People again adjusted to do with less. A meat shortage lasted the entire war, but the Office of Price Administration excluded fish from its price ceiling program. Taxes were raised, again, this time, to pay for the war effort, thereby decreasing after-tax income.

Foley Fish was not immune. The retail sales further declined due to fewer upscale shoppers, the cessation of population migration to the US, the emergence of supermarkets, and Ma and Pa stores selling fish in the suburbs. Individual purchasers decreased their order sizes as daughters and sons of immigrant families abandoned the old-world traditions of frequent fish consumption. Not helping the situation was the increase of retail fish prices to their highest levels. For instance, haddock fillets, Foley's most popular seller, were priced an average 15 cents higher than before the war, increasing from 20 cents a pound to 35 cents. The East Coast fishing fleet was dramatically reduced as many trawlers were requisitioned for war duty as mine sweepers. The remaining fishing fleet was discarding significant pounds of "juvenile" fish (the future parents of the next generation of fish) due to the small-size mesh nets used on trawlers. New, more liberal mesh-size regulations would not be implemented until 1953. Foley's wholesale fish business was hurt by reduced driving and by higher taxes, especially by the wealthy. Affluent families became reluctant to be seen vacationing during the war years. Hotel and resort business plummeted.

Perhaps the only person not worried about sales was FF. The business slowdown allowed him to implement a smoother processing flow. Mistakes owing to haste were reduced.

CHAPTER 33

MISTAKE MANAGEMENT

I have endured ass-whippings (a.k.a. spankings) at my father's hand on my insufficiently cushioned behind causing pain that you don't forget. Before one spanking, Dad said to me, "This hurts me more than it does you." To which I responded, "I won't tell Mom if you don't, and I'll still yell bloody murder so she hears." Dad rejected my idea. Halfway through one spanking, I told him that he had gotten his point across. This plea also did not work. At an early age, I learned, first hand, or was it second hand, about Dad's deep sense of obligation and duty. He wouldn't abdicate.

Dad's whippings at home were called tongue lashings at work. From his anchor desk, FF could view the entire plant in one panoramic glimpse — to the left, the shellfish department and the fish storage cooler room, to the middle, the cutting and packing area, and to the right, the shipping area. He could see everyone and everything. He saw the mistakes that no one reported to him — the debris remaining after the day-end wash down, the insufficient ice on tops of whole fish in the cooler, people returning late from coffee breaks. These blunders and oversights triggered a voice that roared with the sudden force of a tidal wave. Both transgressors and the bystanders would be sucked into his thundering force field. FF's words yelled through clenched teeth were sometimes too clipped to be intelligible, but his anger was nevertheless unmistakably communicated.

Excuses such as, "I'm doing the best I can," were never accepted. He had no tolerance for excuses. Like his mother, FF would never cajole, nor coax — he demanded improvement — no maybes or perhaps — my will shall be done! Transgressors would withdraw limping, weighing less than they had before getting chewing out. FF was never worried about a scolded employee feeling bad. FF knew he was a difficult boss — hard to please and easy to anger. Not a fan of psychobabble, he did not try to figure out what made each person tick. He wanted them to know what ticked him off. His language was not calculated to please. It was calculated to be never forgotten. FF was not a rough man, but was rough on people making avoidable mistakes. His wonderfully blunt manner would stop at belittlement. He did not require to be loved as he never cared about attention for himself. Product delivery was more important than hard feelings. Unfortunately, he never apologized, nor later offered encouraging words. Like his father, no pep talks. He did not perceive his job to be uplift.

Under FF the fish plant was not a fun place to work. The work environment was cold, and a fishy dampness got into your bones and remained the entire work day. No one was gushing with excitement to come to work. He inherited a band of rough, rowdy, hard drinking, blue-collar men. They did not take immediately to FF's disciplinary approach, which was a marked difference to MF's lenient, unflappable, distant management style. Push back was inevitable. I remember Jab Brown, a Boston fishcutter, telling me how much he hated my father. One day he went after FF, unsuccessfully, with his cutting knife. FF told me not to mention it to my mother as it might upset her!

The youngest workers were mostly second-generation immigrants. Unlike MF, their fathers had not moved up the occupation ladder. They were still blue-collar laborers. Fortunately for FF, their parents imparted to them a code of conduct of no whining, hard work, and hope for a better future. While some got to high school, many never graduated. Few job options were available during the Depression. Working at Foley Fish paid for their beer, second-hand cars, and dates. They were happy to have a steady, paying job. This new team of workers was moldable, perhaps leading later to gentler corrections by FF such as calling out a young Jimmy Golden by throwing his own wallet across the floor saying, "You think I can throw away my money like you're doing and still stay in business?"

FF knew no other way to manage. He took no behavioral studies at Harvard. There were no self-help books in the 1940s. His temper was a component of his DNA coming down from his mother's side. Both of them were impatient, intolerant, and insistent. But his enduring temper proved to be instrumental to his success in running Foley Fish. His reflexive outbursts were never causeless. His reactions were as predictable as they were indelible. In time, each Foley employee — young and old — learned never to plead ignorance about what FF expected, which was no avoidable mistakes. His power over people occasionally weighed on him, causing him to ask, "What if I am wrong? He was not preternaturally calm or unflappable like his father. However, like him, FF was fair and mostly not unkind.

Yes, he was the boss, but never threatened anyone by saying, "I will fire you if…" His motives were purely task-driven. He did not need to be loved – just obeyed. Surprising to some, FF did not think much about his temper outbursts, although they were not completely involuntary. He could consciously enlarge the outbursts to convey insistence. His employees often asked if FF was constitutionally incapable of managing his emotions. He would never answer that question because he wanted them to think he couldn't.

CHAPTER 34

ROILING

FF's lack of management training hurt him; he had no handrails to guide him. He felt that too many Foley workers didn't care enough. He showed little understanding of people. Worse yet, he had no human touch. In sum, his managerial style was flawed, but not ineffective.

Why did Foley employees tolerate FF's bullying behavior? For some it was because he was the boss and paid a good wage. But it was more than that for others. Unlike MF, a boss who was dignified, controlled, and distant, FF's manner was perhaps a throwback to his Celtic ancestry. He was an explosive, emotional boss not always in control of his emotions, but he was consistent in his approach. His demands were not capricious. Many workers saw that his emotional commitment to the company was honest, and this recognition led, over time, to begrudging respect. Many realized that he was often correct. If truly misguided, FF could have incapacitated the company. Workers began to internalize his criticisms. In an oddly inspiring way, many workers improved and more importantly, they began feeling better about themselves. His converts saw that his approach worked.

Not a teacher, or an exhorter, FF counterintuitively proved himself to be a talented communicator. Over 80% of his hires started and finished their careers at the Foley Fish. There were a few exceptions.

George Kenneally, the youngest of seven children from Charlestown had four brothers on the USS Harry Lee when it was sunk in the war (after the five Sullivan brothers from Iowa went down on the USS Juneau). He came from good stock. George loved Bill Moloney as his boss. "He had an easy disposition within the sales office. Always nice to me, he would not yell at me if I arrived late after visiting my sick mother during the lunch hour. He always asked, 'How is Mom'? Frank verbally beat you up. I felt that if you did something wrong, you were doomed. "How could I go from a good employee to a bad one when Frank became my boss?" George left Foley Fish after 20 years employment. Ironically, he landed a job at the Office of Price Administration because of the reputation of the Foley Fish Co. for high standards.

The business philosophies of Bill and FF were at odds, resulting in growing tensions between the two. Bill wanted a bigger company. Like a stockbroker, he wanted a double-digit quarterly sales and net income growth record. To FF, Foley Fish Co. was not a public stock; it was a store that he wanted to keep small and manageable. Bill was the big picture guy, too often neglecting the small stuff that FF couldn't overlook. Bill was the careerist obsessed with reaching the top, while FF was the craftsman who loved to get to the bottom of things, not content with his creation if it was still flawed, needing more work, more tinkering.

Inevitable clashes occurred. Bill wanted to get into the historically profitable lobster business. FF was opposed, wanting instead a smaller, more controllable product list that allowed quality delivery to their customers. Lobster supplies were unpredictable, so FF refused to sell them, lest he jeopardize Foley's reputation for consistent quality.

Bill fixated on the bottom line – net profit – while FF focused exclusively on quality which, in turn, he believed would automatically produce profits. If accomplished, FF would also assert that "the bottom line is down where it belongs."

Bill argued for an expanded production line, while FF wanted to keep it small for more control. Like a plumber, FF wanted to ensure that the "pipes" could handle the flows, even if it meant occasionally shutting down the entire line to prevent overloading. An aggressive Bill pushed for 600-pound orders while a cautious FF preferred three 200-pound orders shipped to the same customer three days apart so that whatever customer ate the 600th pound of Foley Fish was just as satisfied as the one who ate the first pound.

Something had to give. Never the politician, FF could not compromise. Given the turbulent and conflicted state of affairs, one of them had to leave.

CHAPTER 35

RESIGNATION/THE COUP

One Friday in the summer of 1947, Bill Moloney suddenly resigned his directorship and management position. Just that morning, he had insisted on being reimbursed for four worn tires. No official good byes, he collected his check and left at the end of the day.

Steve Connolly, recently promoted from the clerical office to sales, describes the next Monday morning at the Foley plant. "Monday did not start well. Normally, you'd see 150 fish orders to start the day. Today there was only one. By 11:00 a.m. there were none as the purchasing agent for Camp Quinnipiac withdrew that order, explaining that Bill Moloney had been her Foley contact for years so she was now switching their account to Atlantic Coast Fisheries of Boston where Bill now worked." At first, the floor personnel thought it was all a joke.

Bill Moloney had taken all the existing Foley wholesale accounts in an act of cold scheming and anger. Bill wanted to put Foley Fish Co., where he had worked 32 years, out of business. He'd first seen his master succession plan begin to unravel with his unsuccessful coup during MF's grave illness, and saw it further deteriorate when FF joined Foley's. The final straw was when MF replaced Bill with FF as the head of wholesale operations. The writing was on the wall. FF was winning the contest for heading Foley Fish. A curdled energy within Bill spilled into a calculated plan to sabotage the company. A bitter man, Bill had been plotting his departure for a year. He would have quit earlier, but companies were not hiring as economists were predicting that the economy would sink back into a second depression after the conclusion of World War II.

His departure was a severe blow. The company's competitors called it a calamity, and predicted that Foley's wholesale operations would close down without Bill Moloney. The "eloquent" Frankie Lynch said Bill had to be from Cork where many were famous for having a "smile on their face while peeing on your leg." Not FF. He reacted with surprising composure. He calmly asserted that Foley Fish would win back these accounts. He rendered no pep talks, nor battle cries. FF knew that Bill would have a very difficult time emulating Foley Fish's performance. It had taken Bill over 30 years to construct Foley's wholesale operations. Atlantic Coast Fisheries was exclusively a frozen fish operation, necessitating that Bill, overnight, establish a fresh fish wholesale operation. Bill would be forced to buy fresh fish fillets from other fish vendors. Without in-house fish production, Bill would have no quality control.

A confident FF must have surprised himself as well as others by his controlled, unemotional response, far different than his patented outbursts when mistakes occurred. Emerging was a paradox in FF's management style. In crisis, he was calm, whereas in good times, he was nervous.

MF kept his own counsel. He patiently and prudently waited to announce his plan until his son had learned the business. MF had to be sure that FF could do the job. It would be easy to suppose that MF's treatment of his son and his brother-in-law was part of a Machiavellian revenge plot. But that was not MF's style. He had a plan all along and was not unwilling to make the tough decisions.

MF had remained the owner without making promises to either one. FF now had a chance, unimpeded by Bill, to prove himself rightful heir to the Foley Fish Co. A few months after Bill departed, MF left for his customary two-month stay in Florida, saying, "My second team with Steve Connolly and Tom Flannery is better than Bill's first team."

For Mother, her brother's betrayal was extremely painful. She had always fostered family unity. It would never be possible now. Out of respect for his mother's feelings, FF never discussed this incident publicly, or at 56 Windsor. For MF, Bill's perfidy may have caused him to regret not seeing earlier the "shifty" side of Bill. Bill was a skillful chameleon, but was finally unmasked.

The clash between Bill Moloney and FF, the Darwinian struggle for leadership, was over. In a historical sense it was a vestigial trace of Celtic clan warfare — the modern version. FF never acknowledged this notion, but it went without saying that he was relieved when Bill Moloney quit, notwithstanding the traitorous manner in which it was done.

CHAPTER 36

THE RESPONSE

FF picked himself up off the floor before the referee finished the ten count. He sat the scared Foley workers down. Neither falsely confident nor totally assured, FF said something like this: "We will win those accounts back. Bill Moloney is circulating rumors that Foley Fish Co. will close its wholesale operations. That will not happen, nor will there be any layoffs. We will not sit back and wait. Our salespeople will be on the phone with every account. No Hail Mary, no miracle passes will be needed. We will continue to deliver products and service superior to what Bill Moloney can. That will be the deciding factor in our ultimate success."

Privately, however, FF was aware of the inexperience of his sales team. Other than Mike Moloney (who was not leaving), it was untested. Steve Connolly was moved up from accounting and Tom Flannery had been recently promoted from the shellfish department. That would bolster the sales staff.

Many of Foley Fish's customers had been won when they realized that they couldn't buy the same quality fish from another supplier. This was the rock on which Foley Fish was built. Consequently, FF stressed to the sales force that when contacting customers who had gone over to Bill Moloney, they should recommend checking Bill's fish on days one, two, and three. Bill Moloney's large promises should be taken with a grain of salt.

FF established a script for the sales force: "Phone for the next order; if no order; reiterate Foley's commitment and urge close examination of Bill's products. Do not push sales on customer. Keep a record of order status. Note any feedback. Should they ask why Bill left Foley Fish, tell them the truth, namely, that he wanted to be head of his own fish company. Do not get into gossip, nor give any hint of resentment on our part. Be classy. No whining. No bad mouthing. If anyone questions Foley's continuation in this wholesale business, tell me and I will phone them to reassure them otherwise."

FF soon learned that Bill hoped to hasten the demise of Foley Fish. To this end, he'd set his prices ten cents less a pound than Foley Fish's quoted prices. Bill was also approaching chefs at bigger accounts with kickback propositions.

FF sat down with Mike Moloney, and asked him straight out. "Did you know of Bill's intentions?" Mike swore that his first awareness of Bill's departure occurred when he came to work that Monday morning, the same as everybody else. He wanted to stay working at Foley Fish. Keeping Mike would be risky, but FF trusted him. Given his sales expertise and knowledge of all the accounts, he was an invaluable employee. FF stated, "This is not a family feud, this is business competition," adding that any hint of less than full loyalty would end his career at Foley's.

FF's confidence that Bill would fail in his attempt to steal many accounts was not unfounded. In the subsequent six months, over eighty percent of the accounts returned. His prediction that Bill couldn't deliver on his promise of delivering fish of quality equal to that of Foley Fish proved accurate. But there was no boasting of revenge or victory. Winning back the lost accounts was reward enough. FF's chewed-up pencils and nails bitten to the quick showed that the effort had been a tough one, his calm exterior notwithstanding.

In December, Mike Moloney came to him. "I can't compete anymore against my brother. He's family, I hope you understand." A month later, Mike received a $10,000 bonus check. Mike Moloney was incredulous and said he wanted to send it back because under the circumstances, it was not fair to Foley Fish. FF's only reply was, "You earned it."

All along, FF was confident that the outcome of the battle hinged on the comparative quality of fish. Foley Fish had demonstrated the superiority of its product. They had won. FF was quietly proud of having succeeded against a devious, talented competitor without compromising his personal values. The power of a superior product would continue to be pivotal going forward against other clever, unscrupulous competitors in the fish industry. He realized that a superior product was the strongest guarantee for continued success. He believed that in the future he could set the rules for buying from Foley Fish — the ordering procedure, the pay terms, and the handling of "his fish." Superior quality meant that he could get and keep customers without them interfering in how he ran the company. Others couldn't tell him what to do. He was now the unchallenged chieftain of the Foley Clan and could do things the right way, his way.

FF was growing more confident. However, there was a lingering question. Had permitting Bill to be the "face" man on so many accounts made it easier for him hijack them? Of course, it did. So, the follow-up question for both MF and FF was: "Will we allow anyone, other than ourselves, act as the dominant representative of M.F. Foley Fish Co. going forward?"

CHAPTER 37

BLESSING IN DISGUISE

Bill Moloney had left intending to destroy FF and the Foley Fish Co., but his plan had backfired. Bill quickly became the enemy — akin to the Yankees for the Red Sox. He had unified a fractured Foley team, making them stronger. As many historians have said, "It's hard to be a hero without a war," so that when Bill went to war against Foley Fish, he gave FF a chance to prove his mettle. FF became the hero, saving the company and its workers. The Foley workers who had formerly resisted him switched from grumbling to willingly complying with his dictates. A once unforeseeable bond between FF and his workers began to emerge, one which may not have been forged without Bill's attempt to sabotage the company. In a subtle but critical way, Bill's actions proved to be a blessing in disguise.

FF had always struggled with compliments as he felt that they softened the recipient. So, he didn't want to listen to talk that he was the company savior. He knew that Foley Fish did not win so much as Bill Moloney's company had lost. Showing a quasi-Calvinistic pessimism, FF realized that Foley Fish needed to get a lot better, or it would be less successful in future battles with competitors more competent than Bill Moloney. "Our company was not nearly as good as people said it was. We need to stop patting ourselves on the back," he said.

Frank had total operating control. He no longer had to bend his people to his philosophy. He did not surrender management decisions to anyone else. There was no chain of command. As President, he would not have a Kitchen Cabinet like MF. He became the head of the wholesale, the head of sales and the head of production. His management style would be a consensus of one.

Nothing now was beyond FF's purview. He dug into corners. Anticipating hidden errors and oversights, he searched every niche. He conducted random inspections of fillet packages to see if they had been correctly identified and properly sized. He removed fillets from the production line and conducted nose-and-taste tests to assess shelf life. He did not, however, appoint himself head of buying, deferring to his long-time talented buyer, Frank Souza. He did, however, substitute as head fish buyer when Frank Souza was on vacation.

FF realized that, unlike the chef who roamed his kitchen constantly checking the sauces, salad and soups, his eyes were not enough, nor the space small enough. He knew that he couldn't spread himself over an unmanageable span of control. Therefore, he deputized several reliable employees to assist him in quality control.

As much as FF disliked compliments, he detested complaints. Paradoxically, the same person who was not reluctant to criticize his own staff, found it very difficult to accept criticism from outsiders. He had always been a fierce defender of his company, and bridled at negative comments. But he knew he had to listen. He established, therefore, the "Customer Complaint Sheet." By so doing, he gave his customers a leverage position that he had never allowed anyone else. It was a tough, but necessary concession. Customers could not be ignored. "I didn't know what I didn't know," he said. "I needed their input."

Postmortems were difficult for everyone at Foley Fish. Admitting mistakes was no fun. But fun was not the goal, getting better was. Egos and thin skins had to be checked at the door. Soon the customers were applauding Foley's for caring enough to pursue complaints, often saying that Foley Fish was the only vendor who did. Collaborative relationships developed. Foley's and their customers were taking more ownership of each other's success. The customers' voices were added to FF's voice in making Foley workers uncomfortable about their performances when warranted, a real benefit for FF as boss. Overconfidence and complacency would become less frequent.

While FF had the helm, MF still owned the boat. Frank was appointed a Director, replacing Bill Moloney. No stock was given to Frank. For

Frank, stock ownership was a premature subject. It was 1948, and Frank was only 35 years old. He had the complete control that he wanted. "I had no right to expect more."

MF was fortunate to be a rich man who had not raised a son as a rich man's son. FF had rescued his company. MF remained on the sidelines, never publicly questioning his son's performance. After Sunday dinners at 56 Windsor, MF and FF would retire to MF's sanctuary bedroom for private discussions.

Every morning MF could be found in the accounting office on the first floor guarding the pneumatic mailing tube which funneled up the completed sales orders from wholesale operations one floor below. MF created a game for himself — SHAMROCKS — which was his nickname for customer's checks. He spent hours reviewing the completed orders (promised shamrocks), and the received checks (real shamrocks). It was a game in which he was always the winner. On his way home, he would often stop at Novak's Restaurant on Beacon Street, one street before Windsor Road, for a celebratory scotch he naively thought Mother did not notice. Having paid off the company's mortgage, he now owned, debt free, the entire premises. A second-generation Foley was in place. Life was very good.

MF in his office at Friend and Union Streets

CHAPTER 38

FF'S SALES PROGRAM

FF met every Monday morning with his new sales team to reiterate his script for phone sales. "Don't wear out your welcome. Don't talk too long as your customer's time is valuable. Call, get their order and get off the phone. Don't oversell. Persuade customers to order only what is needed for the next three days of fish sales. He or she then can reorder. Their fish will be fresher that way. Explain, if necessary, why Foley's needs orders one day ahead of shipping. Their fish will be cut to order. We can't deliver freshness without their assistance. Record any problems on our master "Complaint Sheet." Get back to them within 24 hours with answers and solutions."

FF was a "paint by the numbers" guy. You had to stay within the lines he drew. He didn't want sales to be a mindless following of rules but, early on, given the team's inexperience, he allowed little room for creativity. Tom Flannery was promoted from the shellfish department; Jimmy Barker from the retail operations; Joe Recommendes (a recovering alcoholic, let go by Bill Moloney), was rehired as an order taker (a personal favor by FF to Joe's family); and Steve Connolly, a recent graduate from Commerce High School, was reassigned from the accounting office to sales.

FF was happy that he had an inexperienced sales team; it eliminated the need to have them un-learn Bill Moloney's undisciplined methods. Sales technique for FF was a cluster of traits and skills learned and practiced on the job until they became second nature. There were no shortcuts, no magic, and no overnight success. Foley Fish was about selling quality — quality fish and quality people.

The Foley sales staff was a team with interchangeable human parts. This meant there were few delays occasioned by callbacks. The team was not comprised of independent players paid by commission. FF's thinking on commissions was that if he paid the sales staff a commission for each sale, then he'd have to pay commissions to all the floor workers too, bankrupting the company. He was fully aware that he was taking the fun out of the traditional system in which salesmen could wheel and deal on prices and favors. At Foley's, the salesmen weren't so much making sales, as they there were recording them. Fun was not a reason you worked at Foley Fish. Employees came and stayed on because they had pride in working for an ethical, successful company. At Foley's, the fish was the star.

But after the war, Foley's retail business, while profitable, became less so each year because its traditional customers were emigrating to the suburbs. The Friend and Union Streets retail outlet had become less convenient, and also inefficient. Foley's was sputtering, waiting to stall. Part of the reason was that FF preferred the wholesale over retail. It was more profitable. One wholesale customer would request 100 pounds of fish per order, while the retail customer only bought one pound. But out of respect for MF, FF kept the retail operation open.

With the retail business declining, and the sales staff confined to order taking, how was Foley Fish going to grow? New seafood companies were sprouting up in Boston which created a buyers' market. This was not a favorable development: local restaurants were playing local seafood suppliers against each other for lower prices. FF would not play that game. One price, no bargaining, no discounts at Foley Fish. He decided to capitalize on positive post-World War II developments — especially the new, more efficient transportation infrastructure, which enabled fish to be trucked overnight from Boston to major cities like Chicago, Detroit, and Cleveland. Another consideration was the expanding middle class that could afford a house, appliances, a car and have enough left over to eat out at local restaurants.

FF appointed himself lead salesman in charge of the Midwest prospecting effort. But he was as inexperienced in external sales as his fledgling staff was with retail sales. He had many questions, but few answers. When I asked him what his objective had been, he said, "It was not to sell fish, it was to learn. I had to know the ins and outs of restaurant operations before I could make promises that would help them expand and thrive."

In Detroit, he focused exclusively on Joe Muer's Oyster House on Gratiot Avenue. It was run by Joe Muer, Jr., another son of an immigrant. The restaurant opened on October 28, 1929 one day before the Wall Street crash. Initially, there were only seven tables but by the end of World War II, Muer's couldn't add enough tables fast enough to meet demand.

On his first trip to Detroit, FF didn't make a call on Muer's management, but he ate there: lunch and dinner for three consecutive days. He was doing his homework. He instantly liked Muer's democratic process of seating — first come, first served, including the movers and shakers of the auto industry. Muer's seafood menu was thin — lake fish — and offered zero North Atlantic seafood. Their biggest sellers were Lake Superior whitefish and pickerel. No sauces were used to disguise or enhance their ingredients. Customers could order their fish one of three ways: baked, broiled, or fried. Frank never ate an overcooked piece of fish at Muers. An eight-ounce portion of pike (a.k.a. pickerel) was $2.00, while whitefish was $3.25 for the same sized portion. Foley Fish was selling Atlantic cod fillet for .40/lb., meaning that an eight-ounce portion would only cost Muer's $.20 cents, which after adding the freight charge of $.05 cents per half-pound serving portion, and cost of wrap arounds (potato, vegetable, salad) of .10 cents, resulted in a total plate cost of just $.35 cents. Muer's could charge $2.50, making it the lowest- priced protein (chicken was $2.85, red meat was $3.50) on their menu. Bottom line: a profit of $2.15 per serving of cod.

There were no fish smells. The servers were hotel-trained pros who had emigrated from Europe. The parking lot for lunch and dinner was always filled (FF always parked in a non-customer spot in the back of the restaurant where he could see the names of Muer's poultry, meat, and produce suppliers — all of whom had superb reputations).

Was Muer's account winnable and was it worth winning? An emphatic yes to the latter, but did FF have the wherewithal to win a big chunk of their seafood business with a "foreign" fish called cod? Muer's business was already excellent. Why risk its present cod-free success?

His homework completed FF returned home believing that Muer's menu was ready for the addition of a North Atlantic species. Oddly enough, he felt comfortable with the challenge. First, he met with Muer's butcher, Ernie Zeltwanger. FF was understated without any hint of false modesty: "Your restaurant," he said, "is doing well without Foley Fish Co. of Boston as a purveyor, so I'd understand if you refused to meet with me. In their meeting FF was not boastful, and avoided trumpeting superlatives about his company. Harvard was never mentioned. He was compelling in an unanticipated way, and displayed none of the flashiness of the super salesman. He was anti-sales in many ways, and eschewed "sucker" prices to get an order, He offered no quantity discounts and required orders two days before receipt of fish. No dazzling with a broad array of seafood; he only discussed one fish: cod. When Ernie asked about lobsters, FF replied, "We don't carry lobsters because we can't control their quality."

Frank never talked down the competition. To him the primary competition was Muer's chicken and beef plates. Because he didn't handle lake fish (for the same reason he avoided lobsters), he was not competing with the local fish supplier.

At the conclusion of the meeting, FF left no calling card (he had none), and no marketing material. Marketing had a phony ring to him; it was like sauces on fish: unnecessary with quality fish. He wasn't expecting an order, in fact, he would be uncomfortable if there was one too soon, because "Muers has more homework to do on us." His concluding comment to Ernie was that Muer's didn't need Foley's.

Subsequent visits with Ernie and Joe Muer Jr., the owner, finally resulted in an order by Muer's. It was the first one of over 7,800 orders shipped by Foley's to Muer's over the next 50 years. The total exceeded 7, 800,000 pounds of fish.

"Joe Muer Jr. taught me the restaurant business," FF told me. "Joe said I taught him the fish business." They became the closest of friends — good fish and good people go together.

FF and Joe Muer, Jr. visiting a fishing boat in New Bedford

CHAPTER 39

UNION INEVITABILITY

During World War II, unions were furious because wages had been fixed and food stamps were taxed. "Black market" food prices had skyrocketed. Holders of "A" cards, the majority of Americans, were limited to five gallons of gasoline per week which severely restricted a family's driving.

Sweat shops disappeared, but management still ruled with an iron hand. Businessmen became the villains. Unions strengthened. The non-union shop became a relic. MF saw that a seafood union was inevitable. He was on the opposite side, management.

The majority of Foley workers belonged to the "sacrifice generation." They never questioned MF's paternalistic management style — until now. Acquiescence to MF's wage decisions became a thing of the past. MF did not resist the men unionizing. But it was difficult for him, given his origins, to understand the need for a union. "How can employees insist on job security? I never had it and I'm the owner. Don't they remember that not one Foley worker was laid off during the Depression? Foley Fish has been a successful company without a union."

FF had a broader historical perspective than his father, which allowed him to better understand the inevitability of unions at Foley Fish. Many industrialists had been ungenerous bastards, brutally treating their workers. Legitimate grievances of workers had been ignored. Yes, unions fought back using illegitimate means, but what was their alternative?

The year 1946 was one of fierce labor-management strife. Union workers were fighting for "catch up" pay hikes. Meat packing companies, railroads, as well as General Motors and US Steel were struck again and again. Unions were unwilling to wait any longer for relief. Such was the acrimonious backdrop for FF's negotiations with the International Longshoreman's Association, and its affiliate, the Seafood Workers Union (Local #2). These negotiations were first in the history of the company.

FF was not a raging egomaniac, just raging, someone anonymously stated. He set the standards and enforced them in a brusque, uncompromising way. A consensus of one. No one would dare challenge his decisions until now. How would FF emotionally handle union negotiations that would require conciliations?

FF did not know how collective bargaining worked. "I've got to learn the rules and understand the shoulds and should nots." He would meet with John Donegan, Sr., the Boston Seafood Union's boss. Before contract discussions began, FF's power had been absolute. So, reaching consensus would be a new experience. He was no longer in total control.

John Donegan did not hold back. He emphasized that FF was now dealing with a strong union and a "collective" of his men whom he could not treat as individuals that could be yelled at without consequence. Temper outbursts will not work. Donegan told him, in so many words, "Our workers feel that, bluntly, you are a pain in the ass to work for. Negotiations will be emotional enough, but if escalated, can hurt both sides. Be prepared to hear their pent-up outbursts. You are a frustrating boss to them. You are not easy to get along with. For many of your workers Foley Fish is not a fun place. For you, Foley Fish comes first. For me, the workers and their families come first, but to me, the existence of Foley Fish is a very close second. Your authority will be contested as your men resent your dictatorial ways."

Donegan, apparently, was trying to intimidate. FF listened politely, not contesting Donegan's portrayals, nor disclosing his own reactions. Had there been a transcript of this meeting, Donegan's harsh assertions would endear him to Foley workers. He had really put it to FF, who was, however, unbothered. In fact, he told me that he viewed Donegan's recommendation to stay calm as a valuable piece of advice.

Donegan predicted better than the local Boston weathermen. The three Foley union reps were clearly antagonistic in their prefacing remarks concerning FF's unchecked autonomy. The first item on their list of demands was that FF not to be allowed on the processing floor during work hours. Furthermore, he could not talk directly to any worker, but must communicate through the union steward (Vito Cherissimino). The remaining list of demands read like a Christmas wish list: pay doubled, vacation time doubled, seven paid holidays up from four, seniority rights in layoffs, and a reduction of the apprentice term from three months to one month.

The union had its time at bat. Now, it was FFs turn. He responded not in his customary authoritarian voice, but in a more humane way. "It is not my intent to control the men, but to manage their actions when needed. I set high standards which I know are demanding but are essential for Foley Fish's existence. My control is used as a means, not an end, to insure the ongoing production of quality fish. When Bill Moloney tried to sabotage our company by taking all our wholesale accounts when he left, together we defeated him because of our product superiority. It took both of us to secure this victory. We are a winning team. We have the right line up. No changes are needed."

He then got into the details, stating, "Foley Fish needs more than three months to cull out apprentices who can hurt the company for years to come. We want a six-month trial period for new employees. We will continue with paid holidays, all being official U.S. national holidays. Absenteeism has been an increasing problem. Chronic offenders must be dealt with. We need to jointly establish a penalty that is fair to all. We will not submit a wage response until you return with a realistic proposal."

FF took seriously his role as provider and protector. His father's paternalistic style would not be discontinued. He had an inbred sense of responsibility for providing Foley workers a compensation package that could allow them a decent living. He wanted a decent pay that could enable his men to make mortgage payments on a home, buy a car and needed appliances while providing clothing and feeding the entire family. But he did not stop there. It was not enough. They had earned and deserved more than decent pay. Spending over one half of their waking hours laboring in a cold, wet plant doing physically and mentally demanding work only to return home without status called for a "more than decent" total compensation package for his workers.

Donegan had forewarned that the men would fight him on their pay demands. What was omitted was "except if you pay more than Foley's competition for the next two years." Not only did FF do that, but added, without union pressure, a family medical plan paid by the company.

The union dropped their proposal to keep FF off the processing floor, but insisted that he be the only owner/boss allowed on the processing floor during work hours. The apprentice review period was lengthened to six months. Paid holidays remained the same. Absenteeism wording was saved for the next contract in two years.

Despite the fact that both men began the relationship in a calculating way, Donegan's and FF's relationship evolved into an authentic friendship that made future union negotiations smarter and kinder. FF's relationship with his workers improved especially when they learned that the contract terms regarding vacations and holidays would apply equally to Foley management. They were not second-class citizens. They should not have been surprised; FF owned a modest $10,000 home and drove a car older than those of most of his workers. His car had roll down windows, no A/C, no radio, no whitewall tires, and a stick, not automatic shift. Frank was a "skinny," not a fat cat.

CHAPTER 40

FF'S TEAM

FF looked at the world upside down. He was most worried when things were going well. The early Fifties was an era of phenomenal economic growth. People were making and spending more money – purchasing homes, appliances, and cars at record rates while beginning to eat out in large numbers at restaurants. Yet, FF's Celtic wariness told him something was wrong. He was uneasy. His attempt to control every aspect of Foley Fish's wholesale operation from his "anchor desk," where buying, sales, and production intersected, was not working. Trapped behind the anchor desk, he noticed that the day's events never seemed to go as he had choreographed. "The brown stuff," he often said, "was piled up on my forehead daily by 8:00 a.m. If it wasn't, I knew that I was not involved enough." But too much was hidden by his limited perspective at the anchor desk. He realized that he did not know enough to run Foley Fish alone, not properly. Sales and production were not in sync; in fact, they were going in opposite directions. Sales were outstripping production capability, and the gap was increasing. Every day it was more and more challenging to meet delivery deadlines. The Customers Complaint Sheet was getting crowded.

FF had always been uncomfortable with sharing power, so he hadn't. Fish sales were moving ahead at an acceptable clip, yet Foley Fish was going backwards and quality was threatened. He knew that sales had to be moderated, while production was disciplined. To accomplish this, his one-man, despotic management structure had to be modified. Consequently, in 1952 he formed a new management team. Steve Connolly was put in charge of sales, and Russ Rohrbacher was assigned to head up production. It was a quantum change, a turning point for Foley Fish, as FF had never before sought input from his managers. It would be a challenging time for FF and his two untested department heads. He would still control the company but would increasingly depend on them to implement his plans. Steve and Russ would, however, have to prove themselves before FF would cede to them major decision-making authority.

After graduating from the High School of Commerce (Boston) in 1942, Steve Connolly came directly to Foley Fish to work in the accounting office. After Bill Moloney left Foley Fish in 1948, FF moved Steve into sales, Steve proved himself a quick study, and he did a terrific job winning back many accounts hijacked by Moloney.

FF explained to Connolly that sales orders had outstripped the company's production capability, and this had led to many customer complaints. Under Bill Moloney's management, an unconstrained sales department had dominated, and production problems were given short shrift, or ignored. But with the new management structure, production would no longer be subservient to sales. In fact, going forward production capacity would regulate sales – this was a dispiriting message for Steve.

FF's revised sales strategy began with the assumption that Foley's present daily processing capacity was cutting six thousand pounds of cod, haddock, and flounder fillets, and this work had to be totally uninterrupted by the cutting of specialty fish (mackerel, ocean perch). FF laid down three mandates: 1) sales personnel would restrict sales to cod, haddock, and flounder fillets (plus any pass-thru items like shellfish and sea scallops); 2) "once a week" shipping accounts would shift to "twice-a-week" shipments to streamline production (and double the shelf life of fish); and 3) new accounts would have to agree to receive shipments only on Tuesdays and Thursdays, the two slowest days of the week.

To accomplish these mandates, FF had to rein Steve in, curb his competitive impulses. But slowing down was alien to Steve's deep-rooted methods and ambitions. And so began a complicated relationship. FF and Connolly became an odd couple: Steve, the hare, going all out to sell all he could, while FF, the tortoise, leaned on the brakes, restraining sales. Steve's goal was for Foley Fish to be the biggest, while FF focused on being the best.

FF had a similar task with Russ. He told him, "I'm promoting you from foreman to head of production. Sales are exceeding processing capabilities, causing too many errors." This prompted Russ, true to his blunt German heritage, to reply, "Are you saying that you are promoting me because I am not doing my job?"

The men on the floor respected Russ's leadership. They did what he said. At the last hour of the workday, often behind schedule, he became the heroic coxswain exhorting his crew to up the stroke to an all-out sprint – not for two minutes, but sixty – generating a powerful surge making up the lost time. FF counseled him: "There's no quit in you and your team. It's admirable, but you are blind to the impact on them and the company. Your team is outrunning quality control. They are becoming mistake prone, which leads to more customer complaints. You and Steve are my new lieutenants, but you are also a part of the problem. We need sales to sell what processing can produce without compromising quality." he concluded.

FF presented a revised sales program that would enable production to catch up and reduce errors. Russ, who had a big assertive, and sometimes irreverent personality, fired back: "Did you really graduate from Harvard? These sales ideas are the dumbest I've ever heard. We can up the production capacity without limiting sales. Give me a week and I'll be back with a better plan."

One week later, a confident Russ exploded into FF's office exclaiming, "Thank God you have a drop-out high schooler to give you advice. We can expand production capacity quickly. First, we set up a second cutting room behind the retail room devoted to cutting specialty fish, and move two cutters there; second, we hire two new cutters as replacements; third, we start at six a.m. instead of seven a.m., increasing processing time by one full hour. What do you say?"

FF respected Russ's proposal, but saw that he'd left out the human aspects. His answer was "No, No, No! Those are easy fixes, but they will only prolong the problem. We need a more disciplined, coordinated, and balanced production-sales relationship that will solve our present problem, hopefully forever. And the first step is to reduce sales, and take the pressure off production."

What Steve and Russ had yet to learn was that FF would never agree to more going on than he could control. But both men (both indefatigable) would have to learn. Steve and Russ had become used to operating at only one speed, full throttle. Pressure was their narcotic of choice. They needed detoxing. FF built fences around them to inhibit their exuberance. Unlike them, he would always be clear-headed, cautious, unhurried, resolving matters carefully after lengthy study.

FF's management style had not changed. He still relied heavily on the power of saying no. He was ordering, not listening. Dissenting news was dismissed. Peremptorily, he insisted on stabilizing operations before moving ahead, quality before quantity.

But he still had no one to give him tips on management. His father, the founder, was not his management role model, having allowed Bill Moloney the unfettered freedom that had threatened the company's existence. Eventually, FF turned to Walter Brown, whom he'd known from growing up in Brookline, where Walter owned the Texaco gas station on Route 9. Brown was the first owner of the Boston Celtics. FF had come to admire the management style of Red Auerbach, Walter's first head coach. Red insisted on unselfishness and teamwork. His strategy was a team composed of players who complemented each other, but without any superstars (that came later). The team was the superstar, not any one player. Bob Cousy was his playmaker; Bill Sharman his marksman; Ed McCauley, his rebounding center; Bob Brannum, his policemen under the basket; Bob Donham, his defense specialist shutting down the opponent's top scorers; and Frank Ramsey, the sixth man off the bench who sparked rallies. In the early fifties no Celtic would appear on the top ten scorers' list. But championship flags would line the Boston Garden's rafters. This was the kind of winning teamwork FF desired.

FF initiated monthly meetings with Steve and Russ usually over dinner at Pier 4, Anthony Athanas's landmark Boston restaurant. He had assigned their roles and now, like Red Auerbach, preached teamwork. FF wanted Steve to be as cognizant and concerned about production errors as he wanted Russ to be about sales mistakes that a harried production crew could cause.

In time, FF, with Steve and Russ, initiated what were called "profit sharing" meetings with floor personnel. The premise was that workers at each workstation knew more than management did about their specific task so why not tap into that resource to improve company performance. FF quickly learned that his overbearing, brusque manner had created resentment that led floor workers to resist his requests for input. The workers were fearful of being embarrassed by FF if their ideas didn't suit him. Being a union shop, some were afraid of being critical of a co-worker or, even worse, causing someone to be fired. Others regarded management as their adversary in union negotiations, so why help them.

Monthly management meetings produced some winning ideas. "Take home fish" once a week for all Foley employees was instituted. Soon, the company ethos was enshrined in a slogan: "Sell to our customer only what you'd be willing to bring home to your own family." Russ took a course in time and motion studies resulting in the installation of adjustable cutter stands and special lighting. Both changes significantly improved cutter efficiency. Russ recommended that Bobby Boyd attend these meetings. Bobby, son of George Boyd long-time head of Foley's freezer department, had worked the summer of 1946 and 1947 at Foleys, and in 1948 was hired as a "foreman-in-training" under Russ. But after his first monthly meeting at Pier 4, Bobby, still in the union, wrote in two hours overtime on his timecard after the meeting. The next day FF told him, "We don't pay for stuff like that." Bobby complained to Russ: "I'd rather be with my kids than with you three guys who I see all day long." Bobby did not realize that a major reason for the promotions of Steve and Russ was that five p.m. did not mark the end of their work day. Russ told Bobby that he would never make it to management until he shed his union mentality.

In time, three guys – not just FF — were pushing the rock up the hill. Like the Celtics, Steve and Russ absorbed Coach Foley's upside-down thinking: more (sales) can be less, and less (production) can be more. But it was the unconventional FF, gifted with a "wariness" gene, who pinpointed the core problem: overselling, before it paralyzed the company.

CHAPTER 41

A MISDIAGNOSIS

Years later, FF told me of the agonizing reappraisal of Foley Fish he undertook in 1952. "What I initially thought was just a bad case of indigestion was much more serious," he said. We weren't making good on our promises to our customers. We were making too many mistakes. Our arteries and minds were clogged. But we caught it early enough to not require open-heart surgery. The bottlenecks caused mistakes that should have indicated a deeper problem. I had to drill down to the root cause: me. I was not focusing on our central need: quality control. I was screwing up. We had to slow down our processing, yes, even shrink the operation in order to eventually grow. Operations were too complex, so I cut our product list in half hoping that the reduction would align sales with a more realistically defined production capacity. My new concern was that Steve and Russ were unconvinced that my plan would work. How can Foley Fish get bigger with less sales? The truth was that we would never get bigger until we got better."

With his customary sense of urgency FF initially jammed his plan down the team's throat, but soon realized that he had to persuade, not coerce. Winning the team over would not be easy. To accomplish this, he began to reconsider his management style. It was a difficult decision for FF, a confirmed martinet. He committed himself to carefully, patiently, repeatedly explaining how less is better, how Foley Fish could grow in the future by shrinking in the present.

Steve, unsurprisingly, was unhappy and confused by the new order announced by FF. He had been busting his butt bringing in new accounts.

Now, prospecting was halted because new customers would chafe at being told when they could and couldn't order fish. Present accounts would protest when fewer products were offered for sale. "What happened to the customer is always right?" he asked. FF's contradictory plan was tough for Steve to understand, much less implement. Steve loved selling, was proud of his productivity, and consequently felt stifled.

Ever the counterintuitive contrarian, FF saw things differently. Over 90 percent of present customers' orders were for haddock, cod, flounder, sea scallops, and shellfish. Foregoing the ten percent of volume devoted to other kinds of product would be a sizable loss, but still tolerable. In time, new accounts would compensate for the ten percent loss, despite the "advanced one day" restriction. In taking this action, Foley Fish would be doing the same as meat purveyors who offered a limited number of beef cuts.

FF sat Steve and Russ down to further explain his thinking, a first for the autocratic Frank Foley: "Everyone in the fish business has a gimmick – some have price, some make it by camouflaging inferior quality, others employ volume discounts. Foley's gimmick is quality. With unduplicated quality, the game is rigged in our favor. Quality comes before everything else. It's the reason why profit is always the bottom line of a profit and loss statement – it comes after quality. When Bill Moloney stole all of Foley's wholesale accounts [1948], I told you we would retrieve those accounts in one year. We did. Today [1952], I have the same confidence in today's game plan. I am for sales; I am for profits. I am for growth – but not the erratic type. I want sustainable, uninterrupted growth that we can control. Right now, we are all making too many mistakes. We need to step back and regain our bearings. Stop thinking pounds sold and shipped, think quality."

FF made this same point over and over to his team, but also listened to and deflected objections, patiently and thoroughly. These discussions proved to be a watershed moment at Foley Fish. He'd made a stand for quality, but he couldn't do it alone. He needed Steve and Russ to buy into his approach.

How did FF become so enamored of quality? He had a predisposition for it, ultimately deriving from his father's example. It was in his "craftsman" DNA – a fussiness, an integrity, an obsessive attention to detail, and, yes, his unwavering resolve. FF couldn't run Foley Fish any other way. It defined his intention and shaped all his endeavors. It was his deepest aspiration. Quality was the centerpiece of all his business dealings with suppliers, customers, fishermen, and Foley workers. He strove daily to deliver the best fish. It wasn't all altruism; he expected that quality would have a tangible benefit, profitability. Oaths unbroken led to trust and long-standing relations. Quality commitment gave Foley's a competitive advantage that effectively countered the price buyers and junk merchants. It also made his workers feel better about themselves. Held to a higher standard, they grew in their vocation to being the best, like the Celtics.

FF inherited his father's pragmatism. Out of a desperate set of circumstances he, like MF, contradicted conventional business thinking. In a time of business turmoil, FF imposed structure, order and lasting profitability on Foley Fish. And he succeeded. FF was not only born into Foley Fish, he became Foley Fish.

CHAPTER 42

RESTART

The Fifties and Sixties marked a period of unprecedented growth in the United States. New levels of consumption, unthinkable in the previous two decades, emerged and burgeoned. The transformation from the Depression mentality of sacrifice and frugality was replaced by an optimism best summarized by the notion that "we are earning more, so we can spend more." Self-indulgence substituted for self-denial. Wants became needs. Fueled by higher wages, consumers bought starter homes, cars, and appliances in record numbers. Eating out, once the exclusive domain of the rich, now extended to the middle class. The restaurant industry was democratized. Installment credit that enabled buying now and paying later helped finance eating out. Married couples rewarded themselves, the wife for running the home, and the husband for putting in long hours at work. Restaurant dining soon became ordinary and unremarked.

MF was an immigrant who started Foley Fish, and other immigrants did the same, starting restaurants and the small businesses that supplied them. Diners and hole-in-the wall luncheonettes grew into major restaurants. For example, Jimmy Doulos's Liberty Cafe was enlarged multiple times to become the famous Jimmy's Harborside Restaurant on the Boston waterfront; Anthony Athanas, an immigrant from Albania, owned and operated Pier IV, the number one volume restaurant in the U.S. for years; and the "unpronounceable" Dini Theodoropoulos at Argo Diner in Binghamton, New York was successful enough to afford the electricity bill for his name on the neon sign on top of his diner.

Not all boats were rising with the consumer-driven tide. Foley's was not. Held back by FF's draconian plan, sales decreased. Accounts lost were not necessarily offset by new accounts. Foley Fish's competitors were having a field day claiming, "Foley Fish is difficult to deal with and only offers a few species; they require one-day ahead ordering, and are insensitive to your costs as Foley's only ships in expensive tins. We're as good as Foley Fish but our prices are lower."

Russ knew that Frank would not flinch. He was a rules person who saw the world as it ought to be and was unbothered when his vision collided with the world's reality. Fortunately, Russ loved a challenge. He huddled daily with Bobby Boyd, his new foreman, to analyze prior mistakes, most of which were logistical: ordered but unshipped items, mis-shipments because of incorrect addresses, and incorrect species sent. Corrective action involved adding staff to the packing and shipping departments to double check orders. The loading of third-party independent trucks (Gordon Baker: Cleveland, Detroit, and Chicago; Berman's: upstate New York; and Rogers and Kasper: Pennsylvania) had to be supervised by either Bobby or Russ. Russ (an excellent fish cutter, who could cleanly cut and de-bone shad fish) filled in as a cutter to pace the cutting line. Productivity improved. The Germanic Russ willed it.

Despite these major changes, Foley Fish was still sputtering. The reduced sales figures were unnerving, yet FF adamantly stuck to his plan. He knew that Foley Fish could tolerate criticism regarding types of fish offered, and one-day advance ordering, but if old customers lost faith, the damage could be lasting, and even fatal.

To their credit, Steve and Russ finally took ownership of FF's plan, with no muttering or public questioning. After six months, production capacity edged into synchronization with demand, and soon after, FF gave the green light to solicit new accounts. He also expanded Foley's product scope by adding halibut, salmon, swordfish, cape bluefish, mackerel and shad (only in season). Finally, he also lifted the restriction on when new accounts could order, eliminating the embargo on certain days.

FF was pleased, and vindicated, although he had never seriously doubted his temporary retrenchment. With the crisis behind him, Frank returned to prospecting, first in Chicago. He called on Arnie Morton of Morton's Steakhouse fame, and Don Roth, owner of the popular Blackhawk Restaurant.

FF's pitch to both gentlemen was the same: "You are successful because your beef is the best tasting meat in Chicago. You don't need another signature item; however, I'd like to introduce you and your discriminating customers to Foley's signature item: North Atlantic Cod. I guarantee it will have the same dependable quality and flavor as your justly celebrated meat menu items." He did not cite the lower price of cod compared to meat (even after freight), because he was not selling on price. Further, cod would not compete; it was intended to complement restaurants' meat offerings.

FF also visited the executive chef of the Drake Hotel whose flagship restaurant was named the Cape Cod Room (a misnomer as no Cape Cod fish was on the menu). He hoped the chef might want another fish to complement the Drake's Lake Superior whitefish and imported Dover sole. When the chef rejected cod as a "retail fish," FF suggested North Atlantic haddock as a worthy substitute, arguing that its white flakes and denser texture would appeal to Chicagoans. Showing a competitive flair, he suggested spelling "scrod" on the menu as "schrod," which would signal that it was a member of the haddock family. The chef liked the idea as it could create a bit of drama that would enable their wait staff to demonstrate their fish knowledge and the restaurant's unique offerings.

All three restaurants ordered their "one" Atlantic species. Not a bad week of sales calls. Most satisfying to Frank was that he showed his sales team that the number of species offered was, perhaps, less important than they thought.

Frank's early success with the big restaurants in Chicago and Detroit did not dissuade him from encouraging the efforts of his sales personnel to engage small independents. He frowned on investing too much effort in Boston where many restaurants nickeled and dimed you and some chefs looked for favors. FF believed that, for the most part, people would still buy the best, the ambience and size of the restaurant notwithstanding. Word-of-mouth endorsements of where it was good to eat became the criteria of Foley Fish prospecting. FF preferred ten, one hundred-pound orders to one, thousand-pound order to diversify his risks. In time, Foley's sales increased in this segment, and some no-name restaurants became known.

Steve was the other rainmaker of the sales team. He didn't just sell; he attacked with urgency, trying to make up for lost time. His healthy ego didn't permit the possibility of not winning. Less patient and modest than FF, Steve expected to win over each prospect and monopolize the fish business of each converted prospect by having Foley Fish dominate their appetizer list, as well as the entree sections of the menu.

Steve assigned himself to the Connecticut market, and was quickly successful winning over many hospital accounts such as the New Haven Hospital and St. Raphael Hospital (long before they turned to outside food service vendors), and independents such as the Copper Beach Inn, the Griswold Inn, and many others.

Steve promoted Tom Flannery from head of the shellfish department to chief salesman for upstate New York, New Hampshire and Vermont. In those days, the owners of the small independents — many of them recent immigrants — valued personal relationships with a firm's sales force as much as the firm's products. Often, salesmen were considered to be members of the family. Tom was a knowledgeable, well-mannered gentleman who became beloved by his customers, many of whom "adopted" him in this way. In his territory, many of the small independents started out as luncheonettes. The owner was the guy with the apron on, serving Grandma's recipes, personally ladling chowder into bowls, cleaning tables — the whole house was his domain (much like FF's operation), not just the office. In time, Tom won lots of resort businesses, including White Face Inn (Lake Placid, NY), Inn at Sugar Hill (NH), Woodstock Inn (VT), Four Chimney Inn (VT), Mt. View House (Whitefield, NH), Brewster Inn (NY), Sherwood Inn (Skaneateles, NY), and Olympia Tea Room (Binghamton, NY).

Supporting this sales team when they were on the road was the 'inside' team of Joe Recommendees, Jimmy Barker, George Kenneally, and FF himself. When the wholesale accounts grew to critical mass in key cities, FF and Steve hired "on-site" Foley reps to mind the accounts. These included the following: Gil Klein in Detroit: (Myers, Hudson Stores, Detroit Athletic Club); St. Louis: (Miss Hulling's Cafeteria, Styx, Baer and Fuller Department Stores, Staub's, and the St. Louis Club); Harry

McCarthy in Pittsburgh: (Duquesne Club, Mercy Hospital and St. Francis Hospital); and Gino Pirelli in Florida (Breakers, Vinay Park).

FF insisted on the inclusion of the Foley Fish receptionist as a key member of the sales team. The receptionist's role, in addition to answering outside calls, was to call at mutually agreeable, prescheduled times the company's customers and connect them with their Foley sales counterpart. No waiting or put-on-hold requests with Foley's phone system. The receptionist's position was so important that only Frank interviewed applicants. One time, FF interviewed Agnes Taggerty but rejected her. "I'm not hiring that lady. Too damn pretty; no work would be done by the gawking employees." He did hire Louise Christianson who filled the position from 1952 to 1960. Perhaps Foley customers' favorite was Kay Bombard (1960-1980). When out-of-town customers visited Foley's, they would always ask first for Kay.

Kay was class personified, well mannered, well dressed, and always cheerful. The year Kay retired, was a poor year for Foley's profit sharing. Frank paid out of his own pocket an amount equal to the average salary in a normal year. Loyalty begot loyalty. To this day, a Foley receptionist will greet you — no punching in extensions.

CHAPTER 43

PROFIT SHARING

MF had it right in the beginning: quality rules. Bill Moloney lost this vision, and lost his position. FF re-founded the company on this rock of quality. New to management, Steve and Russ were now adherents. At first, they had resisted FF's decree that prioritized quality over growth. The strictures he imposed on both sales and production seemed wrong-headed to them…until they didn't. The light went on, and stayed on. Both men became converts.

With the right team in place, FF lessened his grip on the management reins. He stopped hovering, and allowed them to do the necessary micromanaging. There would not be another power struggle like the one involving Bill Moloney. Neither Steve nor Russ aspired to become the next boss at Foley Fish, partly out of personal choice, and partly because they learned, when they substituted for FF, that the top job was time-consuming and nerve-wracking.

FF had agreed with Russ's recommendation to have all the floor workers start one hour earlier in order to create additional production capacity. Frank was surprised when Donegan, the union boss, initially refused his request for the early start unless workers received overtime pay (one-and-a-half time's hourly pay) for the first hour of each working day. FF acquiesced. It was a bitter price but necessary.

Foley Fish had no retirement plan for its employees. New retirees like Frank Souza, the legendary buyer, found that Social Security was insufficient for a decent standard of living, as it provided on average only thirty percent of an annual wage. This was not acceptable to FF. As he told me later, "It's more than a job, it's their life, and I was accountable to them for their lives after their work ended at Foley Fish."

Behind the scenes Frank quietly began studying profit-sharing plans. Neither the workers nor the union had ever discussed profit-sharing. Frank attended monthly meetings of the New England Chapter for Profit Sharing, read all the extant literature, and visited with chief financial officers, including Paul Kinnealy at Roche Brothers, a family-owned supermarket chain in the Boston suburbs.

Profit sharing provided employees a stake in the company. Workers who had a stake in the profits of a company would necessarily become more invested in its success, adopting "an owner's instinct." Previously, FF had failed miserably when asking for employee input to improve Foley Fish. So profit sharing was a leap for him, especially since he was uncertain that unionized employees would shift their allegiance more to the company. Additionally, some workers groused that FF should increase wages instead of putting money into their retirement funds. All these reasons made it seem unlikely that FF would institute a profit- sharing plan at Foley Fish to buy labor peace.

But ever-contrarian FF did just that, perhaps to his own surprise. Here's how he explained it to me: "Working at Foley Fish is more than just a job; it is a commitment which makes it stressful. Our workers spend more of their non-sleeping lives here than at home. I am accountable to them and their families after they retire. They've earned the right to a profit-sharing plan. Social Security won't provide enough income when they retire. It's not good enough. Profit sharing will close the gap."

There was another component to his thinking. Frank did not want Foley workers to be distracted while they were at work. Reducing their financial security concerns might allow them to better focus on their work. He hoped that the creation of a profit plan would communicate loudly that workers mattered. He was well aware of the priceless benefits of motivating loyalty, mutual trust, and cooperation. Profit sharing would stabilize Foley Fish.

All Foley workers already participated in a benefit package covering medical benefits, vacation days, sick days, and bereavement days. Now, all workers (including clerical) would participate in the profit-sharing plan. Each Foley's share distribution would be equal to their annual wages as a percentage of the total wages paid. Annually, the CPA's report would be mailed to each participant. No early withdrawals would be allowed for vacations, home purchases, or tuition. The Foley plan would be a pure retirement plan, allowing no withdrawal until retirement. An independent trust administrator, paid by Foley Fish, would be hired to assure total compliance with federal and state tax laws.

The Foley profit-sharing plan would never become part of the union contract. FF knew some malcontent would attempt to revamp or otherwise sabotage the plan. Of course, many Foley workers were not thinking about retirement. They, like many Americans, assumed that their mortgage would be paid off before retirement, creating an ample nest egg. But there were always multiple reasons why mortgage payoffs were delayed. The Foley plan was another leg of a retirement stool. Unlike many American workers – certainly none in the seafood industry at that time — Foley workers became partners of a sort; they had "skin in the game." Each Foley worker would benefit from creating a bigger financial pie from which came bigger slices of profit. Each distribution would be tax-free until liquidation, which meant that share profits were reinvested in safe havens, and were compounding, further enhancing each worker's account.

On December 19, 1955 the Foley Board of Directors adopted the profit-sharing trust. Before that date, all profits redounded exclusively to MF; after it, a significant portion went to the workers. Fifty years later, over fifteen million dollars was in the Foley Profit-Sharing Trust. FF had put his workers ahead of his heirs and their descendants. It was not a difficult decision. The workers had earned this money, while his heirs had yet to do so.

The decision to put his workers on a proportionately equal profit footing was entirely FF's. He knew it was not only the right thing to do, but for him the only thing to do. FF had already given a big part of himself, now he was giving a big part of his future net worth. The average Foley worker stayed over forty years at Foley Fish (ten, over fifty), and the plan fostered an owner's instinct in each worker. The commonweal created by FF's foresight was invaluable to the success and longevity of the Foley Fish Co.

CHAPTER 44

MF STILL PRESENT

Few founders remain at work three quarters of a century after they started. Most founders fail and fade away. But not MF. He never lost touch with the business. Neglect is a silent killer in any business, but especially at a company that processes perishable products and values its workers. Most successful founders labor mightily, and then step back, assuming all is well. MF saw it differently, and remained involved over the decades, albeit at a slower pace. MF could not be overlooked, or presumed. He was not. He was the founder and no one could take that away from him. He had created the owner's quality mindset that would endure. Fifty years from the 1906 inception of Foley Fish, MF was at the Foley plant every workday. He was not retired, nor was he tired of being there.

How did the Foley workers see MF? Perhaps as a non-threatening presence, a bit out of reach, courteous, but not big headed despite still being the owner of this successful second-generation company. No airs. There was incomplete understanding of his role, which was part of the fascination about him. He floated between his retail and his wholesale operations, appearing every noon at the shellfish department for his daily lunch of four Wellfleet clams, his four meaty Cockenoe oysters, washed down by a neat whiskey across the street. His presence was a subtle and steady reminder of tenacity and commitment. He was unique and quietly revered.

His customers and friends saw him as a gentle man as well as a gentleman. How was it for MF? He was where he wanted to be, observing and absorbing from his unique perspective. His privacy was not absolute;

he greeted workers he'd known for decades, interacted occasionally on small matters, and otherwise kept to himself, excepting when his daughters came to put the touch on him. At the plant he was unbothered by changes, having complete trust in his son's stewardship. A contented man, he did not have to put on a good face. An interior narrative might reveal his enjoyment of being Granddad, and his sense of permanence, as if tomorrow would always be there. He was not worried about aging, or becoming irrelevant. He lived in the present, not contemplating the years ahead. Everything else he kept to himself.

How did FF feel? He liked the plot line. MF's founder's presence symbolically reinforced daily the company's core value of winning with quality. His message was not obsolete; it endured. He lingered behind the scenes leaving FF to embed this core value in a deeper way. After Sunday family dinners at 56 Windsor, father and son would retreat to the privacy of MF's bedroom. What they talked about was unknown to all others, including other members of his family. One subject not discussed was closing the unprofitable retail operation. FF respected his father, and the company's legendary launching so much that he kept the retail operation going until 1956, when it had its 50th anniversary. MF's longevity and his pride in the retail operation all those years ago were irretrievably entwined. FF knew this and honored it with a son's respect and forbearance.

MF revealed more of himself inside the business office located in the retail fish area, especially after Tom Colbert was hired in March 31, 1952, two weeks short of his eighteenth birthday. That Tom's family was from Tramore – one county over from Tipperary – elevated Tom in MF's eyes. In effect, MF treated Tom as a grandson. MF loaned him $2,400 for a new car, and was properly dumbfounded when Tom paid him back (previous borrowers had not). Afterwards, MF would often ask Tom if he needed another loan for a newer car. Tom went to Ireland annually for his vacation weeks. MF entrusted him with checks to be delivered to the Foley relatives. Once, Tom was out sick for a few days. On the day of his return, he asked MF if he had missed him. MF replied, "I was not worried. Only the good die young."

MF had a child-like reaction to his "shamrocks," the customers' checks that Ms. Oberson, the bookkeeper, gave to him every day. But in his later years, after he had lost an eye due to an unsuccessful cataract operation, he was unable to continue this habit. Tom became his protector, watching over him. Tom would follow MF down the steps of Union Station to ensure that he got safely onto the correct trolley to Brookline. One day MF had put his glass eye back in upside down. Tom immediately noticed and made the adjustment.

Tom would coordinate MF's doctor appointments with Mother. At least twice a year, Tom would arrange for Mr. Lepie, "the" tailor in Boston's Financial District, who custom made suits and hand tailored lapels, to come to Foley Fish to measure MF for a new garment – the only customer who received such regal treatment. Steve Connolly once said of Tom "there is no more loyal employee than Tom Colbert" (nor more loyal "grandson"). Tom worked at Foley Fish for fifty-one years, the second longest term (after Frank Souza) in the employee history at Foley Fish.

CHAPTER 45

CALM BEFORE THE STORM

Another day at Foley Fish. Fish arrived, were filleted and boxed, and went out to customers by truck and train. FF focused on the usual production bottlenecks, a few customer complaints, and past due receivables. One thing he didn't worry about was whether there would be enough fish in the ocean for his customers. He and everyone else in the industry took for granted that there would always be a rich harvest. They were wrong. In the 1950s there were no federal regulations on what and how many fish could be caught. Because a plentiful supply had always existed, a laissez-faire conservation philosophy pervaded. There was a federal fisheries management vacuum, and state governments had limited jurisdiction over marine wildlife within the three-mile offshore boundary. On the rest of the vast terraqueous globe, all nations were free to do whatever they wanted.

No problems, so no solutions needed. No threats of overfishing, or over-utilized species. No scientific evidence of declines in fish populations. No pressure from environmentalists. No harm, no foul. Abundance continued; scarcity was unimaginable. Government officials pushed to increase the capacity of fishing fleets in order to exploit this fish abundance. Thus, the "pounding" on the plentiful fish resource began. Unbeknownst to all involved, the 1950s marked the start of the fishing industry's resource problems.

Fishing fleets expanded beyond what the fisheries could sustain. The Fish and Wildlife Act of 1956 established a Fisheries Loan Fund. From 1957 to 1973, $31 million dollars in loans was approved, enabling a rapid modernization of fishing fleets. In 1962 Congress facilitated private capital investment. Tax laws were changed to encourage investments primarily through an investment tax credit that allowed ten percent of capital investments as a credit against taxes. In 1970 Congress established the Capital Construction Fund. This act allowed commercial boat owners to defer income tax on projects from vessel operations, but only if the money was placed in a special fund for later renovations, construction, or purchase of fishing boats, thereby allowing fish owners to acquire boats with pre-tax dollars. In effect, the government was providing interest-free loans (in its first 25 years the fund established 7,000 accounts, sheltering more than $1.8 billion).

Few storm flags were raised in the face of this unprecedented expansion. But the quadrupling of foreign fishing fleets' effort in New England waters did eventually lead to the 1976 Magnuson-Stevens Act, which created the two-hundred-mile limit that removed foreign trawlers from U.S. waters. The "Americanization" of this vast expanse of the ocean resulted in an estimated 20 percent increase in the annual catch of the combined U.S. fishing fleet. After Magnuson-Stevens, many in the fish industry felt more secure. They shouldn't have.

Almost overnight the New England fishing fleet began overfishing. This was the result of enlarged optimism, and the new tax incentives, which led in turn to a modernization frenzy. Steel-hulled stern trawlers, modeled after factory ships, were built in record numbers. These new trawlers were far more efficient and technologically advanced than the older boats. New navigational aids such as satellite instruments, Loran (long range navigation) systems, and depth finders were added. Engine rooms now sported new 720 horsepower diesel engines. Fuel tanks were enlarged allowing longer fishing trips. This new fleet of high-powered "vacuum cleaners" could sweep up more fish per day than the eight-day catch of older vessels.

The federal fisheries biologists at National Marine Fisheries (NMFS) were the first group to argue for a scientific, rational fisheries management plan. No one else – processor, fishermen, and even conservationists — recognized that overfishing was getting out of hand. Shame on us, we were still asleep at the wheel.

NMFS biologists asked many technical questions, which ultimately boiled down to one: "What is the maximum sustainable yield of all species on a continuing basis?" The scientists hypothesized that the existing population of fish would annually produce an amount equal to half of its unexploited, uncaught population, thereby ensuring an acceptable continuity in the supply of fish.

A daunting task, as no one knew the exact size of the fish populations caught annually, or (a more difficult question) the rate of depletion. Data gathering began with extrapolations made from samples retrieved by biologists on research vessels. The scientific community struggled with spotty information. What was missing was the impact that age distribution amongst species (year classes within each species); size, age, sexual maturity by species; and mortality rates that should include the "predatory" impact of some fish-eating other fish, would have on overall fish population.

NMFS turned to recording landings (number of fish taken aboard vessels) to capture mortality figures. Misreporting by some fishermen undermined some of the data gathered, and "discards" (fish caught but not landed), and juvenile fish that did not escape passage through the net's meshes, were impossible to ascertain. Lastly, scientists were not able to consider fish losses due to fluctuations in environment and interaction between fish and other sea creatures, for example, seals and other sea animals feeding on fish.

The fisheries had grown much faster than the information about them could be gathered. The necessary biological information was thin and unreliable and, therefore, the fisheries management vacuum continued. The alarm that sounded for resource conservation went largely unheeded because the scientists couldn't definitively prove fish population declines. Precautionary notes were published, but few read them. Overfishing – if it existed – would continue uninterrupted; actually, it accelerated. A little too late could become a lot too late. The imbalance between too many boats and, perhaps not an unlimited fish supply, was not accepted, except by the scientific community. Nothing would be done until "urgent" became an existential crisis, and it eventually did. This occurred as scientific findings furnished more definitive, reliable proof on declining fish populations. Fish shortages would imperil the existence of many fish processors like Foley's, as restrictions on the size of catches were imposed.

CHAPTER 46

RUSS ROHRBACHER

The graveyard of fish companies is crowded with failures caused by fish buyers who were either unscrupulous (on the take), lazy, just plain stupid, or all three. Whichever quality standard of fish you choose, you are only as good a buyer as the fish you buy relative to that benchmark. Your mistakes can't be camouflaged, nor can the fish that you buy be improved after death. There are no second chances.

Successful fish buying is so important to the survival of a fish company that, in the early days, the owners were often their own buyers, for example, George Berkowitz, of Legal Seafood, Mr. Wolf of Wolf Seafood in Brookline, and Mr. Grier of Grier Seafood in Belmont. They only trusted themselves.

Frank Souza was not an owner, but he possessed an owner's mentality of winning with only quality fish. He bought as if he was spending his own money. For 52 years Frank handpicked Foley's fish, scraped off the ice before weighing, and insured that the quality went in before the Foley name went on the purchase ticket. Frank was Foley's rock star, and a Hall of Famer in the fish industry. A mystique of omniscience and endurance followed Frank Souza to the age of seventy-five, when he retired. Excepting MF, Frank holds the longevity record at Foley Fish with his 52-year tenure.

In looking for the second buyer since the start of the company, FF initially tried Bobby Boyd, but early onset of an eye disease ended this appointment. FF then turned to Russ Rohrbacher, who was heading up production. Replacing a legend was made more challenging for Russ because the modernization of the fishing fleet allowed fishermen a longer time at sea. Hence, more fish were landed, but less Foley-quality fish were available. The typical two-day trips of Souza's era became ten-day trips. These extended periods created a new purchasing burden. Foley Fish wanted, needed, only last-day-caught fish, not older-caught fish, of which there was much more. A majority of the fish landed were not acceptable to Foley's. Russ had been pressure tested during his years running Foley's production. Despite being saddled with diabetes, he was a man of great energy who thrived on challenges. He had to face a situation that Frank Souza never had to confront.

Russ lived north of Boston, near enough to Gloucester, the third-largest fishing port after Boston and New Bedford, to stop each afternoon (including Sundays) to inspect the fish landed by the "day-boat" fleet which, up till then, would be sent out to the Boston auction the next morning for sale. Russ initiated a partnership with Madruga's Fish Co. of Gloucester built on a single premise: Russ would pay the Boston auction price – no questions asked – for all Madruga's one-day old (bullets, as they were called) fish. A hassle-free relationship with Foley Fish replaced the run around that an "outsider" like Madruga's faced when dealing with the Boston pier. Instead of going to the pier and waiting around for hours, Madruga's truck drivers would now deliver the fish directly to Foley's plant by 6:00 a.m. and return with a check for the previous day's catch. A win-win situation.

From his days in production Russ knew Foley's needs by heart. But Madruga's could only fill a portion of these needs. Russ also needed a reliable source on the Boston Fish Pier, and he was starting from scratch. Enter Vito, no last name, as he never disclosed it ("Who's asking"), the head fish buyer at Great Atlantic Fish Co. On the Boston fish pier, Great Atlantic was strategically located at the most spacious end of the fish pier for ease of managing purchases from the most trawlers. An elusive, enigmatic gent, Vito had laser-like eyes that could see through you. But peering out from his weather-beaten face, his eyes revealed nothing. Vito was as formidable as FF in getting his way. As stern and humorless as Russ was smiley and good-natured, Vito was the one that Russ, the new kid on the block, targeted to form a special buying alliance. Odds were very much against Russ winning over Vito. No one ever had.

Russ had more than once stood up to a cantankerous FF, but a hard stance would not work with Vito, who held all the cards. Instead, Russ played up to Vito. On weekends Russ, calling on his prior experience running a landscaping business, helped Vito improve his sparse lawn in Revere. Vito was a car buff, and Russ sold him his souped-up classic Chrysler sedan at a discount. These gestures wouldn't be sufficient, but were good start.

Russ knew what was in the proposed partnership for Foley Fish: access to a substantial number of boats controlled by Vito; insider information on which pens held the latest caught fish; not paying a 2.5 cent premium over the auction price; and extra weights (free fish) from the lumpers who worked for Vito.

Vito had to sell a certain amount of lower-grade fish, and Russ was handicapped by not being able to accommodate him at all. This created a seemingly insurmountable hurdle. Russ countered by announcing to Vito, "Unlike the bastards you deal with, you can trust Foley Fish to honor its commitments to you. We will bring to you an unequalled A-grade customer group who will not be scared off in a higher price market. We will support your boats in tight markets when fish scarcity drives up auction prices, which is a major difficulty for you given your penny-pinching supermarkets customer base." In essence, Russ was offering Foley's buying strength in exchange for Vito's supply strength. "We both win. Our growth will be your growth. We don't compete in your market; we work for you, not against you."

Whether Vito saw a chance to enlarge his buying empire, or just because he liked his lawn becoming the envy of his neighborhood, he said, "We'll see how it works."

Russ had still to sell the arrangement to FF, always a skeptic. For every ten new ideas that Russ came up with, FF said, seven were crazy, two were maybes, and there was one a good one. This was one of Russ's good ones. Frank's response echoed Vito's "We'll see how it works."

Russ's alliance with Vito gave Foley Fish a legitimate chance of realizing the same absolute standards of excellence to which Frank Souza had adhered. The new arrangement Russ had orchestrated allowed Foley Fish to adjust to the new realities of ten-day fishing trips, and proved to be a turning point in the company's history. The end results were dramatic. Foley Fish significantly widened, on the buy side, its comparative advantage over the competition.

CHAPTER 47

RESEARCH TRIPS

Technological advancements powered innovations in the methods of catching fish, but this was not the case on the "processing" side. Little had changed from MF's time, other than no longer cutting fish on an overturned wooden barrel. The majority of sea food companies were happy with the old ways.

FF was an exception. He was in his words, "still catching up, rarely getting ahead." He needed answers. He constantly sought new tools for his toolbox. He initiated field trips to pick the brains of people way ahead of him. He traveled to England and Scotland to visit research stations, to the Maritimes to learn from fishermen and processors, and to shell fishermen to learn about scallops and quahaugs. He listened and took notes, just as he had when he studied profit sharing. Gladly would he learn, and gladly teach.

FF loved Nova Scotia. He would call home to tell his wife Rita he had found the perfect burial site there. She was neither amused nor entertained by this suggestion. He called on National Sea Products, a behemoth fish processing company located on the historic harbor of Lunenburg, N.S. His notes read, "They were way ahead of us; very mechanized; scientists and engineers running the company; emphasis on efficiency, not quality; motorized conveyors from their ships' holds to the cutting lines, most of which were cutting machines that replaced hand cutting of fish; they were the General Motors of the fish industry. Only one big problem — the machines beat up the fish badly; fish quality became secondary to production goals; lots of fish were downgraded to fish sticks (frozen) and/ or salt cod for the West Indies. I was surprised; I learned what not to do."

At the urging of MF, who loved smoked "Finnan haddie" (fish lore had that it originated when a local fisherman in Findon, Scotland awoke to a fire in his barn where his "split" haddock were hanging and, consequently, getting smoked). FF's notes read: "Traveled to the Torry Research Station in Aberdeen, Scotland to study the fish-smoking process; not one, but two choices, hot smoking and cold smoking; both methods utilize a salt brine, hot smoking at 158°F to 176°F, cold smoking not above 90°F; hot smoke technique was best for cod and haddock; sawdust containing high proportion of hardwoods that burn in the kiln imparted a pleasant flavor and color; no room in present plant for smoke facility; MF will have to wait."

While at National Sea Products, FF also visited with their scientists who specialized in the study of freezing fish. His notes read: "Don't freeze fish too quickly, else dehydrate the product; start with well-iced fish (target 35°F); opt for method that would chill down product to 28° F in reasonable time (two to three hours); choice of IQF method (individually quick frozen) or by plate freezing; problem with IQF for fillets is their uneven size such that the thickest part of the fish (shoulder) could be unfrozen while the thinnest part (tail); would be over-frozen; recommended plate freezer at minus sixty degrees Fahrenheit; need to study packaging that will allow plate compression without injuring the product; not a high priority product at Foley Fish; plenty of fresh fish; U.S. consumer regard frozen fish as inferior to fresh; not want to jeopardize Foley's reputation."

FF's notes ended with "No postponements! No more seat-of-our pants conjecturing." The "founder's" mentality was still alive in the second generation. Unfortunately, the installation of a smoker, a freezer, and a special bacteria retardation system would have to wait until a larger, new plant could be built.

CHAPTER 48

PREP FOR A NEW PLANT

One day FF asked Bobby Boyd if he could create ten percent more production capacity in the Friend and Union plant. Bobby replied, "We could add a refrigerated trailer, a second shift, and more overtime work, otherwise, we can't. We've hit the wall; we're at full capacity. Our plant's aisles are clogged. Our system of pitchforking whole fish to the cutting line is archaic. Lifting 250-pound-packed barrels of fish up one flight of stairs when the elevator is not working (often) is crazy," replied Bobby.

Capacity wasn't the only problem. Bobby added, "We're only a half-step ahead of the competition technique-wise. We need more advanced procedures. It's not my money, but I would build a new, state-of-the art, more spacious plant incorporating new technologies."

FF knew Bobby was spot-on in his analysis. Foley Fish's growth would stall out without a new more technologically advanced plant. The search for a new plant site commenced immediately. FF wanted to build the very best, a state-of-the-art facility. However, FF had little mechanical aptitude.

Saddled with this handicap, FF couldn't be his usual assertive self, as he didn't know enough. His do-what-I-say autocratic style had to shift to a more democratic modality. He had to listen to his "think tank" composed of Steve, Russ, and Bobby. They worked together asking hard questions such as, "Can it be made?" "Is there something still missing?" "Are we overreaching?" FF needed this kind of probing questioning. The effort to build a new plant initiated a pivotal change to the democratic in the management culture at Foley Fish.

"We'd been doing things by the seat of our pants. What worked in the past, hunches and educated guesses, wasn't good enough going forward. It was time for me to get under the hood, to devise a production system that was scientifically based," FF recalled to me.

He realized that he needed more than will and persistence. He needed to get smarter like his hero, Vince Lombardi, iconic coach of the Green Bay Packers. FF had similarly drilled his team over and over again on the fishy equivalents of blocking, tackling, and teamwork. Now he had to go back to school to learn about fish perishability.

FF drove two hours north of Boston to meet with Lou Ronsivalli, Director of the New England Division of National Marine Fisheries Service, in Gloucester, Massachusetts. It was the first time that a fish processor had ever come to his office for advice. "I need to pick your brains. Why doesn't fish hold up as long as meat? What causes fish spoilage? Can I slow it down, or is it inevitable? Treat me the same way as Vince Lombardi did his veterans and rookies at the beginning of training camp. I need facts, not hunches, for my playbook. "What," FF asked, "is a fish?"

He learned the following from Lou: "The shelf life of fish starts when fish die. A race against bacteria growth starts then. The rate at which fish spoils depends on sanitation and how well the fish is iced." Lou explained to him that time temperature tests showed a linear relationship between temperature and bacterial spoilage of fish based on the following perishability rule: Fish loses one day of shelf life for each day it is stored two degrees over 32 degrees. Therefore, fish held at 42 degrees for one day lose an additional five days of shelf life, and at 52 degrees, ten days. But storage of fish at 32 degrees produces a potential shelf life of over eight days. This maximum shelf life, however, is not guaranteed. Lou created the "Fish Spoilage Clock" based mathematically on hundreds of time-temperature tests that he and his staff had conducted. This clock told time in terms of days lost rather than hours. Its internal mechanism ticked according to the two-degree rule of fish perishability. The clock tracks the passage of fish from hook to skillet, assuming a temperature of fish at 32 degrees (fish are not frozen at 32°). The adoption of this clock was a pivotal moment in the history of the Foley Fish Co.

FF was alarmed by the thin error margin in Foley Fish's daily race against the spoilage clock. He knew that his Midwest sales push would be jeopardized without an overhaul of the company's current handling procedures. The spoilage clock was ticking too quickly at Foley Fish. Even before the new plant was built, Frank implemented time temperature checks at each critical production control point, starting with the pier, followed by the plant's fish storage, the cutting line, and the shipping department.

Foley's switched from wooden to insulated, sterilized barrels at the pier. Frank Souza now brought extra ice in his refrigerated truck for newly bought fish. Whole fish had to be immediately laid down in insulated containers in a layering process that continuously surrounded all fish with ice. The elapsed time for whole fish cut and packaged was 20 minutes maximum. The average "fish" temperature at Foley's would remain close to 32 degrees. A new refrigerated storage bin was constructed for fish packages before shipment. Barrels were thoroughly iced. Baker Trucking checked all Midwest shipments, and topped off barrels with more ice on route during the warm months. Foley's salesmen called customers for temperature reports on Foley orders, recording complaints on the customer complaint sheet, and noting corrective actions taken.

Armed with an enhanced understanding of the relationship between temperature control and spoilage, FF flew to Seattle, Washington to meet with the North Star Co., maker of a new ice machine that produced 27°F salt-water flake ice for West Coast Halibut producers. This super cold ice would chill fish faster and keep it cold longer. Because it was flaked it would "embrace" the fish rather than crush or dent it. Installation of the North Star machine posed a problem. It worked on a gravity-feed basis that would necessitate a roof-top installation. FF went to the Landry Refrigeration Co. of Boston. Mr. Landry proved to be exceptionally talented in his field. Armed with information provided by Lou Ronsivalli of NMFS, and the North Star Co., Landry immediately determined that Foley Fish would need to create an "insulated" ice-holding bin refrigerated at 15°F, due to the warmer weather in Boston (than Seattle), else Foley's goal of achieving 32°F would be jeopardized. Landry also warned of an ice "clogging" problem, which would necessitate a set of churning paddles in the bin. Later, Bobby, and Russ recommended two ice chutes, one for use by the shipping department and the other for the whole fish department.

An on-off switch at the production floor would enable distribution of the flake ice on an as-needed basis.

A new cutting line looked simple: enlarge the present one to allow five cutters on either side of a conveyor belt. Bobby and Russ insisted on a new system of feeding fish to the cutting line that no longer used pitchforks. The new system was more complex. A mechanical hoist system geared to lifting over 500 pounds of fish in large insulated boxes would need to be well anchored for safety reasons. The larger challenge was to construct a hoist system with cables that allowed adjustable heights, because feeding a scaling table would be higher than the whole fish conveyor line underneath and in front of the scaling table.

The design for the new cutting line was still not finished. Lou Ronsivalli had pushed for a chlorinated spray system to be affixed strategically along the entire processing line that would lower bacteria counts of Foley's processed fish. No one in the seafood industry had such a system. If Foley Fish installed a chlorinated spray system through which whole fish were fed to the cutting line, the chlorine sprays could remove the bacteria lodged in the eviscerated innards of the fish. Another bank of sprays could be situated on the cutting line, after filleting, for further bacteria reduction. A chlorinator would apportion appropriate amounts of chlorine in water circulating through a network of pipes and nozzles for spraying on the fish. Various dosages of chlorine were studied culminating in the decision to set the chlorinator at twelve parts per million, well below the levels of chlorine in city water, and undetectable in taste tests. To accomplish all this, FF hired Will Pierce, the owner of Pier Sheet Metal Co. of Boston to construct the system from scratch. There was no model, no blueprints, save his crude configurations and measurements.

CHAPTER 49

MONKEY WRENCH

FF planned to sell the Friend and Union Streets building to finance the new plant's land acquisitions and construction. One minor stumbling block remained: a letter from the Boston Redevelopment Authority (BRA) informed FF that, as part of the new government center plan (1959), the Foley Fish Building was to be demolished under the rule of eminent domain. Worse yet, the offered compensation was tens of thousands of dollars below the building's appraised value. FF sued the BRA, and hired Charles Hamilton, the best real estate lawyer in Boston. The government representation was formidable. It included Mayor Collins (who had defeated the iconic James Michael Curley), and Edward Logue, a Yale Law School graduate specializing in city planning, the head of the BRA. To that date the BRA had already razed 22 buildings, mainly in the Scollay Square area.

Charles Hamilton was an imposing man at six feet, seven inches and 300 pounds. Wearing his signature ten-gallon hat, he was bigger than life. At the jury trial, Hamilton stacked the jury with Irish Catholics, many of whom had been recently dislocated from their homes in the Dock Square area (adjacent to Scollay Square). Hamilton's next-door neighbor in Scituate was Mr. Lou Perini, head of Perini Construction, and the owner of the Boston Braves and, more importantly, the largest donor to the Catholic diocese, so it was helpful that he arranged for Cardinal Cushing to write a letter on behalf of the Foley family who, he noted with Joseph Kennedy, had donated heavily to St. Aidan's Church in Brookline. Architects wrote letters attesting to the unique architectural design of the world famous flat-iron building. Valuations were presented to substantiate the appraised value of the building.

Pressure was mounting on Mr. Logue to keep the tax-providing companies inside Boston. He had scuttled 46 tax paying entities (including the famous Joe & Nemo's), causing substantial losses in city tax revenues. Hamilton let it be known that Foley Fish would be forced to leave Boston unless a satisfactory settlement was made by the BRA.

In his summation Hamilton laid it on. The jury trial became a stage for the witty, acerbic lawyer, who was attuned to the importance of performance. Playing to his handpicked jury, Hamilton spoke of the historical value of the Foley building starting with ownership by the grandson of President John Adams, who later bequeathed the property to Harvard College. It was now owned by MF, he continued, a six-grade-educated Irish immigrant who came to Boston at 16 years of age, working 14 hour days, seven days a week that enabled him to earn enough money to buy this landmark across from Faneuil Hall, a building renowned as a venue where voices against tyranny were raised, tyranny much like that Foley now faced. "Is this progress?" asked Hamilton, "to leave only a park bench atop a paved sidewalk. Is this urban renewal or urban recklessness?"

Sarcastically, he conceded that Scollay Square had added to the cultural life of Boston, while Boston Foley Fish Co. couldn't make a similar claim. The Foley Fish plant, however, was not a bawdy burlesque house populated by drunks and hookers with sinful grins betting on which tassels (the left or the right) would stop first on the "Old Howard" stage. Unlike these places where parents told children never to go, thousands of Bostonians unhesitatingly recommended Foley's to their neighbors.

Summing up, Hamilton asked, "Where is the fairness? MF, unlike many other owners in Boston had never asked for tax abatement. He paid his taxes fully. The BRA never complained about the appraised value until now, when they offered a cowardly compensation significantly below value. Raising his voice in defiance, he said, "Where's the respect? Where's the fairness?"

Foley Fish won a financial settlement that was three times the original, now discredited, BRA offer, enough for a new plant. For years afterwards, Charlie Hamilton came to the new plant to buy fish. He never had to reach for his wallet.

CHAPTER 50

NEW PLANT

Chlorinated spray system in new plant on W. Howell Street, Boston

After more than a half century, Foley Fish workers had a new work place. On August 23, 1963, the company moved to its new digs. Years later Bobby Boyd recalled its smell of newness, like that of a new car. The new plant was located on West Howell Street, not viewable from Dorchester Avenue, the main thoroughfare connecting Dorchester to downtown Boston. Its low profile was not accidental. FF wanted to avoid prying eyes, so he did not choose to relocate on the Boston Fish Pier, home to most of his competition.

The Foley workers were happy to see a more than ample, meterless parking lot, although a few veterans groused that there were no bars nearby for their "coffee breaks." They did appreciate the new men's locker room, which featured a sizable shower room. The boss's office did not display his Harvard degree, or any family pictures. There were two chairs, FF's and another wedged between a wall and his desk. The latter conveyed a message to visitors: "Don't overstay your welcome." There was a small, second-hand recliner for his brief afternoon naps. It was spare if not Spartan. The office's one window offered a view of the barb-wired fenced side property. No distractions were the keynote of the plant's general ambience.

FF parked in the same parking lot as everyone else, and the workers often joked that given five choices, an outsider could not pick out FF's car. The men never lost. His six-year old Mercury, fronted by "bandaged" fenders and lacking air conditioning, deceived everyone except those who knew this humble man.

Not changed was the location of FF's glassed-in "anchor desk" that gave him a clear view of the entire production floor. It also permitted the workers to see FF, like them, at work.

His management style underwent as much modernization as his new plant. It was as if an alien-self had appeared. His radical truthfulness ("I'm the least mechanical guy in the seafood industry)" echoed his starting day's pronouncement 27 years earlier: "I'm the least street-smart guy in the fish industry." He had come to recognize the efficacy of giving his knowledgeable brain trust more of a say, more power. He let others lead, and held back comment so as to listen better, and see through the eyes of key staff. Meaningful relationships grew, resultantly, which strengthened the creative process. Consensus was not coerced, it evolved. Bobby Boyd remembers these years, the early 60s, as the most enjoyable of his career. His mind was still bursting with ideas after work. He loved the free tuition post-graduate education provided by Lou Ronsivalli, Will Pierce and Mr. Landry. FF's research was still used. Boyd relied on FF's notes when implementing the new fish smoker and the plate freezer. Bobby Boyd and the management team knew there would be no cutting machines replacing the men. Machines could not judge the quality of the fish they cut, could not reject subpar fillets. When being complimented on the new plant, FF would say, "I was just smart enough to know what I didn't know and turned to experts like Lou Ronsivalli, Will Pierce, Mr. Landry, and the

North Star Ice Co. engineers who are underappreciated and who deserve the recognition, not me."

The National Oceanic Atmospheric Agency (NOAA) later published a pamphlet on the proper handling procedures for the fish industry. Foley Fish Co. was the model. While proud of this recognition, FF downplayed Foley's accomplishments: "We were not taking processing to the next level as much as to a level that we should have always been at."

Years later, FF would be referred to as the Dr. Deming of the Seafood Industry. Deming was an acclaimed quality control expert who had taught hundreds of Japanese engineers, managers, and owners including the founder of Sony, Akio Morita. But FF stated, "The hero who justified such accolades is, Lou Ronsivalli. His work and instructions represented a turning point in the history of the M.F. Foley Fish Co."

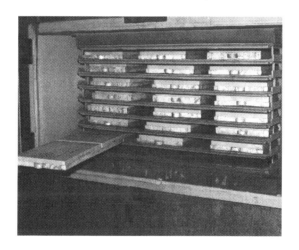

Boxed fillets in trays in new plate freezer, W. Howell Street plant

CHAPTER 51

IN MEMORIAM

In 1956, retail operations closed, exactly 50 years after MF had founded the M.F. Foley Fish Co. For years, old customers and friends asked how MF had taken the news. In response, the family said that it was not as wrenching as the shock when the flatiron building was demolished in 1964. The heavy lead ball swinging at the end of the crane crushed this historic six-story flatiron building as quickly as Mohammed Ali disposed of Sonny Liston in the first round of their 1965 championship fight in Lewiston, Maine. The lead ball caught the iconic, imposing building square on its chin, and MF watched as chunks of masonry and steel tumbled down. His building was counted out in less than 15 minutes. Before MF's eyes, his work place for decades dissolved into nothingness, with no tombstone to mark its location, an inglorious ending.

Traumatized, MF felt hollowed out. He limped home. He knew he could never return to the old patch, the spot where he had launched Foley Fish 50 years before. It was a short bereavement period, however, as he had too many tomorrows to get ready for in FF's new plant. Temperamentally, he had never been one for rage, or depression. MF moved on with no whining. And he made no valedictory statements. That would have been untoward, and as undignified as the buildings end. The flatiron building died without a wake.

Time would be now freed up for healing reflections. MF had greeted thousands of customers, and knew most of them by name, as did his workers. The extent of personal attention by Foley countermen extended to the names of spouses, children, and grandchildren. MF used to say that if a counterman received ten cents each time he patted a baby's head, he would make more money than him. No longer would he be checking the cutting boards for cleanliness before the start of business, nor removing fingerprint smudges from the showcase. His countermen were not only knowledgeable about fish, they were also showmen, full of hyperbole: "This fillet is the prettiest fish I've ever sold," and "This fish is only for you; It's too good for my family." The staff made the customers feel that Foley's was doing something special for them. It was a firm that internalized the belief that more than fish was being exchanged for money at Foley Fish. The Foley retailors – Danny Lamott, Jimmy Barker, Davy Friedman, George Kenneally, George Brown, Charlie Knones, and Joe Pitts — would not be forgotten. They would be missed, not only by MF, but by their many loyal customers.

MF's decision to start the retail operation had far-reaching consequences. Its success enabled Foley Fish to secure a stable, debt-free financial footing, which underwrote its wholesale operation in the 30s. MF was willing to risk his retail earnings by starting up a wholesale operation, despite knowing little about the wholesale market. Nevertheless, his business acumen told him that if quality fish won in retail, it could also win in wholesale. Without the success of retail, and MF's confidence in launching wholesale, there might never have been a second Foley generation at Foley Fish.

The long-time workers were now gone. Danny would not be answering MF's usual morning question of who died, and what was his or her age. Foley retail had died at age 50. It had a great run!

MF's eyesight had been steadily declining. Finally, like his old plant, it faded almost entirely. Fortunately, he would no longer have to manage the steep steps in his old plant. In time, he developed mental handrails to guide his movements in the new plant, a map that included the number of steps and turns to the shellfish department, the location of the office manager's desk where he received his daily shamrocks, and the order desk on the work floor.

His hands replaced his eyes. He devised a personal ATM system using the same hands that had so reliably worked on the farm. He placed his ones, fives, and ten-dollar bills on the left inside lining of his hat, and the fifties and hundreds on the opposite side. No one would cheat him.

MF would not surrender; his time was not up. He would take more of life at a time where there was less time to take it.

CHAPTER 52

A DIFFERENT KETTLE OF FISH

By the early seventies Foley Fish began pulling ahead of its competition. In a *Boston Globe* interview John Koniares, President of the Massachusetts Restaurant Association, spoke of the Foley Fish advantage in this way: "I've been dealing with Frank Foley and his company for many years. He has the best fish in Boston, there's no comparison. He's number one, the king of them. His stuff just stands up so much better than anybody else's. Never once have I had a short weight and you can't say that about any other supplier. And there are all kinds of tricks in the fish business, and he doesn't play any of them."

Russ Rohrbacher was buying "bullets" from Madruga's day boats of Gloucester and from Vito on the Boston Fish Pier. Bobby Boyd and his team were producing much better shelf life for their fish than any of their competitors. The other companies lacked Foley's chlorinated anti-bacterial system, and its super-chilled flake ice machine (both unique on the East Coast). Foley Fish was consistently winning the race against the bacteria spoilage clock. Actually, it was its only real competitor.

FF was forcing his competitors to seek cost advantages to compensate for their quality disadvantages. Foley's competitors opted to buy lesser quality cod, paying, for example $1.60 per pound for whole cod that would translate to a quoted cod fillet price of $5.00 ($1.60 x 2.5=$4.00, plus $1.00 standard markup) while Foley's, on that hypothetical same day, bought the highest quality cod at $2.00 per pound that equated (same formula) to a $6.00 per pound cod fillet price. This meant that the competitors' price advantage came about because they had paid less for lower quality fish.

The competition's strategy only worsened their competitive disadvantage. They might begin their sales pitches saying they sold the same grade of fish as Foley's, but this assertion was belied by their $1.00 per pound lower price. FF had only one daily price for customers (per species), whether they were a prospect or a confirmed customer, irrespective of the size of the order (no discounts). His only gimmick was quality.

Aiding the company's financial stability was the fact that it didn't have a bloated expense structure. FF was more frugal than most of the Brahmins in Boston. Paper clips were never thrown away; memo notes were written on both sides. Assertions from competitors that Foley prices were higher only because their non-fish expenses were excessive did not hold water.

FF had an undeniably unique style. Many said that you couldn't invent him. Asked how he could say "no" so readily, he replied, "By just saying no." Traveling back to his "ridiculous" sales mandate of not offering more than four fish species to his customers until production caught up with sales, FF issued a string of dramatic nos: no debt, no second plant shift, no fancy car, no over talking on sales calls, and no non-working family on the payroll.

Perhaps his most legendary "no" came in the mid-1970s when he made a decision not to accept any new customers for seven years. Initially deemed a wacko idea, this decision turned out to be a marketing gem. FF had learned that the Minister of Fisheries for the Canadian Maritime Provinces (Nova Scotia, Prince Edwards Island, Labrador, and Newfoundland) had decided to close down the entire Canadian fisheries until fish stocks, especially cod and haddock, had substantially rebounded. In response, FF announced, "No new customers at Foley Fish until further notice. We'll keep a waiting list and when a customer leaves us, we will add a new one. Why? Because we will dance with the customers who brought us here, and will never put ourselves in a position of shorting any customer in order to supply a new one."

After returning from one of his Midwest sales trips FF announced the first opening for a new customer. Here's how this happened: One day while travelling, Frank arrived unannounced at six a.m. to inspect a customer's fish cooler. It was not in good order, and he told the customer, "You don't need Foley Fish; you can buy fish from others for less. You don't handle our fish properly so it ends up the same as everyone else's." Goodbye to that customer. The next Monday morning FF called Jay Haverstock, owner of the famous Jay's Restaurant in Dayton, Ohio to tell him that he could start buying from Foley's. Jay has repeated this story many times, adding, "I was so excited by this news that I went on a bender for three days."

Bobby Boyd, Nick Martin and FF taste-testing
product, W. Howell Street plant

CHAPTER 53

MISMATCHED EXPECTATIONS

FF-Rita Martin wedding, Ritz-Carlton, Boston,1940

In 1940 FF married Rita Martin in a ceremony at St. Cecelia's Catholic Church in Boston. The newlyweds enjoyed a sumptuous reception in the Grand Ballroom of the Ritz Carlton of Boston. Each had eleven attendants. Both felt that they had married someone special. Being devout Catholics, the permanence of their marriage was never in doubt. Divorce in those years was not an option for Catholics.

Raising three children, difficult me, and my sisters Pat and Rita Jr. (the oops baby, born eleven years after Pat), was, with housework and cooking, a full-time job for Rita. She was a highly intelligent woman, but never utilized that intelligence outside the home. She played a mean hand of bridge but charity work did not interest her.

Marriage to FF was an economic step up for Rita. Her father,

Joseph Leo Martin, had been personal assistant and confidante to the infamous Mayor John F. "Honey Fitz" Fitzgerald, Jack Kennedy's maternal grandfather. Joe lost considerable investment money during the Depression, but held onto good paying jobs within Boston's Democratic Party. He provided his family a comfortable style of living, but it was not at the level of FF's privileged home at 56 Windsor. Rita's brother, Joseph Jr. went to Harvard and the Harvard Business School. The Martin family could not afford room and board at Harvard, so Joe Jr. day-hopped to Harvard from his nearby Belmont home.

Rita, the second oldest, was the "favored" daughter, coming ahead of two sisters, Betty and Ella Mae. She had been accepted to Smith College, but the double tuition would have overstretched the Martin budget. Subsequently, Rita earned a secretarial degree from The Katharine Gibbs School in Boston, which allowed her to find work in the city.

FF did not want to replicate his parents' lifestyle. He was not seeking wealth, maids, luxury trips abroad, and, most importantly, spoiled children. Dad often said it was more difficult to raise children in upper middle class Newton, Massachusetts than in blue-collar towns like Roslindale or West Roxbury, where one's next-door neighbors might be a policeman on one side and a teacher on the other, occupations whose values he felt to be more compatible with his own.

FF wanted his family to live a thriftier, considerably less flashy life than he had lived at 56 Windsor, so he created a world with no allowances, no outside help, two pairs of shoes only (one for Sunday Mass, the other for school), no air conditioning, and so on. Pat, Rita, and I did not feel deprived, but we certainly did not feel we were living in affluence.

Life at 151 Neshobe Road did not allow for spoiled children or spoiled wives. What FF did not realize was that this lifestyle fell short of Rita's expectations. Rita was envious of her mother-in-law's comfortable life — the cook, the maids, the European trips. Rita had to run the home according to a plan that called for a simpler, scaled-back lifestyle than the one at 56 Windsor. Affluence, to FF, was meaningless except in a negative way. Rita quietly disagreed.

FF would run Foley Fish, while Rita stayed home to manage things according to his plan. She was unprepared for this job, because growing up she'd lived a relatively pampered life. Her mother had done all the household chores. Rita depended on FF for her sense of identity, and learned to be a scrupulous housekeeper, earning the moniker of "neat as a pin." She kept a tight grip on family finances. There were no credit cards, no extravagances, and a rainy-day fund, should another Depression occur. A tight budget precluded luxury such as jewelry, expensive clothes, and fancy vacations.

I was born September 14, 1941; Patricia, August 2, 1944; and Rita, ten years later on March 20, 1953. Raising us was a full-time job for Rita. With FF gone from six a.m. to six p.m., and we children usually absent from seven a.m. to four p.m., life became un-busy for Rita. Maintaining spotlessness in the house was no longer sustaining. The hours alone became untenable.

Rita eventually grew tired of her husband's frugality. She could not scale back her aspirations, and kept hoping that he would change. He didn't, and Rita realized he probably never would. She then sought an escape from the reality of FF's rigid rules and the long lonely hours. She found a new companion, Mr. Alcohol. The family tried to convince Rita that this was not a good solution, but Rita proved as intractable about alcohol as FF was about finances. Her brother-in-law, a recovering alcoholic, offered to take her to AA meetings. She declined. She had too much pride to acknowledge that she had a problem. Her father was an alcoholic, and one of her two sisters was using drugs. She was fighting a genetic disposition to substance abuse.

I tried to be a go-between for my parents, and encouraged them to talk to each other about the situation, but I failed. Neither had any deep understanding of the other's problems. Eventually Rita was admitted, against her will, to McLean Hospital, a preeminent psychiatric facility in the Boston area. The doctors there attributed her alcoholism to severe depression. At a family meeting that I will never forget, the lead psychiatrist told FF that he needed to spend considerably more time at home with Rita. FF said, "I can't run the Foley Fish Co. and take care of my wife." It was the first time I had ever seen my father helpless. He seemed beaten.

McClean tried shock therapy on Rita, which made her an unrecognizable shell of her former self, catatonically numbing. She continued to drink, which furthered her shame and melancholy. FF was burned out, and taking heavy doses of belladonna for his ulcers. His close friends worried that the stress he was under could lead to a stroke or heart attack. Both at home and at the business, there were major worries.

FF had surrounded himself with the highly talented team of Steve, Russ, and Bobby. All three subscribed to his script for a successful business, but it was not clear that any one of them could replace him. Would Foley Fish continue beyond the second generation, especially if it was dependent on me, a kid who had to be sent to military school to shape up? Years later, I wondered if my father could have spent more time at home. But I concluded that Dad could not change his ways, and should not be blamed for Mom's illness.

Eventually, Mom came home from McLean, still denying that she was an alcoholic. She was able to function better at home and managed to get her chores done and prepare dinner before she blacked out. Dad never complained, despite often carrying her to the second floor to bed. In later years, Dad's evenings became vigils, because Mom would wake to have a cigarette, and her emphysema required a canister of oxygen next to the bed.

Dad was not demonstrative in public, but it was evident to the family that he was devoted to Mom. He never criticized her to anyone, including family. He didn't wallow in self-pity despite the inescapable pain. When I asked why he had stayed married to Mom, Dad said," Our marriage had good years, and we are now living through some bad years. Your mother would throw herself in front of a bus to save me and I would do the same for her." In retrospect, I believe their devotion to each other was more than religious duty. They did the best they could for each other within the limits of their own capabilities. They loved each other deeply in the old- fashioned way. In their last years together, they enjoyed each other's company.

CHAPTER 54

WAS HE ALWAYS LIKE THIS?

MFF enters 8th grade, La Salle Military Academy,
Oakdale, Long Island just after his 12th birthday

MF and FF, first and second-generation fish mongers may occasionally
have pondered whether a third generation Foley would want to continue
the business. As FF's only son, I, MFF would be the natural successor.
(No consideration would be given to my two sisters, both very able,
because they were women.) Given my early years, both MF and FF
probably despaired of me ever having the maturity to successfully operate
a challenging business.

As a child, I was predictable. I did what people said not to do. FF had
resorted to spankings to amend my mischievous ways, which I still believe

to be an act of unwarranted coercion. This father-son confrontation was my first exposure to authority, teaching me that I never wanted anyone above me, especially if he had a belt in his hand.

On Sundays the Foley clan often met for a family dinner at 56 Windsor. The ground rules were explicit: keep negatives to yourself, no public squabbles, confine conversation to safe subjects such as school, sports, and the weather. Kids were excluded from the "big" table; they had to dine in the kitchen's back room, the breakfast nook. The youngest grandchild, MFF, protested: "Who said that I'm unfit to eat at the big table?"

There was never a blowup at 56 Windsor until I, too familiarly, raised a fish business question to MF — my feeble attempt to become my grandfather's confidante. I was abruptly dismissed. "It's none of your business, Michael." I will never forget his words, the expression on his tightened face, or his narrowed, piercing eyes. This remonstrance was followed by the rapid closure of the valves of his attention.

Unlike MF, Mother (Nanny to me) was my champion, always exhibiting endless patience with me. She often said, "Michael, you are sometimes naughty, but you are never bad." I always wondered if she truly believed it or was saying it to bolster my spirits. Either way it worked. She was always in my corner, but once I almost lost her support. One Good Friday afternoon I went to the movies instead of attending the Stations of the Cross at St. Aidan's Church. Nothing got by her. I was truly ashamed. My punishment was nine days of prayers and devotions, a full novena. I never crossed her again.

My elementary schooling was at the all-boys Walnut Park Country Day run by The Sisters of St. Joseph. I needed structure, boundaries, and rules, but detested the school's regimentation. During my seven years there, I found the nuns to be imperious, severe, and humorless. While they respected their vocation, they didn't seem to like themselves, which kept them from forming close bonds with their students. The sisters that I encountered appeared to have a bi-polar mindset, alternating between caring and coldness. Once, a nun asked me to tell her in strictest confidence the name of the student who had started a food fight. I did and, unfortunately, she repeated my information to her superior, making me feel like an informer, something the Irish hold to be a cardinal sin. It was a teaching moment that I've never forgotten. I could not forget this deception, and it reinforced my loathing of nuns.

I spent seventh grade at Warren Junior High School. Released from the controlling nuns I ran amok. Three of us, an ex-con, a nineteen-year-old football star who had flunked multiple times, and me, were the only students required to have a form signed in each class attesting to our attendance and behavior. That year, I became the first Foley brought home by the Newton Police for something I did.

For grades eight through twelve, I was "sent" to La Salle Military Academy on Long Island, run by the Christian Brothers. It felt like a jail. Calling it a school was a euphemism, unless you added the adjective "reform." My father had no other choice for I was willful and defiant to the point of maddening obstinacy. I quickly learned that I was to be locked in jail for the next five years. I was the protruding nail that had to be hammered down. At La Salle I was pounded, but never broken, as I refused to give in. The Christian Brothers (a misnomer), were as sadistic as the nuns at Walnut Park. On my first day I met Brother Bernard (a.k.a. Rocko), who FF had urged to toughen me up. He guaranteed no parental interference.

Unlike MF or FF at 13, I was rebellious, feisty, and totally lacking in diplomacy. I would miss out on the normal life of a teenager. Fitting in and liking La Salle were stretch goals. I never said, "I give," even to the older, hairier, more muscular Italian bullies. Backing down was not in my vocabulary.

There was no real chance for a high-quality education due to many factors: inferior teachers (Brothers Matthew and Michael were the exceptions), weak curricula, and the absence of mentors to encourage intellectual aspirations. Classroom time was devoted to telling, not explaining, memorization, not analysis. English was taught as if it was a second language. There was no Steinbeck, Faulkner, or Hemingway. Religion, History, and Psychology brooked no expanded debate in class.

La Salle Military Academy was the only accredited secondary-level military school in the country. Modeled on West Point, its daily schedule (except Sundays) was: 6:00, reveille; 6:30, march to breakfast; 7:30, inspection; 8:30, classes; 12:00, march to lunch; 1:30, classes; 2:30, drill; 3:30, sports; 5:30, march to dinner; 6:30-8:30, study hall; 9:00 lights out.

Just as the Tipperary farm had armored MF, La Salle similarly toughened me. I was a good student (top 10% of my class), and earned highest honors. But I was a bad cadet. Military positions were awarded at the end of my junior year based on three equally weighted metrics: grades, faculty opinion, and demerits. If grades were the only benchmark, I would have been one of the top ten ranked cadets. Instead, I was 36th. Why? Because I had accumulated more demerits than any of my peers. Always rebellious, I resided at the bottom tier of faculty assessments. The Christian Brothers hadn't knocked obstinacy out of me. I remained an insufferable, predictable pain-in-the-ass to them. I finished my La Salle career busted from master sergeant to private for hitchhiking home in my uniform. At graduation, my classmates gave me a standing ovation when I received my diploma. Nanny proudly noted that I was the most popular in my class. I never corrected her. I couldn't wait to leave.

The question arose: Will he always be like this? I was not one of La Salle's success stories. That I had survived was a point of great pride that has stayed with me, and has sustained me during future bad times. I never dwelt on the time stolen from me. I used my hardships to motivate me to keep moving ahead. Much later, I realized my no-concessions policy to the La Salle totalitarian regime was wasted energy.

FF gave me a get-out-of-jail card. I was accepted at Holy Cross, but he decided that since I was just sixteen years old, I was too young for college. He didn't know that I was, also, intellectually unprepared. I was interviewed and was a late acceptance into a one-year postgraduate program at Browne and Nichols (B&N), an esteemed private day school located in Cambridge, Massachusetts. It was a turning point in my life.

I still did not know what I wanted other than to leave La Salle. My self-knowledge was incomplete, to say the least. I had learned how to study, but not how to learn. A window to another, more embraceable, thought-provoking world would now open.

B&N was welcoming, supportive, and encouraging, yet considerably more challenging academically than I expected. I was way behind my classmates. I quickly learned that none of my courses were repeats. In fact, I knew that I would need two, not one, years of post-graduate work. FF agreed.

I was blessed with outstanding teachers: Hal Melcher (English), Mr.

Denny (Math), Doc Walters (Sciences), and Mr. Brisbois (History), the smartly dressed Brooks Brothers man, who was never out of sorts, always serene, not a yeller or scolder, Mr. Brisbois quietly and subtly coaxed us students, asking the whys, not the whens, of historical events. I knew I had to be a challenging student for Mr. Brisbois, unlike the "brainiacs" in my class, McCloskey, Smith, and Caplan. At first, I was a note taker and did not try to answer his prodding questions, but later in the term I began to catch on to his teaching style.

I began raising my hand in his class and asking probing questions that revealed to him and to me I was learning how to think, and how to analyze and evaluate choices made by historical figures. He was not just a teacher; he was a great teacher. I began to extract new and fuller meanings from his assignments. Beyond verifying that I had listened, I was proving that I had learned. Mr. Brisbois was a psychologist who patiently and successfully tilled the landscape of my mind.

Most influential was Mr. Edwin Pratt, B&N's Headmaster, a scion of the Standard Oil Family, and graduate of Harvard College. This prominent Brahmin took a liking to this Irish Catholic kid. He went above and beyond whatever I deserved. He literally walked across the Harvard Bridge to Harvard College to convince Dean Bender, Harvard's Admission Director, to accept me. Fortunately, Dean Bender was a big football fan, and the Harvard football team had just been walloped by a Yale team headed by the All-American Mike Pyle. As a football player all five years at La Salle, and two years at B&N, I had "football" typed all over my application form. I was a legacy applicant as well, and I got accepted. It was the greatest day of my life up until then. Mr. Pratt became a hero to me. Finally, I was on the way to becoming the hero of my own life.

CHAPTER 55

HARVARD YEARS

MFF, Harvard football photo, 1962

An article appeared in the *Boston Globe* on May 15, 1960 entitled, "Many Are Called, Few Are Chosen." The gist of the piece was that more than 5,000 young men had applied to Harvard that year; 1,400 had been accepted and 3,600 had been refused. Headmaster Pratt had forewarned me, unnecessarily, of Harvard's educational demands, suggesting that I would have a good education and more fun if I went to the University of Pennsylvania instead of Harvard.

I knew that many of my new classmates' SAT scores and GPA numbers were off the charts. This caused me some apprehension. My numbers were okay, but not outstanding. I knew how others got in, but was wondering how I did. I wanted to meet "admits" whose profiles aligned with mine, freshmen who were a mixture of not-as-smart but hard-working. One of my roommates, Charlie Bardelis, was a "P.G." from Suffield Academy who was aggressively pursued by Duffy Daugherty, football coach at Michigan State University. My other roommate, Arden Doss, was on a full, need-based scholarship. His other credential eclipsed mine and Charlie's: he was High School National Debate Champion in 1960. Starting his first year, he would be taking only Advanced Placement courses.

My search continued at the freshmen football tryouts. With 130 freshmen trying out, I felt considerably less uncomfortable, except for one guy sitting directly behind me whose neck was as big as my thigh. The intimidating fullback candidate was Paul Choquette, an All-American on Brown's 1959 football team, now at Harvard Law School, and volunteering as an assistant football coach.

Settling in proved to be not as hard as I'd feared. All freshmen were required to pass a writing course. My teacher read a submitted paper that he thought represented analytically strong writing. As he began reading, the sentences sounded familiar. When asked who the writer was, the teacher declined, but I knew. It was me.

I never missed a lecture, a class, or a reading assignment. I wasn't worried about exams. When necessary, my classroom strategy was to ask a question that reiterated the professor's theories, on the assumption that the prof would be flattered sufficiently to give me a passing grade. It worked, and my grades were sufficiently good to be accepted into the honors economics program my junior and senior years.

Socially, I was still unwise and un-adult. One day I reset Arden's clock two hours forward; his six a.m. was actually four a.m. He was always the first to have breakfast at the Harvard Union, as he was that day, but he couldn't explain the solar eclipse.

I did make an academic list, but not the Dean's list. In my sophomore year I was put on the Social Probation List for what I humbly thought was an ingenious idea. To promote intercollegiate social relations in the Boston area, my pals and I posted flyers on the bulletin boards of local women's colleges, inviting the coeds to fall social mixers. This allowed us to meet lots of eligible woman from local schools: Endicott Junior College, Emerson, Babson, Mt. Ida, Garland, Simmons, Wellesley, and Pine Manor junior College. We plastered mixer invites on the bulletin boards of each dorm of these colleges announcing a Harvard-sponsored mixer at Leverett House, specifically at F-65, which happened to be our dorm room. It worked. Three hundred women showed up. We had lots of dates for our entire sophomore year! Leverett House Master John Conway, however, was not appreciative of my entrepreneurial move, and exempted us from "parietal hours" (having dates in our rooms) for three months.

Despite a faltering academic start in my freshman year owing to an undeserved D in calculus (I deserved an E as differentials totally eluded me), I did finish my first year with a good grade average, bolstered by an A in Professor Havelock's Latin course on Ovid, the Roman poet and philosopher. I was fortunate to be able to pick from a sumptuous smorgasbord of classes offered by learned (some famous) professors whose lectures were later deciphered by future professors. Most memorable was Hum 2 taught by the iconic Master Finlay of Eliot House who put on Oscar-winning performances when reproducing scenes from *The Aeneid*, and *The Iliad*. Professor Alfred taught English 10. A playwright and specialist in Old English literature, Alfred inspired me to minor in British literature wherein I devoured Jane Eyre's *Wuthering Heights* (Heathcliff became a favorite of mine), Thackeray's *Vanity Fair*, and many works of Charles Dickens. Lectures by John Kenneth Galbraith, the preeminent macroeconomist of our times, by Otto Eckstein in Econ 1, and John Dunlap on labor relations in America, influenced me to major in Economics. Harvard allowed auditing of classes (no class credit), which connected me to lectures by such giants as Henry Kissinger, Arthur Schlesinger, Jr., and Oscar Handlin, that further sated my boundless appetite for learning.

Athletics continued to be an important outlet for me at Harvard. Playing football allowed me to forge multiple friendships overnight. I was one of 130 frosh trying out for the freshman football team. These athletes, and the others I met in classes and via my roommates, meant that I had access to approximately 30% of the class of 1964.

I made Harvard's freshman football team as starting left end. I scored the winning touchdown on a scoring pass from Bill Humenuk (so well thrown I couldn't drop it!) beating Holy Cross, a Division 1 power at the Varsity level. It was quite a thrill. I lettered on the varsity team the next three years. Thanks to an outstanding team highlighted by Captain Pete Hart, All-East Bob Boyda, All-Ivy Bill Swinford, All-Ivy Darren Wyle, Q.B. Ted Halaby, Billy Taylor, fellow sophomores Bill Grana, Scotty Harshbarger, and Rich Beizer (another roommate) Harvard won its first Ivy League Football Championship my sophomore year.

Ironically, my fondest memory was of our football practices that gave me a chance to earn the respect of my teammates. We were student athletes, not jocks, especially not "dumb" jocks. I was blessed to have senior teammates (Jeff, Scott, Rick, Dobie, Cleo, Stephenson, Neuenschwander, Southy, Humenuk, Guzzi, Bob Stringer, Lozeau, Minotti) who graduated in 1964 and attended prestigious graduate schools: Harvard Med (2); Tufts Med (2); Harvard Business School (4); Harvard Law (2); Michigan Law (1); University of Virginia Law (1); University of Chicago (me); and Columbia Business (1); UPenn Law (1).

My life at Harvard was mostly confined to the Harvard campus locales such as Leverett House, Lamont Library, Mem Hall, Fogg Museum, Dillon Field House, Harvard Yard, Pi Eta Eating Club, Hemenway Gym (where I played JV basketball my sophomore year), Harvard Stadium, The Rugby Playing Fields (rugby team for three years). I reached out beyond to Cambridge's local commercial enterprises: Tommy's Luncheonette on Mt. Auburn Street, Elsie's, the Coop, News Kiosk in Harvard Square, the T, Hayes-Bickford, Worsthaus, Cronin's Bar, Hasty Pudding, the *Lampoon*'s building, Brine's Sporting Goods, the Andover Shop, Brigham's, and the Varsity Liquor Store.

Not to be overlooked was the learning by osmosis gained by associating with smart people. In my tutorials in the economics honors program, I studied with other economics majors from other Houses who could have lectured at Harvard, and later did. They were that advanced. Dave Sacks was a neighbor of mine in Leverett Towers who lectured in the toughest pre-med course, Chem 20, as a junior! At subsequent class reunions, I met many classmates for the first time. Recently, at my 55th reunion I met more classmates who epitomized the uniqueness of the Harvard student: smart, approachable, hard-working, and a joy to be with.

One of these was Jim Wynne, co-discoverer of excimer laser surgery that laid the foundation for the laser refractive surgical procedures known as LASIK and P.R.K. The visual acuity of over 40 million people (me included) were improved because of these procedures. Another was Michael Droller, Chairman Emeritus, Urology Department at the prestigious Mount Sinai Medical Center.

These are just two of the 32 summa cum laude graduates in my class. As a footnote, my roommate, Dave Carroll would have made the total 33 had I not persuaded him to take an Economics course that gave him a grade that kept him from becoming the first ever summa cum laude in fine arts at Harvard.

A serendipity event occurred in the last semester of my senior year. Four of us, Tom Piper, Ken Nahigian, Chip Stuart, and I decided impromptu to go to the Mardi Gras during our spring break. We stayed in a Tulane dorm courtesy of Chip's cousin. On our last night we met and befriended a guy who needed a place to stay before returning to Southern Illinois University. Grateful that I got him sleeping space, Bill Raasch suggested that I phone Linda Johnson, a fellow graduate of his at Arlington Heights High School, who was attending Smith College in Northampton, Massachusetts. After returning, I invited Linda for a weekend at Harvard. Not knowing my prior history, she accepted sight unseen. "How will I know you? She asked. I replied in my smart-alecky way, "Don't worry. I'll know you by your inquisitive look!" We had a wonderful weekend, attending the Hasty Pudding Show, Pi Eta party, Sunday at the Isabella Stuart Museum. Linda was (and still is) a knockout, smart, attractive, sound, and personable. I was smitten, but I didn't know if she was, so I phoned her at Park House to see if she arrived back safely. The balance of power quickly changed. "Not here," said the person on the other end, "Linda is out on a date at Amherst College." Subsequently we dated, frequently attending my rugby matches and post-game parties. At one memorable match against the Royal Canadian Navy who had just finished fighting in Cyprus, I arranged for Linda to be "locked in" behind the bar to ensure her safety at our post-game party. No commitments, but she agreed to introduce me to her parents that summer.

I graduated cum lucky: lucky for the education, friendships, and my pure luck in meeting Linda. I was eager to move on to the next place of my life, but I still didn't know where that was.

CHAPTER 56

THE NAVY

MFF-Linda Johnson wedding, Arlington Heights, IL, August 1967

For the first time in my life I was deciding what I wanted to do, not acceding to what my mother, my father, the nuns, and the Christian Brothers wanted me to do. Tired after 18 years of school, I did not want to go to graduate school. Unlike my father, who 28 years earlier, after graduating from Harvard, went immediately to work at Foley Fish, I had no desire to become a junior Fishmonger. I needed time off before wrestling with a career decision. In addition, I felt I had to get away from a life spent entirely in Massachusetts. There was much more to life than what the Bay State offered, or so I felt at the time.

My parents and I had not discussed my plans after Harvard. Most Harvard graduates did not join the Armed Forces, but things were different in 1964. The Vietnam War was happening, and the draft was still the law of the land. At Harvard I had been exposed to the Camelot script and JFK's clarion call for service: "Ask not what your country can do for you; ask what you can do for your country." It resonated. I enlisted in the Navy, not merely out of a sense of duty, but because I desired to be liberated, to be finally and unequivocally on my own.

I applied and was accepted into the "90-day wonder" Naval Officer Candidate School Program in Newport, R.I., which required a three-year commitment. This obviated making any career decisions until 1967 at the earliest. Commissioned as an Ensign, I was assigned to the USS Thomas J. Gary (DER-326), a Destroyer Escort Radar ship as an MPA (Main Propulsion Assistant). It was a laughable assignment as I didn't know a piston from a cylinder. On my first day, I met with Chief Dormer, the highest-ranking non-commissioned officer in the Engineering Department, for a never-to-be forgotten woodshed talk given by him to me, his new boss.

"I have great respect for your accomplishments that far exceed mine; however, for our relationship to work you must let me run the engineering operations below deck. I'm very good at my business so until you learn more please don't interfere. My men and I need you to support us grease monkeys. In return you can count on us supporting you, 100% percent," so said the 30- year veteran Chief Petty Officer to me the three-month boot Ensign.

On our 1965 cruise to Dunedin, New Zealand, home base for what was called Operation Deep Freeze in Antarctica, our diesel engines broke down in Lima, Peru. For three days and nights I stayed below deck with Chief Dormer and our men, the so-called Black Gang. The Chief was impressed and said, "You're a quick study, even for a kid out of Harvard."

In Barcelona some months later, I repaid the compliment. Chief Dormer had too good a time ashore and failed to return by sailing time. I led some of my sailors on a rescue operation and found the Chief, a bit worse for wear, and brought him back for our "delayed" departure. His woodshed talk stuck with me, and became a teaching moment that stayed with me later.

While not very helpful in engineering, I did step up as the ship's education officer. Drawing on my education at Harvard, I used our year-long cruise to prep our many non-high school grads in a General Education Degree (GED) program. Eighty of our servicemen earned their GED certification, which meant they could now take advantage of the G.I. Bill and go onto college.

Upon our return to Newport a year later, I was asked to return for a second Operation Deep Freeze, this time as the Navigation Officer responsible for circumnavigating the globe, a tempting offer. Unfortunately, I became ill with an arthritic virus and was still hospitalized when my ship sailed. The good news was that Linda Johnson was still interested in me. Another year apart might have sunk the relationship.

I was given shore duty and, after a brief stint on the staff of "COMCRUDESLANT," the massive U.S.N. unit that oversees all cruisers, and destroyers the Atlantic Fleet, I lucked out with a job teaching at my alma mater, Officer Candidate School in Newport, Rhode Island.

After a full-court press dating Linda during her senior year at Smith, we became engaged to be married, which was happily formalized in Arlington Heights, Illinois on August 19, 1967, the summer after she graduated from Smith.

In 1967 Linda, making more money than I did, taught at the John Clarke School in Newport, allowing us to rent a nice house in Newport on Gibbs Avenue. Due to be discharged in November of 1968, I extended my Navy stay by six months to enable me to retire the same time that Linda finished teaching. I was promoted to Lieutenant, an unexpected bonus as my "unused leave pay" would now be determined at this higher pay scale. This enabled us to spend the summer in Europe using Frommer's "Europe on $5 a Day" as our Bible. I started working for my father at the Foley Fish Co. in the fall of that year.

CHAPTER 57

APPRENTICE FISHMONGER

Upon returning from Europe, we learned that Linda was pregnant. We rented a one-bedroom apartment in Quincy, a few miles from the Foley Fish plant in Dorchester. Rising early, leaving Linda to care for baby Laura, I began to work there in September 1969. It was my intention to spend my entire career there. But very quickly I became frustrated.

No family consideration was accorded me. I was treated like any other trainee off the street, and assigned to the same menial duties I had as a summer worker years before. This pained me. Despite my Harvard economics degree, four years as a Navy officer, experiences that I felt justified a more significant assignment, I was ensconced at the very bottom of the totem pole. Dad said nothing about my progression, not a word about timetables, rotations, or ultimate placements. There was no goal, no reward, in sight.

After seven months, I met with FF, and told him, "I am not happy; I can't decipher your thoughts or plans for me. I expected you to ask me for feedback during my initial rotations, but you didn't." To which Frank responded, "It's the only way I know how to teach you the business." He offered no specifics or encouragement.

I realized that I had mishandled my start. I had not sat down with him beforehand to discuss mutual expectations, a grave mistake. In retrospect, I realize that I had naively blocked out any potential problems about my path upward, relying instead on unrealistic scenarios. By entrusting my future blindly to FF, I'd trapped myself, and he dealt with me in the only way he could conceive. When FF started at Foley Fish, he said he was the least street-smart guy starting in a business that prized street smarts. Michael Francis Foley, MFF, was no different. I had flunked my first test.

It would be incorrect, however, to assume my brief time on the lower rungs of the company had been wasted. For instance, I learned that I did not share Dad's love for the business. I did not want to work for such a narrow-minded boss. FF's autocratic, rigid management style, however successful, was not mine. Recalling my spankings, I realized that Dad still held the belt over me. Because of the nuns, and the Christian Brothers, I disliked ceding control over me to anyone. I could not foresee a partnership with FF. He couldn't change; neither could I.

My father-in-law had come to visit us and meet his first grandchild. He perceived how frustrated I was and privately suggested to Linda that I look into other opportunities, including graduate school on the GI Bill. I had 48 months of eligibility under the Bill. I applied to the University of Chicago Business School, which offered the option of evening classes, and was accepted. I had no job yet but I had lined up interviews with the three largest banks in Chicago: Continental Illinois Bank, First Bank of Chicago and Northern Trust.

I quit Foley Fish. It occurs to me now that in so doing, perhaps I was taking the same route as my grandfather, who left his brother's business because he wanted more than that life could furnish. He wanted someday to run his own company. FF did not try to dissuade me. We parted on good terms. No harsh rebukes; Dad never said now or never. The door was still open. He was gracious about my decision, kindly saying, "Work hard and win."

On my way to Chicago, I felt an exhilaration much like MF must have felt when he had departed Tipperary almost 70 years prior. I sensed that an exciting though challenging part of my life was about to begin.

CHAPTER 58

NEW CAREER

"Why should we hire you?" asked Bill Staples at my Continental Illinois National Bank (CINB) interview. "You probably shouldn't," was my response. "I have no accounting background and am so green that I can't tell a deferred asset from a long-term or short-term liability, nor am I equipped to perform basic credit analysis. I have a body of work, however, that will show how all my life I have found ways to catch up and, eventually, get ahead. I have applied and been accepted at the University of Chicago Business School, in fact, I start tonight. I hope my story helps you decide why you should, or should not, hire me. I'm ready to prove myself, again." They took a big chance, and I was hired at $5,000 dollars above what I had made at Foley Fish, plus moving expenses.

My first two prerequisite courses at University of Chicago were in advanced calculus. At Harvard, I received a gift grade of D in this subject. To my amazement, I received two As at Chicago. I also made honor grades in all 20 courses (except cost accounting), while working full time at CINB, first in a training program, and then as a lender in the National Division of the Commercial Lending Departments, where I was responsible for dealing with accounts and prospects located in the Mid-Atlantic states.

My promotion to company officer was one of the fastest in CINB's history, although I know that part of the reason was being in the right place at the right time. My ascent came right after Penn Central Co. declared bankruptcy, the largest in bankruptcy history until the 2001 Enron bankruptcy. Every major national and regional bank in the U.S.

had substantial loan exposure. At a meeting in the boardroom of Citibank, Penn Central's lead lender, the discussion focused on whether to inject new capital, or to seize collateral for repayment. I was easily the most junior person in a room populated by the heads of most of the commercial banks in the U.S. Only my second year at CINB, I was a bag-carrying subordinate. I asked the top-ranking CINB representative, Don Myers, if I could make a statement. Not knowing who was scared the most, my boss, Myers, or MFF, "Based on my homework we should opt for the collateral package." When the Treasurer of Penn Central admitted that the railroad could not compute the cost of running a train on a given route, I concluded that new loans would be pouring good money after bad. Additionally, my valuation of the railroad's collateralized stock package (mainly Penn subsidiaries such as Buckeye Pipeline, Aruida, Six Flags), was in excess of the company's debt by a large margin.

Word about my boldness circulated. I received disproportionate praise when, in actuality, I'd merely demonstrated I had more testicular courage than brains. I still did not know enough about depreciation, off-sheet borrowing, or basic accounting tools critical to credit analysis. I had yet to make a loan myself until Don Myers, the brilliant head of our East Cost territory, assigned Dave Handy and I to evaluate the creditworthiness of a manufacturing company in Michigan, a subsidiary of one of the division's largest accounts. We made the loan and the company didn't survive. My glory days were transient. It was a powerful experience, one sufficiently sobering for me to avoid any further bankruptcies during my eight years of lending.

I ascended the ranks from Trainee, to Officer, to Assistant Vice President, and to Vice President, head of the Mid-Atlantic States lending group, all in record time. My performance reviews were stellar. Often, I was the junior-most member of long-term strategic planning teams. CINB picked me to be its first interviewer of applicants from Harvard Business School, and later sent me to the Harvard Business School executive finance program for two summer stints.

I was not prepared for what happened next. Without any forewarning, I was relieved of my management position as head of the Mid-Atlantic States lending group. The cited reason was that I drove the train too fast, making it difficult for some of the newer members to stay aboard. I was perceived by those reporting to me as unapproachable and intimidating (could this be genetic?) But there was no questioning of my loan portfolio quality, or account growth, or new business development under my management.

The suddenness of the decision suggested to me that there was another, larger reason for being relieved. I had my suspicions, but kept them to myself as the decision was fait accompli; it was pointless to challenge. The reasons were revealed years later when my suspicions of a power play above me were confirmed.

I was put on waivers. A painful week of sleepless nights followed. Should I fight or flee? I was too proud to resign, however. I was determined not to leave on a sour note. It was important for me to leave, if and when I did, on my own terms. Looking over my shoulders at this setback for the rest of my life was unacceptable. Tightlipped, I did not seek vindication, so much as a new start in a different area of the bank. I was not beaten, in fact, I remained self-confident. I would prove, again, that I was best when coming from behind. Within one week, Joe Anderson, Senior Vice President, hired me. I lucked out; I had found my niche.

Joe Anderson was (and still is) the most dynamic manager, and the brightest (actually co-brightest with Don Myers who tragically died of cancer the year before) I'd ever met. Graduating with high honors from Notre Dame, Joe moved up the ranks in the Operations Department and now was the chief troubleshooter for George Baker, the head of CINB's Commercial Bank. My assignment was to research loans principally lodged in Continental Illinois Ltd., a subsidiary of CINB. Soon, Joe rewarded my work by getting me assigned to the Bank's task force focusing on product development under the guidance of the consulting firm McKinsey & Co. Like other banks in the late 1970s, CINB began focusing on fee income sources to improve its return on assets at a lower risk basis.

We presented a recommendation to Roger Anderson, Chairman of CINB, that called for the formation of a new department for product development and management that would feature a corporate finance division focusing on private placements, financial advisory, and mergers & acquisitions, all on a fee basis. The proposal was a major departure as it legally skirted the Glass-Steagall Act by assuming functions (collecting fees) heretofore the exclusive province of investment banks.

I was appointed co-head of the private placements and corporate finance divisions (with Bob Williamson), and a short time later was promoted to head of both divisions. John Porta, a seasoned commercial banker from Citibank, former CEO of a major Cleveland bank, and then head of Continental Illinois Limited, became my boss. John was a great supporter of the group and me; he successfully fought for key players that I wanted in the group: John Dancewicz, a standout Harvard Business School grad, Michael Smith, a seasoned commercial lender, and Jim Dalton became the core group. We enjoyed incredible success in private placements, 12 in our first year.

I was promoted to the division head pay grade sooner than if I had stayed in the commercial lending. I had come back. I was doing what I was best at: new and ambitious ventures, in this case, competing against investment bankers. I had survived by swimming upstream again.

Those years were crucial because I had proved myself to me. Something changed in me. For the first time in my life I felt settled. I was 38, much older than when MF (15) and FF (21) experienced the same feeling. Better late than never.

CHAPTER 59

STEVE CONNOLLY DEPARTS

In the spring of 1979, after returning from a two-week vacation, Steve Connolly hand delivered his letter of resignation. It was inconceivable to FF that Steve would quit after spending 37 years at Foley Fish. But Russ and Bobby were not surprised. FF had been a hard boss, and Steve had chafed at his overbearing manner and arbitrary restrictions, especially when FF decreed that the company would not accept any new accounts for the foreseeable future. FF's confidantes and business associates tried to explain the fallout from this decision: "You can't hold back a racehorse. You hired and developed a high-performing executive, so it was inevitable that someone would try to recruit him away from you."

Steve had never forgotten his modest start growing up on Henry Street in Dorchester where his mother worked in a local bakery to supplement her husband's wages. A psychologist would later tell FF that Steve was "shooting for the moon," with his plan to establish his own fish company, a venture that he believed would provide him wealth not known in his family.

Like Bill Moloney, Steve was the public face of Foley Fish. He possessed the keys to every lock; he knew every account. Unlike Bill, Steve was going to a company that had an established fish processing line. He was going to F.E. Harding Fish Co., located on the Boston Fish Pier, a firm that sold primarily to retail and supermarket accounts.

F.E. Harding was counting on Steve to exploit his connections to Foley's accounts. He would become Harding's hired gun, and target every Foley account. FF was concerned and asked himself some hard questions.

Would Connolly, like Bill Moloney, attempt to cripple Foley Fish by raiding accounts, and also try to hire key personnel? Had his, FF's, suffocating restrictiveness alienated Steve to the point of seeking revenge by raiding his former company? Foley Fish did not have a "star" system. If it had, Steve would be a superstar. It was a major loss, but it was fated. Years later Steve told me, "I hated every day of my 37 years working for your father."

FF in his favorite Charles River Country Club hat

FF met privately with each key manager to address Steve's departure. The divorce, he concluded, would be portrayed as amicable. FF did not want to provide fodder about feuds or grudges to the rumor mills. FF's first action was to increase each manager's pay. He then appointed Tom Colbert to replace Steve at the anchor desk. Finally, he decided to become more active than ever in generating new sales.

Another complication arose from Steve's departure. The IRS had been pressuring FF under the IRS excess profits statute to reinvest more of the company's accumulated profits. If not, the IRS under the code, would tax these profits a second time. FF had met with his managers, including Steve, to discuss possible sites for a second processing operation. The Boston Fish Pier, Gloucester and New Bedford were considered. FF decided on a new plant site in New Bedford, Massachusetts. FF had offered Steve the head position at the New Bedford plant. Steve, however, felt strongly the plant should be in Gloucester. This was another element in Steve's departure. With Steve out of the picture, FF needed someone else to manage the New Bedford plant construction and its subsequent operation.

FF expected unconditional loyalty. In his scheme of things, Steve, by resigning, had created an unforgiveable breach of trust. FF felt that the Foley's management team, its account, its plant, and its technology, were all covered by an imaginary patent that protected these proprietary assets from infringement. FF felt robbed, concluding that Steve's departure was tantamount to betrayal. He pushed away any thought that his leaving was merely because Steve wanted to become his own boss, just as MF and FF had. A glacial silence followed. FF would never again speak to Steve Connolly.

CHAPTER 60

DECISION TO RETURN

FF (2nd generation) teaching Laura Foley
(4th generation) to fish, Cape Cod

Shortly after Steve left, FF phoned us (not a regular occurrence) and said in his inimitable style, "Ha-Ha. The damnedest thing happened. Steve Connelly just resigned. I'm coming out to Chicago for sales calls. Can we meet?"

Afterwards, Linda asked me, "Do you think there was a hidden message? Do you think he wants you to come back to Foley Fish?" Unbeknownst to us, Rita had urged her reluctant husband to make the phone call. If he was open to hiring me after I had abruptly quit ten years earlier, I would have been surprised.

As I had been earning my MBA and making my way in the world of banking, Linda had been home with our first two children, doing occasional substitute teaching and putting time into several volunteer organizations. After a while she was not a happy homemaker. She craved more mental stimulation, and so, as our daughter, Laura, started kindergarten, Linda started as a full-time student at DePaul College of Law in downtown Chicago. We rode the train together, Linda studying and me working on banking matters. Linda was on the Law Review and graduated magna cum laude. She was hired by the prestigious Chicago law firm, Bill, Boyd, Lloyd Haddad and Burns.

Our future paths seemed well-etched. We were settled in Linda's hometown near her family. Our children were happily settled in the neighborhood and loved their schools. In spite of our "settledness," however, Linda and I had days where thoughts of riding the same train, trekking across the Chicago river and on to LaSalle Street, doing the same jobs, for the next thirty years felt stifling. We knew we had complementary talents and talked of one day starting a business together. Foley Fish was never considered an option.

When FF came to our home in Arlington Heights, I asked him if he was asking me to return to Foley Fish and, if so, in what position. Dad said he wanted me to be in charge of a new venture, M.F. Foley Inc. of New Bedford, a startup operation focusing on sales to supermarkets, a market we had never tapped. He laid it out plainly, "We have no plant, no customers, and no employees, and will need debt financing. You would be in charge of overseeing the new plant's construction, securing financing, hiring personnel, and researching and prospecting for potential new supermarket customers. You would be expected to establish a new business model because supermarkets are very different from the institutional customers that we have at Foley's Boston."

Linda was uncomfortable. Wired differently than me, she possessed an objectivity that I lacked. As a lawyer she was trained to analyze legal documents for flaws. Every "I" had to be dotted, every "T" crossed. Dad's plan, she found, lacked the specificity needed for us to properly assess the risks involved. I had not asked enough questions the last time I'd gone to work at Foley Fish, so I found merit in her studied skepticism.

Nevertheless, she said that she would support any decision I would make, provided that there was agreement on salary, moving expenses, full medical coverage, and a Buy/Sell agreement, in place, meaning that we could eventually purchase the new company.

I had never thought about returning to Foley Fish, not once over ten years. Things were going well at Continental Illinois Bank. I had formed a talented team headed by John Dancewicz, Jim Dalton, and Mike Smith. We had exceeded everyone's expectations, and the Corporate Finance Division could become an increasingly important part of CINB. Plans were underway to strengthen the corporate finance consulting division, now in its infancy. Why had FF chosen me? Linda answered, "Because your father naturally wanted the Foley Fish Co. to stay in the family. He had heard enough to know of your success at CINB. He knew that you were competent, or else his proposal to you would never have happened. Time will solve issues between you and your father."

There were many "unknowns." I would be starting way behind but Linda knew that I'd always been at my best in such uncertain situations. We felt confident that I could do the job simply because I would will it to happen. Unlike at CINB where I would always have bosses above me, at Foley's I would ultimately be my own boss. Linda and I would eventually run the business together.

Working out the financial aspects and the terms of the Buy/Sell Agreement were easy compared to the task of telling Linda's parents, Norma and Dick, of our decision. They had become a second set of parents for Laura and Michael, feeding them breakfast, walking them to and from grammar school, and babysitting them until we returned from work. Laura and Michael had become their children too, and tears of sadness flowed. Norma was upset, and couldn't be consoled.

CHAPTER 61

BACK TO THE FUTURE

FF and MFF: a meeting of the minds

My biggest struggle after returning was figuring out how to manage my father, which included, I learned, managing myself. He had to change. I had to change. The success of our personal relationship was pivotal, a *sine qua non* for success of our New Bedford business. Dad and I had to be a team. I knew that it would be pointless to copy my father. He was idiosyncratic and inimitable. I needed to eliminate competition between us. I also had to lower my personal expectations so that I would be less likely to be disappointed. I sought his support, while not expecting agreement. I truly felt that if I was half as good as my father in the fish business, I'd be two times better than my competition.

While driving from Illinois to Boston, I had ample time for further self-analysis, starting with inescapable truth that I was starting again. The task before me was certainly not below my qualifications; the opposite was true. Echoing my father's "least street smart" statement when returning to Foley Fish, I was the least "fish smart" guy in the fish business. I knew so little that I had no preconceptions. But Dad did. As he often said, "American consumers were fed up with fish that, when cooked, stunk up their homes. They were ready for Foley-quality fish."

I had to manage my impulses. My overwhelming instinct was to just throw myself into the job, bring my all. Such mantras sound good on paper, but could be dangerous in the real world. As with crossword puzzles, a hurried response could result in failure. Self-restraint, self-questioning, not leaping before looking — these were not my strong suit. I had to summon new powers.

My first task was the business of negotiating a term loan to finance the Foley New Bedford plant. I opted for a tax-free Industrial Revenue Bond (IRB) in order to receive the lowest possible interest rate. New England Merchants Bank of Boston, Foley's long-standing banker, insisted that my father personally guarantee the proposed $1.47 million, seven-year term loan, since the borrower, M.F. Foley Inc. of New Bedford, a subsidiary of M.F. Boston, was a startup with a chief executive lacking a track record (they were too polite to say, "no fish experience"). I refused, saying that if the guarantee was required, I would be forced to take my banking business elsewhere. I counteroffered with a negative pledge covenant, thus guaranteeing they would have a senior (superior) position to my other creditor, FF, in case of bankruptcy, plus the usual default covenants with safe cure periods relative to timely payment of interest and principal when due. The bank's loan committee balked, wanting more protection. Consequently, I offered a new covenant calling for our parent's company's working capital to always exceed the term loan amount (in existence) by 1.5 times.

Not only did New England Merchants Bank agree to these terms, they dropped their requirement for FF's personal guarantee. They generously agreed to a single-digit fixed rate at a time when Paul Volcker, then Secretary of Treasury, was hiking interest rates to combat inflation, which peaked at 14.6% on March 1980. The agreed-upon loan rate proved to be a museum piece: 8.0%.

I never forgot FF's response when I told him that he would not be guaranteeing the loan, "I knew that; it was your loan, not mine." He was correct that it was my loan. He had fully entrusted the new venture to me. I was the chosen one. It was then that I realized that my decision to return to Foley Fish was motivated by a much deeper emotion than a desire to run my own company. Outranking everything else, was MFF's desire to earn the esteem of FF. FF's ultra-conservative business approach of retaining all profits in the company triggered the IRS requirement to invest these funds in the New Bedford plant, without which I probably wouldn't be in New Bedford. Additionally, the bank financing, without Dad's personal guarantee, would not have been acceptable to the bank without the company's substantial plowed-back earnings. This infusion made the working capital coverage ratio work. Indirectly, FF had guaranteed the loan.

During the credit negotiations, I studied the financials. Ed Rogers, a new partner at the CPA firm, Sullivan Bille and Co., became our account manager, and a key advisor to me. I was very impressed by Ed's technical knowledge, but even more so, by his desire to help Foley Fish succeed. His personal commitment to Foley's was demonstrated early on. Ed proposed to file for a "manufacturing classification" exemption to the personal property taxes imposed by the state on our fixed assets. Heretofore, we had been classified as a "wholesaler," making us subject to these taxes. We filed a seven-page brief to the Massachusetts Appellate Tax Board, in an attempt to validate our petition to be classified as a "manufacturing" entity. We won, saving thousands of dollars that year, but, more importantly, in all future years.

Secondly, Ed urged me to opt for a subchapter "S" tax classification, even though Foley New Bedford would be taxed at a slightly higher personal rate than would be the "C" Corp tax rate that Foley Boston had, because future earnings of Foley New Bedford would be tax free. Dad had preferred the "C" classification for Foley's Boston because he didn't plan to distribute dividend earnings. I liked Ed's optimism!

So much for the easy stuff; it was time to move on from loan negotiations and tax matters to building a plant and doing so while becoming re-immersed into Foley Fish. The responsibilities of finding a new home, new schooling for Laura and Michael, and finding new friends fell solely on Linda's shoulders. Her Midwestern toughness and resilience would be greatly tested.

CHAPTER 62

NEW PLANT

Cutter at measurement bench, New Bedford plant

The site FF had purchased in New Bedford was in south terminal where most of the other seafood plants were located. Unlike the others, however, FF had chosen a site about a block inland from the waterfront. This made the land more affordable but was also necessary because of the way the fishery operated. Processors located dockside bid on a boat's catch at the auction. If the bid was won, that boat's catch was unloaded at the winning processor's plant. The processor took all the fish from that boat, newest, oldest and everything in between.

Foley only sold the best fish and had no outlet for the less fresh catch from a boat. Therefore, Foley's became the customer of the existing processors, paying them a small premium over auction price for the best off the boat. This made the other processors more comfortable with Foley's, the new player in the neighborhood.

FF's extensive research regarding temperature control and sanitation done when building the West Howell plant only needed to be updated and adapted for the New Bedford location. The chlorinated spray system was a given. New Bedford would use an ammonia-based refrigeration system rather than freon. The plant would be larger than Boston with room on the property for expansion. The cooler would have a special system which would provide more moisture. There would be a North Star salt water flake ice machine on the roof, same as West Howell with an additional ice chute in the plant.

It had been almost twenty years since West Howell was built with its focus on preserving fish freshness through temperature control and sanitation. Yet at the time the New Bedford plant was built, most processing plants still were not refrigerated. The Foley production areas were maintained at about 50°F. Most other processors operated at room temperature or above, greatly increasing the spoilage rate.

Perhaps the most significant upgrade implemented in New Bedford was the measurement bench. Foley's had always kept its eye on yields but the new production line in New Bedford would have a much more precise reading of the "cost of goods," fish. Yield would be measured at every step, from receiving, to filleting, to skinning to packing. Selling price could be adjusted to reflect lower yields, such as when fish are in spawn. Cutters could be rated, skinning machine blades sharpened, vendors assessed, all based on the information provided. It was an onerous task to stay on top of the numbers, pre-computer, but it assured us we'd have no delusions about profitability.

One critical decision made about New Bedford was that we would continue shipping in tins as Foley's in Boston always had. In the 1960s, processors other than Foleys switched to shipping fish in plastic boxes. Plastic was cheaper and lighter than the tins. Processors maintained that it insulated the fish better. This might have been a benefit if the fish was near 32°F going into the plastic but coming from a cutting line in a 70°F or warmer plant it was far above that, spoiling at a rapid rate. Ice on top of the plastic in delivery totes did not cool it. The plastic was acting as insulator to keep the cold out.

Foley fillets being packed in tins were close to 32°F. For truck shipments, tins were nestled in 15°F flake ice which maintained or even lowered the fillet temperature and maintained it to destinations like Chicago or Florida. For air shipments, tins were buried in ice to lower fillet temperatures before being packed in insulated air cartons with super cold frozen gel packs and topped off with a small amount of dry ice. (Airlines had disallowed dry ice in the cargo hold so that the amount we added was calculated to have dissipated before cargo was loaded.) Yes, we were fanatical about maintaining shelf-life, i.e., freshness and flavor for our customers.

Tins in ice prior to being packed and shipped

CHAPTER 63

THE LESS-TRAVELED PATH

Plant at 77 Wright Street, New Bedford (ice machine tower on roof)

While I had spent a lot of time working in production at Foley's-Boston, I had never been the one in control of the whole operation. As we prepared to open the New Bedford plant, I felt like a Chevy driver who had been gifted a Ferrari. How do I avoid crashing it?

FF invited Russ Rohrbacher to teach me to drive the Ferrari. Recently retired after 50 years at Foley Fish, he was pleased to be enlisted as my personal mentor at Foley Fish Inc. of New Bedford. He knew the fish business thoroughly. Russ set the bar high from the get-go, telling me, "We can't just duplicate Foley's Boston; we have to be even better. We need a sturdier product than FF is selling, because our fish will be held under less favorable conditions, and for longer periods before sale. Fish in a retail display case are subject to more temperature variations and more handling and thus more opportunity for spoilage. We must cut 'sculptured,' eye-catching fillets since they will be on display. There will be no do-overs or second chances. Our fish must be the newer, better fish from the get-go."

"We must hire employees from other fish companies. We must undo their bad habits, and remake them into Foley work habits." Russ's narrative to prospective mentees was compelling: "I started behind where you are now. I had no fish experience. I've done every job in the fish business of Foley's: cutting, shipping, buying, and production. I will be your teacher, sharing with you everything I know."

He went on to articulate a philosophy that I began to call The Foley Way. "We have a winning formula that puts quality ahead of price, unlike other fish companies you know. We will strive to do all the little things better than our competitors. You've come at a good time. We're starting a new company here in New Bedford. Our goal is to build a unique fish business to supply supermarkets. We will make mistakes, but we always learn and grow from them. We're not a sweat shop, but I will insist on good work habits until they become second nature. You will make a difference."

Just after our new plant was constructed, we got lucky in the hiring of production personnel. The local New Bedford seafood workers union struck the New Bedford dealers for higher wages. The port was closed down. All seafood workers were laid off. After two months the union ran out of money, forcing workers to settle for pay decreases averaging $1.50 per hour. We were able to cherry pick the best cutters, who are born, not made. Russ smelled potential in John Williams and offered him a starting job in production.

We also lucked out by not having a union shop. After the New Bedford strike, new employees were drawn by the promise of a guaranteed eight hours work, five days a week, at a wage considerably above then union rate. We were able to attract other outstanding cutters. Bobby Boyd marveled at our cutters' dexterity and speed. John Felix, Horacio Gouveia, Rick Cunha, Joao Silva, and Anabel Duarte were cutters with the skill of a surgeon. They learned their craft in the Azores.

Russ, knowing that the New Bedford dealers would be suspicious of our new company, became the perfect ambassador to the community. His wonderfully engaging manner broke down many barriers. He met with each seafood dealer and explained that he wanted to become the best possible customer.

Russ taught Rick Cunha how to be a fish buyer, obsessive about buying only the top-of-the boats catch. One day Dad called Russ saying that some of the large New Bedford seafood houses were squawking about Rick being too demanding. Russ then knew he had picked the right guy.

Unlike Dorothy in *The Wizard of Oz*, who searched for the Wizard only to find out that he was a human being, Russ was the company's real wizard. Just being around him, inhaling his insights was a privilege. He had a magical way about him that motivated us to become better than we thought we could be. His largeness of spirit, his ebullience, was as infectious as his energy. I loved that man. He was my mentor, my confidante, and my cheerleader. He became a unique friend whom I will never forget.

Icing down newly received fish prior to cutting

CHAPTER 64

SUPERMARKET RESEARCH

While the New Bedford plant was under construction, I travelled to reacquaint myself with our Boston accounts and to visit supermarkets in various parts of the country. I also spent time at the Boston fish pier and other processors to get a better sense of the supermarkets' current suppliers. I needed to see what was working and what was not working in supermarkets relative to seafood. What I found was demoralizing.

The reception to my proposal to provide them with a better grade of fish generally brought a response as follows: "I've never heard of Foley Fish. I already have four suppliers from New Bedford. They all know that they must have the lowest prices to get my business. Quotes for special store sales have to be given to me four weeks ahead of my newspaper seafood ads. They truck my fish directly to me four times a week, irrespective of the volume. I don't pay for freight or for shipping boxes, which means the quoted prices are automatically delivered prices. Our seafood departments are profitable. We don't have any product shrink; we sell everything. We have well-trained personnel who source both the meat and the seafood counters. I'm not interested in taking on a new supplier. I always get the best fish and the lowest quoted prices. You can fax me your delivered prices. I'll tell you if you are in the ballpark. If you are, I may give you a try. I'm aware of the usual fish scams, so don't try any on me."

I learned that this was malarkey. My due diligence over six months revealed that most fish programs were not profitable. Follow the math: 15% gross profit margins, minus 8% shrink (difference between pounds bought and sold), minus 13% labor and overhead, meant a 6% net loss on every pound of fish that they sold. He hadn't done the math.

To meet "lowest price dicta," the suppliers had to buy discounted "seconds," the oldest fish that they camouflaged by soaking the fillets in vats of weight-adding sodium tri-poly solution, water weight that would camouflage the age of the fish and seep out at the store. Additionally, sales of throwaway fish, defined as fish not saleable in four days, were rampant. I remember sitting in the office of a New Bedford seafood boss overhearing a conversation with his customer: "For the price I charged you, did you expect aces?"

The majority of supermarket prospects were not worth winning, nor were they winnable. It made no sense to ask the frogs to drain the swamp. The existing seafood programs were seriously flawed because there was no commitment by the owners and managers to quality seafood. There couldn't be because supermarket seafood buyers had no understanding of the variability of fish quality, its highly perishable nature, and how easily poor fish could be disguised by brining. There was little or no education and training on proper handling and displaying. Incoming fish that should have been rejected were blindly accepted. There were no icing procedures for proper temperature control. To them, fish was a commodity not a perishable food product that needed special attention. Clerks knew nothing about fish species or cooking methods. Most seafood departments were under the aegis of the meat manager. To the meat manager seafood was a stinky stepchild. Supermarkets needed to reboot and I needed to reboot my thinking.

To have any hope of selling Foley Fish to supermarkets, Linda and I realized we needed to devise a fish education program. A new script had to be written. The cornerstones of a successful seafood program as we saw them were absent. A fish program worthy of customer loyalty required the owner's commitment to quality, the presence of a knowledgeable fish czar to replace the meat men, quality seafood suppliers, training programs for seafood handlers, and fish education programs for consumers that explained quality detection, proper home storage, and cooking instructions. The *sine qua non* was, is, high quality fish.

Was I crazy? How were we going to motivate seafood prospects to make such a daunting commitment?

I had not unlearned my habit of not backing down since my days at La Salle Military. I remained as defiant and willful as ever. We would create the Foley Fish retail program that no one presently wanted. Yes, I was crazy!

CHAPTER 65

SAVED BY THE PHONE

Roche Bros. ad introducing Foley Fish to its customers

One morning I received an unexpected phone call from Bud Roche, co-owner with his brother Pat of Roche Bros., a four-store supermarket chain located in the Boston suburbs of West Roxbury, Westwood, Needham, and Natick. Bud, whom I'd never met, said in a booming voice, "I had an interesting conversation with your father. I told him that I am looking to upgrade my seafood program starting with my newest store in Sudbury. FF said you might not be interested since in your experience, most supermarkets' fish programs are run by meat men who care nothing about fish quality. Nevertheless, I'd like to visit with you if you'd consider supplying our stores."

At that time, we were on life support at Foley's New Bedford. We were in the red every month with no major turnaround prospects. FF had even begun to question the wisdom of our decision to sell exclusively to supermarkets, and whether we should jettison the original game plan.

What was my father thinking when he met with Bud? Dad responded, "Well, Bud may think that by spending a few more pennies for fish, it would instantly upgrade his fish program. I told him that he would have to make major adjustments, beyond who he selects as a vendor. So, before you get ahead of yourself, test his commitment. You'd better discuss the realities of the seafood industry regarding fish perishability, limited shelf life, pricing and processor scams, with which, as a meat man, he may be unfamiliar. He can't expect a new seafood program to become successful overnight, as you have painfully learned yourself."

My first reaction — wanting to shoot my father — soon gave way, as was often the case, to understanding his wise, counterintuitive guidance. Dad knew that I would be overeager, so he wanted to balance the scales. Dad had never entered a sales call in an unequal position. He felt Roche Bros. needed Foley Fish, as much as we needed their business.

I met with Bud who told me at our first meeting, "I am dissatisfied with my fish. I have the best meat, the best produce, the best deli spreads, but just average fish. I'm opening a new concept store in Sudbury that will be my version of a food emporium, emphasizing the best perishables sold anywhere. I would like to feature your fish in my Sudbury Farms store which opens in one month. This store is my baby. You'd be working directly with me with no interference from other Roche managers. Your father forewarned me that Foley Fish's reputation is also on the line, and that you would require my understanding and cooperation to do it your way," said Bud Roche.

Out of respect for FF, Bud, and myself, I stifled the urge to jump over my desk and hug him. Bud was a saint. In subsequent meetings with Bud, meetings that I termed "the gulps" because the changes proposed caused one or the other of us to gulp in astonishment. The most difficult issue we confronted was price and the volatility of fish prices. Bud could understand that fishermen are paid more for "the top of the catch." More upsetting to him was the volatility of fish prices due to abrupt shifts in supply and demand. I empathetically told Bud that it must be mind-boggling for people coming from a meat background, people like him. Meat and fish are priced radically differently. Meat prices don't change often and, when they do, it's only in pennies. Conversely, fish prices change daily at the seafood auctions, and by dimes, quarters and more. Many processors buy multiple grades of fish in order to average down their prices. Foley's only offers the best fish so cannot buy cheaper grades in order to lower our average prices. Published fish auction prices never cite the lower prices incurred for sub-par fish. The industry does not want you and other store owners to know this fact. No fish company ever advertises having mediocre fish at the right price. Foley Fish has only one grade of fish and just one pricing formula for all its customers. Namely, the cost of fish purchased plus an honest markup to cover labor, overhead, and a small profit. I told Bud that he can expect to pay, on average, thirty cents per pound more for Foley Fish. Gulp.

Bud asked about "price specials" to attract new customers at Sudbury Farms. My turn to gulp. I presented an alternative to price specials. I committed to working at the Sudbury fish counter every day until Bud was confident that our program was working. Furthermore, I promised to provide weekly fish demos to prove the superiority in taste and flavor of our fish. A complaint sheet would be kept. We would follow up on each complaint. Bud said okay, but with the caveat that we would further discuss this subject should Foley be asked to sell fish to his other stores.

Another thorny issue was the fish display procedures at Sudbury Farms. I had visited the other four Roche Bros. stores to study how fish were displayed at each. Roche did it better than their competitors, but improvement was needed. The fish cases needed to be refrigerated, and fillets were piled too high. Storage of fish at night was needed. We needed to overhaul their display system. Gulp.

To solve the problems of inadequate refrigeration and excessive fish handling, we devised an alternative fish display system. We would sell Foley's fish directly out of Foley's aluminum tins which would be nestled in the case surrounded by Foley's super-chilled, salt-water fed, flake ice. This would eliminate double handling, which always damaged quality, especially by untrained personnel. Closing down the fish case would be dramatically easier and quicker, requiring only covering tins and thoroughly icing the fish case. Opening each morning would entail merely brushing off the ice atop the nestled tins, and re-icing as necessary.

Bud had assigned Paul McGillivray, his top trainee, as head of Sudbury's fish department, and I was pleased that Paul took immediate ownership of the new fish program. Paul and I took Bud to one of his stores to demonstrate the proposed display system. We timed setup and close-downs. We measured the temperature differences of the fish between the old and new systems. Our findings proved conclusively, in fact, overwhelmingly, that the new system was superior. Bud concurred. But it was a controversial decision, and the old guard preferred the older, conventional system because it would be more eye-appealing. We opted for preserving quality and efficiency over appearance.

Because Roche Bros. is in New England their customers had some familiarity with fish. The large Irish and Italian Catholic populations had grown up eating it weekly. However, there was a lot the Roche customers didn't know about fish. Paul and I were on a mission to prove to customers and prospects that not all fish is the same, that fish shouldn't smell fishy, and that Sudbury Farms fish tasted better. We agreed that a positive, helpful attitude toward customers would tilt their attitude toward the new fish program at Sudbury Farms. We asked them to store their fish in the coldest part of their refrigerator, the bottom shelf. We asked them to try baking their cod and haddock fillets at 450° for ten minutes per inch of thickness. At this time most fish, even in many restaurants was being seriously overcooked.

The fish demos I did introduced customers to fish cooked medium-rare, with all of its moisture and flavor intact. Perhaps most impactful, we were able to demonstrate that quality fish doesn't smell "fishy." I could say to a customer, "I have been cooking fish in the store for three hours, can you detect any fishy odors?" And, of course, they couldn't because there were none. Forty years later, Foley Fish is still doing cooking demos in Roche Bros. Stores.

Bud Roche took a chance on me, partly because he knew Foley's reputation for selling the best fish. Bud was savvy, and knew exactly what he was doing when he made his disarming phone request to come see me, not the opposite. Unlike many of his fellow supermarket owners, Bud dared to get better in seafood. It was done out of pride. That's why he and his brother Pat prominently stated their commitment by putting their family name on the line. After my dismaying experience with other supermarkets, I had begun to wonder if other owners like Bud Roche existed. Without him our venture would have been much more difficult. Bud's strong bias toward excellence underscored the success of this new partnership and made it happen. Bud was a hero to me.

Sudbury Farms' seafood department was so successful that Bud established similar programs in his other four stores the following year. To my knowledge, Roche Bros. became the first supermarket in Massachusetts to feature an outside vendor as their in-store fish brand.

CHAPTER 66

A SCHOOL OF FISH

Chef Scotty Gray cooking for Saunders family, owners of Park
Plaza Hotel, Boston, at a mini-seminar in the W. Howell plant

Bud Roche had given us their fish business in all five stores. Even better the
fish department would carry the Foley name. I could sense a turnaround
at Foley's-New Bedford. Further, our solicitations of prospective
supermarkets outside Massachusetts were starting to bear fruit.

All seemed well. But then, Steve Connolly started his own fish
company. Rumor had it that Chuck Muer, successful owner of over fifteen
restaurant units in Michigan and Florida and a long-time Foley Fish
customer, was financially backing Steve. Worse, Chuck moved his entire
fish business from Foley's to Steve, a major loss. Steve would be coming
after more Foley accounts using the Muer account victory as validation.

The Muer account loss energized my plans to take Foley's at both locations to another level. It was time for a reappraisal of our strengths and weaknesses. There would be no changes, of course, in the core principle of quality. Nor were any changes made with production. No other fish company had the buying and production capabilities of Foley's. But our sales were lagging. This was the next big challenge.

The Foley sales team, Nick Martin, Tom Colbert, Mike Doheny, Tom Kenney and Mike Maloney had been well-schooled in the characteristics of "top of the catch" fish. They knew the importance of temperature control and sanitation to fish quality. Our customers, mostly, did not. Poor quality fish, its age and odors masked by brining, and soaked sea scallops, with up to 25% water-weight, were always available and substantially less costly than the "top of the catch." We believed that our customers would be more loyal if they understood what differentiated quality fish, i.e., freshness, flavor, shelf-life, no fishy odors, etc., from cheaper fish. In order to sell we needed to educate. The lessons we'd learned from National Marine Fisheries Services needed to be shared with our customers.

We established the Foley School of Fish, a two-and-a-half-day fish seminar at Foley's in Boston. It was the first of its kind in the fish industry. The initial curriculum, presented by industry members, NMFS scientists such as Bob Learson, and Foley Fish staff included: an introduction to the concept of the "spoilage clock," a visit to the Boston fish pier to see the varying grades of fish being unloaded, species information and taste tests, a visit to the New Bedford auction, a visit aboard a fishing boat, and time spent on the production floor of both plants to learn about everything from candling, to cutting, to bacteria control, to shellfish storage and more.

Foley Fish had never employed an on-site chef. But I soon realized that we needed one to share his cooking knowledge with us. At that time, too much fish was overcooked, harming flavor and texture. I wanted a professional who could explain proper technique and, because he would be a chef training chefs and egos were involved, who was also a gentleman possessing friendliness and approachability to match his culinary skills. Chef Stuart Grey ("call me Scotty") was the perfect candidate. From his youth, Scotty had always aspired to become a chef. After professional cooking school in Scotland, he apprenticed in Germany. All non-Germans were ordered out of the country in 1938, and Scotty boarded a cargo ship to South Africa where he became a British Army cook during WWII. After the war, he emigrated and spent twenty years as executive chef of the renowned Coonamessett Inn in Falmouth, Massachusetts. In the early 80s, Foley Fish brought him out of retirement and hired him as our first chef.

Seminar attendees touring the New Bedford plant cooler

Chef Scotty belonged to the old school of cooking, humbly believing that the essence of his profession was finding the best ingredients, and properly cooking without any sauces. He always said, "Good fish doesn't need sauces, laddie." His goal was to cook fish to medium-rare doneness. "You'll witness the flavor depart if you overcook fish; too much fire unmakes fish." He taught Foley's staff as well as our seminar guests how to properly sauté, bake, and broil fish.

All seminar attendees received "The Foley Green Book," a three-ring binder filled with information on all the topics presented. Over the forty years that Foley's has been presenting seminars, the Green Book has grown and been updated to include topics such as seafood safety, fisheries management, menu planning, wait staff training and more. After the seminar, Foley customers use these materials for in-house training.

The first seminar group came from our biggest Midwest account, the Real Seafood Co. in Ann Arbor, Michigan. I knew that Steve Connolly had set his sights on taking the Real Seafood account from us. So, the seminar had to be effective; we had to prove its merits.

On February 10, 1981, a few weeks after the seminar, we received a letter from one of the three owners. He wrote, "I don't know what you did, but my people can't stop talking about their trip to Foley Fish. They were thoroughly impressed with what they described as the best seminar they had ever attended. Roy, our kitchen manager at Real Seafood-Downtown had, within one week, implemented fish classes for all his personnel."

This letter was followed by messages from hundreds of other attendees thanking us. The Foley School of Fish was later accredited by the American Culinary Federation Education Institute. Even after retirement, FF, when out to dine with Rita, would tell anyone who would listen about the Foley Seminars. Many of the listeners — Francois Prevost, General Manager of the Copley Plaza; Jacques Gasnier, General Manager of the Park Plaza; Joe Rebas, Executive Chef of the Parker House; Henri Boubee, General Manager of the Ritz Carlton-Boston; and Rob and Madeleine Ahlquist of the Sole Proprietor Group sent their entire staffs to the seminars as a result.

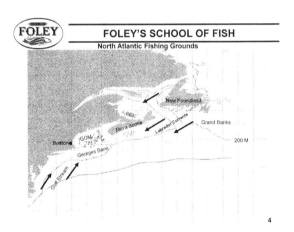

Page from Foley Green Book with diagram explaining
Georges Bank nutrient-rich tidal upwellings

Because many restaurants couldn't afford to send all their people to Boston, we eventually took the seminars to their work place, instituting mini-seminars at the restaurants. We had benefitted from the instruction provided by the fish scientists at NMFS, and it was our turn to pass on this knowledge to our customers. The seminars marked a major turning point for Foley Fish, and also for the fish industry. Foley's was the first fish company to provide such formal training.

I phoned owners of our major accounts. "We need to do a better job for you. We are offering at-the-restaurant classes put on by your Foley account manager to help you identify and correct any handling procedures that are reducing your shelf-life or causing you to serve less-fresh fish. This information-sharing session is designed to help you reduce shrink and preserve flavor. And, you will gain an edge over the competition because you will be serving better-tasting seafood."

We earned their trust. We began being invited to their menu planning meetings, a rare honor for a supplier. In time, mini-seminar subjects were extended to wait-staff training, menu writing, and seasonal fish promotions. We had gone beyond selling fish. The new training and education programs had redefined our entire seafood program. We were not teachers, but sharers — an important distinction because many restaurant workers hated school.

Needless to say, after our seminars were so favorably received by our Foley's-Boston customers, we hastened to develop a comparable one for our New Bedford retail customers.

Our seminar guests brought some unforeseen benefits to Foley Fish. The attendees spent time on the production floors of both plants. Our production workers enjoyed the spotlight as they explained processes, answered questions, and demonstrated cutting techniques. This attention and respect from Foley customers was appreciated, and it added to the feeling of being part of a team.

Our sales people, buyers, and production managers each led a part of the seminar. In the beginning those not accustomed to interacting with customers were nervous, but they quickly grew into their roles. They were proud to speak on behalf of the quality product they produced. While Foley employees were tired at the end of a seminar, there was an afterglow from the attention and complements of the attendees.

We often heard from our seminar guests that North Atlantic fish seemed to have the best flavor. Chef Scotty would tell them that "you are what you eat" is true for fish too. Fish, like wine, owes its flavor, beyond freshness, to its "terroir." The best fish "terroir" is the Georges Bank. The Georges Bank—just off Massachusetts and protected by the 200-mile fishing limit— produced the most nutrient-rich fish of any ocean because of the intersection of the Labrador currents and the Gulfstream. This nautical melding created tidal upwellings that produced an enormous supply of photo-planktons, on which juvenile fish fed. Georges Bank was a unique vineyard. A majority of Foley Fish came from there. Thanks to our visitors' observations, we realized that Foley Fish could be differentiated, not only based on freshness and shelf life but, equally, if not more importantly, on flavor. We began a new marketing approached centered on comparative taste tests. Our Chef Scotty-trained Foley salesmen would cook our fish and offer it for comparison with what chefs at restaurants were presently using. We developed a list of Signature Items, seafood selections harvested from the Georges Bank and shellfish from places with great tidal flows and rich nutrients. The flavor differences were discernible. The "Taste the Difference Campaign at Foley Fish" began. It would propel us forward in 1980s and 1990s.

CHAPTER 67

THE 50/50 PROGRAM

FF was not as pleased as Bud Roche and MFF about the use of the Foley name in the fish case. FF had spent a lifetime building the procedures that ensured the consistency and superiority of Foley fish. To put the product into the hands of a seafood/deli clerk, even if the clerk had been Foley-trained, worried him. He also worried about other cheaper, inferior fish being sold under the Foley name. Although some Foley's-Boston restaurant customers' menus touted that their fish came from Foleys, had they asked FF's permission before the menus were printed, he would have declined the endorsement.

FF trusted Bud Roche to protect the Foley name, after all Bud's name was on the store. After Foley's-New Bedford seminar attendees had toured the Roche stores they wanted a branded program. I knew that while it was a great way to get our name out there, we needed to take steps to protect the value of the brand.

LF had been working as an Assistant General Counsel for a Rhode Island Corporation. On my 41st birthday, she gave birth to our third child. With a new baby and two middle-schoolers to care for, LF resigned her corporate position. The good news for me was that she was now more available to Foley Fish. Her first big project was development of the 50/50 Program. This branded program defined a 50/50 partnership between the retailer and Foley Fish. Foleys would provide premium quality seafood, education and training for seafood employees, Foley-branded marketing materials at nominal cost for use in ads and in-store, including: species brochures, recipe cards, leak-proof fish bags with home storage instructions, Foley aprons and hats and ad slicks. Foley's also agreed to provide additional training and trouble-shooting as well as complimentary fish for seafood demos. Very important to the retailer was that they would have exclusive use of the brand within a mutually-agreed geographic area.

The retailers committed to having a seafood "czar" to oversee the program and ensure that seafood employees were following sanitation and temperature protocols. They also agreed that any species sold which Foley offered would come from Foleys. Substitution of lesser quality fish was not permitted. If the retailer offered species which Foleys couldn't provide, for example, fresh water species, those species must meet Foley quality standards.

The program was very ambitious. The goal was to educate not only the seafood personnel but, most importantly, seafood consumers. We wanted them to experience eating truly fresh fish, to learn how to properly cook great fish without destroying its flavor and texture. We wanted our customer's customers to learn about less expensive and underutilized species. We wanted to give them value for their seafood dollars

The 50/50 Program requirements eased FF's concern over use of the Foley name. As we expected, the Program was adopted by smaller, privately owned retailers. The supermarket giants would continue to sell on price.

CHAPTER 68

NEW TEAM, OLD TEAM

Nick Martin and Johnny Bettencourt with Boston Fish pier
employee waiting for loading of Foley refrigerated truck

Of generational ownership, it has been said: "The first generation builds
it, the second generation enjoys it, and the third generation destroys it."
As I assumed ownership of both companies in 1986, my goal was to make
Foley Fish III better than Foley Fish II, just as Foley Fish II had advanced
over Foley Fish I. The success of the Foley School of Fish was a major
step toward my goal. The team Russ had molded in New Bedford was
maturing nicely. Foley's-Boston was still the engine of the train, however,
and I needed not to mess too much with success. As I took over ownership
of Foley's-Boston, I felt fortunate. While I didn't financially inherit the
business, I did inherit FF's varsity team, namely, John Bettencourt, buyer,

Nick Martin, sales, Mike O'Connor, production, and Tom Colbert, anchor desk and seminar leader.

John Bettencourt always tells our seminar guests, "My family comes from the Azores, from one of nine islands in the middle of the Atlantic Ocean. We were very poor; we never owned a pair of shoes growing up. You don't go to college. You go to work in the fish plants. I came to the U.S. in 1970. Frank Foley met me at my house. He talked to my wife who spoke more English than I did. I only knew how to say "ef-you," which I kept from Frank. Frank hired me and a language tutor."

John instinctively knew good fish, but he was tested by the sellers on Boston's docks who would try to slip in fair fish with good fish. They would quickly learn John's no meant no. He would not be intimidated: "I was a pain in their ass because I was a cherry-picker. I bought the fish I grew up with in the Azores: hours old." If they didn't like me — so what — I let them know how I felt with the few swear words I knew in English." John was another standout in the grand history of Foley buyers.

Mike O'Connor came to Foley's as a summer intern from a program that FF had established at his alma mater, B.C. High School. He knew the O'Connor family well as his best friend was Jerry O'Connor, Mike's father, who with his gracious wife Anne had raised nine fine children. Without an interview or resume, Mike joined Foley's on June 4, 1974 after graduating from Holy Cross. He was instantly beloved by his fellow workers. From his rugby days, Mike had learned how to move the scrum forward and grind it out. I needed Mike's leadership as I was viewed as anti-union on matters like overtime. Mike became a major reason why people liked to work at Foley's.

Tom Colbert addressing seminar attendees on
production floor of W. Howell plant

Mike O'Connor hefts a striped bass for seminar
attendees at W. Howell plant

After graduating from University of New Hampshire, Nick Martin
(FF's nephew/MFF's cousin) joined Foley's just seven days after Mike
O'Connor. They knew each other from an overlapping two-year stint
as summer interns at Foley's. Like Mike, Nick's motor was always in
overdrive. He was a grinder, and like FF had an active worry-meter. As
demanding of himself as others, Nick was temperamentally the opposite
of Mike. He managed by yelling. Like FF, he expected perfection. While
often causing consternation to his co-workers, he had an owner's instinct.
I relied on him to be my eyes and ears in Boston when I was on the road

or in New Bedford. Nick's strong belief in quality made him an excellent salesman for Foley Fish.

Tom Colbert started work at Foley's on March 31st, 1952, 22 years before Nick and Mike began. He was the only employee who had also worked for both MF and FF. He respected FF, but loved MF. He was somewhere on the adopted-son-to-favorite-grandson spectrum. Tom replaced Steve Connolly as anchor desk man. He was also responsible for account development in Connecticut, Upstate New York, and Pennsylvania. Eventually, his biggest role became heading up the seminar. Ever the genial man, he was beloved by all.

In a meeting with these four men, I emphasized that one of our biggest challenges was to stop looking to the boss to make all the decisions as they had under FF. I said, I "If we individually are half as good as our predecessors, we would be way better than any of our competitors." From the get-go, I stressed the importance of their decision-making. Sometimes you will fail, but fail better, learn from your mistakes. Take ownership of your outcomes. I am not a "second-guesser," but don't make me a "third-guesser" (which was my way of saying that I was democratic, up to a point). The team all needed experience, including me, to improve. My plan was to see how sound their judgements were, then, I could decide how much latitude to give them. I was fortunate that each member of this team believed that Foley Fish was a unique company.

Meanwhile, back in our New Bedford plant, sales were increasing and our prospect list was expanding. I had lucked out with Russ Rohrbacher's mentoring, effusive presence, and experience. He had done an excellent job of staffing and training the buying and production team. Staffing the sales, management and accounting offices were my job. I had to build a team from scratch. Those that I hired as a starting team came from disparate backgrounds and had no experience in the fish business. No one knew more than the other about how to make a success of this venture. There was a great sense of camaraderie. The Boston plant was 60 miles away so there was no one second guessing our decisions. Much to my surprise, FF left it totally to me to sink or swim.

Despite my banking background, my focus had to be on operations and sales. I hired an accounting professional, Bill Lancelotta, to manage New Bedford's finances. He oversaw everything from the Industrial Revenue

Bond, to taxes, to payroll and interfaced with Ed Rogers, our outside accountant. He also set up all the procedures for payables, receivables, kept tabs on costs, inventory, and more.

Certain early hires left indelible imprints. A young woman, Mary Basler, was only with us a few years but LF still recalls what Mary brought to the team. Incredibly, without any seafood experience, she became our go-to person at the anchor desk. When taking customers' orders over the phone, she would wax poetic about the fish she had just seen the buyer bring into the plant. LF, working in the sales office with Mary, was inspired by her enthusiasm and her knack for getting customers to try something new or to increase their orders. LF was always looking for that kind of enthusiasm when interviewing future sales hires.

John Williams, hired by Russ as a floor worker, was not part of the original management team but his outstanding performance in all areas of production led me to promote him to Production Manager. John is intelligent, soft-spoken, organized, diligent, occasionally stubborn and always loyal. He listened stoically as I yelled at him about overtime (shades of FF). LF eventually became a sort of intermediary between John and me, pleading our respective cases. The fourth generation was fortunate to have John on the varsity team when they took over.

I was the only experienced salesman in New Bedford. Finding new accounts to fill our production schedule was up to me. FF had taught me about fish. Bud Roche had taught me what could be achieved in a quality-minded supermarket. Now I needed to put it all together and SELL FOLEY FISH! I hit the road.

271

CHAPTER 69

CHECKERS TO CHESS

LF was raised as the older "son" by Norma and Richard Johnson, head of research for Stone Container. She worked beside Dick repairing leaky faucets, mowing lawns, and wallpapering walls, all the while absorbing Dick's mantra. "A job worth doing is a job worth doing well." Linda's acute legal mind wrapped itself around every gritty detail, absorbing, delineating, and then extrapolating and synthesizing into the big picture.

LF thrived on problem solving. She was continually finding things that needed to be corrected or upgraded or new procedures to be implemented in all areas of the plant. LF would bring these problems (opportunities in her mind) to me to discuss and to seek approval for her proposed changes. I was busy being the sales leader, building a book of business and did not want to hear about problems. Finally, I told her, "Your name is Foley, if you don't like something just change it."

One of the changes LF made was a total redesign, reallocation, and remodeling of all the office space in New Bedford. (It would have been much less costly to listen to a few problems!) The new layout included a kitchen and a space for seminars. It also included, for the first time, an office on the production floor where the increasing paperwork of buying and production could be handled. LF has a probing, unquiet intelligence. She regularly challenged me: "How do you know you're right? You don't have all the facts. You won't improve our decision-making without a better information system." At the outset, she had voiced her major concern to me, which was that she was too much of a pleaser to be a manager. Responding to this self-observation, my good friend Mickey DeFanti,

Managing Partner at Hinckley, Allen, said, "Linda should get a second opinion on that."

Foley Fish had to move on from a labor intensive, redundant, handwritten data recording system. The only software programs that then existed for seafood-processing companies were essentially warehouse applications: boxes of fish in, boxes of fish out. None addressed yields. Foley's lacked an in-house computer geek, we — I mean LF — started from scratch. Fortunately, she had already mastered the warp and woof of Foley operations in New Bedford during her first two years at the company. She contacted Cranberry Computers, owned and operated by Mark Benny, who had devised a unique software program for the cranberry industry. While this consultation was helpful, our business was more complex than cranberry production because of the multiplicity of seafood products. LF taught Mark the seafood business and Mark, developed the necessary software. With full confidence in their analytical prowess, I absented myself from the software creation. A smart move, as it turned out, because it was a daunting task, one well beyond my competence. But they were successful, and Foley Fish moved out of the dark ages, information-wise.

The cornerstone of Foley's software program was the digital measurement of yields. Unlike the cranberry industry which had only one yield to measure, our system was challenged by the fact that each of our whole fish products could be multiplied into as many as ten or more products, depending on the differing cuts (e.g., skin-on, skinless, scrod, etc.). Designing a comprehensive, detailed software program to track the varying costs of raw materials was a challenge, but well worth the effort. We had previously developed cutting benchmarks, but the manual recording process was cumbersome. Let me explain: when ten Foley cutters are cutting the same whole fish, there will always be some variance in cutters' yields. If the actual yields are below the assumed or projected yields, then Foley's actual costs would be higher than assumed costs. Consequently, we would be selling fish at a loss. Under our old system, these losses could continue undetected. The new Foley system created a diagnostic tool that isolated which cutters were under-performing, allowing corrections to be made in minutes, not days.

The new system, potentially, made us smart. The computer became our mentor. It was like having a chess grandmaster on our side. Foley Fish buyers could now instantaneously access sales orders (taken one day ahead of shipment), match them against current inventory to determine their buying needs. Each Foley salesperson had access to numerous reports reflecting and analyzing their account activity. Hand-written orders were computerized, thereby freeing salesmen to do more planning. Production now relied on the computer to prioritize the fish-cutting process.

Accounting no longer was inundated with handwritten reports. Accounts receivable, accounts payable, and data input for financial reports were streamlined. The accounting personnel were overjoyed that their "forgotten" department was upgraded to equal standing with the other departments at Foley Fish.

With foresight, LF first introduced the new software program to the New Bedford plant. Later, after she and Mark Benny worked out the inevitable kinks, they implemented the new system at Foley's-Boston. Initially, unsurprisingly, there was resistance from the entrenched Boston management team. They remembered and deified what had worked for them for eighty years. Linda reminded them that the historical growth of Foley Fish was predicated on the belief that our product was never good enough. LF sent a clear signal that Foley's third-generation leaders were moving ahead, just as their predecessors, MF and FF, had done in their times.

FF's reaction to the proposed changes was not exactly supportive. Grudgingly, he offered this: "It's okay as long as it doesn't interfere with us turning out quality fish." LF reassured her father-in-law, "I will not tamper with your manual system. You can keep your rolodex, your well-thumbed, personal account files and other financial reports." This approach was successful, and later on I noticed FF studying the computer reports.

The computer system gave Foley Fish another competitive advantage. I made LF a fifty percent shareholder of Foley Co. She was too capable to lose in a divorce, and deserved becoming the first non-Foley owner. Looking back now, it seems patently obvious that Linda reinforced a critical factor in Foley Fish's longevity: we must never forget that we are constantly swimming upstream.

CHAPTER 70

FISHERY MANAGEMENT

By the early 1990s, the fishing industry's attitude on fish supply and scarcity had moved from overconfidence to concern, and eventually to dire warnings. Our earlier presumption of fish abundance proved to be as false as it was naïve. National Marine Fisheries (NMFS) for the North Atlantic region imposed severe fishing cutbacks as trawl surveys indicated a sudden decline in fish stocks, especially in our revered cod population.

In May, 1994 NMFS mandated a "days-at-sea" (DAS) amendment which ordered each commercial fishing vessel to reduce its DAS by ten percent per year over the next five years, effectively limiting DAS to half of the 176 days previously allowed. Additionally, large acreage of the prized Georges Bank was closed to any fishing. Dissatisfied with early results, in 1996 NMFS further reduced DAS by another 50 percent for the next two years, and also closing a large portion of the Gulf of Maine to commercial fishing. In 1998, the Gulf would be completely closed. A "species" quota system was introduced and given the name total allowable catch (TAC) by species.

Unsurprisingly, tensions between invested parties – fishermen, NMFS, marine scientists, and environmental groups — created unproductive negativity, preventing those involved from doing their best work. NMFS's blaming of overfishing as the root cause of the problem made fishermen the scapegoats. It didn't help that NMFS used the term "overfished" when a stock was low, rather than "low stock." Accusations swirled; environmentalists were accused of selfishly wanting to turn the ocean into an aquarium. Scientists were branded as stick-in-the-mud intellectuals who talked over everyone's heads, and NMFS was under fire for their "draconian edicts." Remedies were viewed, in part, as vengeful, and disproportionate blame was placed on the fishermen, with some justification, but imagine if your business was forced to cut back to only working 60 days a year. Not to be ignored was the U.S. government that had "bribed" fishermen to buy modern "vacuum cleaners" with essentially "no interest" loans, not required to be repaid for many years. Unfortunately, the warring factions had ignored Buddha's famous teaching on anger: "Holding onto anger is like drinking poison expecting to kill the other person."

Fishery management was fraught with disagreement between the fishermen, the regulators, the scientists, and the environmental lobby. We needed our fishermen to provide ongoing fish intelligence, just as we needed the scientists to provide their intellectual quotient to extrapolate solutions. Both are vital to the process. Understandably, fishermen complained that NMFS changed the rules too often without the outcome of the previous regulations being thoroughly evaluated. In early 2000, stock improvements were heralded, the haddock stock had exploded, hake was improving, and Acadian redfish was strong. But there were still too many mistakes. One year there was believed to be a lot of yellowtail flounder, the next year they reversed that verdict. Similarly, with pollock – one year bad, the next year good. A whipsaw of findings showed that the proverbial population assessment nail was still sticking up, and needed to be hammered down. The prognostications of fish populations were still flawed. There was no industry buy-in.

Historically reliable, trawl surveys had become outdated. You can't measure what you're not counting. If models were dependent on landings, they needed to account for the fact that landings were suppressed by new management measures, not necessarily a lack of fish. After the government boat buyback program in 1995, the fishing fleet was decimated. Trawl surveys with observers from NMFS and Woods Hole Oceanographic were incomplete, as now only 80 boats (compared to the heretofore 2,000) could not survey a statistically significant area(s). The ecosystem in the North Atlantic exceeds what could be canvassed by these few boats with observers available only four times a year.

By 2010, NMFS dropped trip limits and DAS as fishing restrictions. Trip limits were useless. For example, fishermen were restricted to catching, say, 300 pounds of cod in a five-day trip. If the fishermen caught that limit on the first day, all cod caught in the remaining four days were required to be thrown overboard. Landings were reduced, but fish mortality increased. DAS restrictions reduced mortality through less fishing, but the cost to the fishermen of only being able to fish the equivalent of one day a week was steep.

The concept of "catch shares" (by species) was introduced by the George W. Bush administration, which allowed commercial fishing at any time (not anywhere, as rolling and permanent closures remained to protect spawning fish and sensitive habitat). The underlying assumption, and hope, was that by privatizing a segment of the catch exclusively for commercial fishermen, their ownership would incentivize them to do a better job to combat overfishing.

At Foley Fish, we knew our success was dependent on to the state of the fishery. We also knew that we needed to get better to be informed about the health of the various stocks we were selling. Bill Gerencer, who served as our Portland Fish Exchange buyer, was deputized as the fishery management person for Foley Fish. Bill sat on the New England Fishery Management Council ground fish advisory panel for 20 years. He also sat on the ICATT Highly Migratory Species Panel – the governing body that dictates regulations regarding species like swordfish, tuna and shark. Bill's deciphering of the information helped Foley Fish to steer customers toward the most abundant species and to counter media reports of reckless fishing and habitat destruction. His shared knowledge lent further credibility for the Foley Fish account management team. A section on fishery management was added to the Foley School of Fish so customers could see just how the oceans were being managed and the results of that management.

At Foley's we were keenly aware that the severe fish shortages resulting from the management efforts had brought about major increases in the price of fish. Some supermarket customers could no longer afford their favorite New England species. This was a major challenge for Foley's-New Bedford and our sales volume was adversely affected. We worked with our supermarket customers to encourage substitutes for cod such as pollack, hake, and ocean catfish. Our New Bedford sales team did numerous in-store demos, cooking less popular species for customers to sample. Some fish stocks have recovered nicely but because so many fishermen had to give up their boats, fish is still in short supply and prices have remained at higher levels. This remains a challenge for the fourth generation.

CHAPTER 71

GROWING THE BUSINESS

Foley Fish display at Boston Seafood Show

Thanks mainly to the Roche Bros. account, we had become a legitimate player in the supermarket field. Other major supermarket accounts followed: Schnucks (St. Louis, MO), Buehlers (Wooster, OH), La Bonnes (Watertown, CT), Highland Park Markets (Manchester, CT), D&W Food Stores (Grand Rapids, MI), Sunset Foods (Northbrook, IL), Insalaco (Western PA), and Market Place (Bermuda).

In the mid-eighties we exhibited at the Boston Seafood Show for the first time in decades. We were targeting supermarket buyers. LF and Betsy Szell of Articulations, who had designed our 50/50 Program promotional materials, designed our booth. It was like nothing anyone had seen before. In one section of the booth we had a supermarket display case demonstrating the optimal display process we had introduced at Roche

Bros. with the fish displayed in their gold tins nestled in our super-chilled ice. At the other end of the display we had spotlighted, free-standing seven-foot-tall fish forms with display boards explaining how we could manage to produce such a superior product. Our slogan, across the top of the booth — "An Open and Shut Case, Foley's: Fish that Stand above the Rest!"

The investment in the display proved worth it. Visitors to the booth became Foley's-New Bedford customers. We enjoyed long relationships with Clemons Markets, Laneco Markets, and the McGinnis Sisters all of PA, Tops Markets of upstate NY, Butsons Markets of NH and VT, and Ukrops Markets of VA, among others.

The seafood show also brought us a different kind of business. A California broker introduced us to two wholesalers in the San Francisco/ Oakland area, Chris Svedise of Vince's Shellfish and Steve Pucci of Pucci Seafood. We also met Johnny Nalbandian of J&J Seafood in the LA area. Around the same time, we were introduced to Nick Vitalich of Chesapeake Fish in San Diego and Bill Merry of W.R. Merry Co. in LA.

Orders from these wholesalers were on a scale that was entirely new to us. We were shipping thousands of pounds to them rather than hundreds, the fish and shellfish packed in gigantic LD3 containers, a first for us. Much of what we shipped was New England shellfish, especially mussels. Our dry-pack, all-natural Georges Bank scallops and Georges Bank cod fillets were also in demand. These were not weekly orders but generally went out several times a month to each wholesaler. We enjoyed this business for several years. It was great while it lasted!

Our New Bedford sales office was not nearly as experienced as Boston's. Bill Doyle, Fred Weckman, Chris Knowles and Rance Gillespie were there for most of our tenure. This team led seminars, managed accounts, and did in-store education and cooking demos. Finding new customers remained my role and I relished it.

I had convinced myself that I was the go-to guy at Foley's, the heroic leader for sales development. But my success as a sales leader was threatening my primary role as chief executive. I saw that I needed to step back and become the mentor, trainer, and teacher of our sales teams so that they could cohere and grow. My habits had to change. This recognition was a turning point for me and Foley Fish.

I was particularly eager to work with our Boston sales team, as our wholesale accounts were still vulnerable to Steve Connolly's solicitations. I told them that I was doing a lousy job servicing and training them. Going forward I needed to become their mentor and partner. FF had created the one-leader culture by telling his sales force what to sell and not sell. In my own way, I had been following in FF's footsteps.

I addressed our sales team: "A new, proactive, collaborative approach will replace the passive practices of the past. It is time for you to get your voices heard. The new sales model will take time to implement. The change is equivalent not to a mere outpatient operation, but rather to an organ transplant."

Turning to sales trip preparation, I explained that the sales team would use the new software system to focus on "share of menu" analysis. For instance, sales of appetizer fish items such as sea scallops, smoked salmon, oysters, calamari, mussels, and clams will be delineated to usage patterns. Our ultimate goal, I said, will be to be invited to join our customers' menu planning sessions.

Trip planning, I continued, will include meetings with me to review strategies and tactics such as taste tests, field seminars, and new product suggestions. Upon returning, post-mortems will be recorded on written sales reports, the most important section of which will be planned follow-up actions. Copies of each salesman's reports will be distributed to all other salesmen.

I instituted written annual performance reviews to be used for salary and bonus decisions. FF had always paid his salesmen well, but had never reviewed their performance with them. Our new software program helped make the review system more credible. Reports generated by the computer system gave me and the salesmen objective measurements of what they had or had not achieved. In the reports, actual sales were compared to sales objectives measured in poundage and individual product sales. Prospect development was measured by profit contribution, as well as lost versus new accounts. For the first time, the sales account manager became responsible for accounts being paid up according to terms. This approach gave Foley salesmen full responsibility, from goal setting to collections, for each assigned account.

My final judgements on each salesperson's performance review were slanted somewhat to the subjective. Qualitative factors of effort, attitude, and cooperation were all noted. Effort was measured by number of seminars, trip preparation, follow-up work, and taste tests conducted. Attitude meant no alibiing or scapegoating, but resilience. I wanted to see them fail well, learning from their mistakes and putting newfound wisdom to work.

Lastly, I studied their savviness, an attribute I define as knowing what is winnable and what is not worth winning. On this subject — a true story — we were approached by a hotel consultant whose assignment was to locate the best seafood purveyor for his client. He chose us. I explained our pay policy on any new accounts: seven days payment. He said no problem. One week before the first order he called to say there was a slight change. His customer insisted on 30-day terms. His "slight" change was a major change for me. I said no. Later I learned I had turned down a future President of the United States! It was not worth winning.

The Boston sales team embraced the challenges somewhat warily, but was energized by their enlarged role in the success of Foley Fish. Nick Martin, Tom Kenney, Mike Doheny, Mike Moloney Jr., and Tom Colbert exceeded my expectations to the dismay, I'm sure, of our competitors.

Because the computer system had been installed first in New Bedford, the New Bedford sales team was already using various reports for trip planning, etc. I was using other system reports to monitor their progress. There were no bad habits to "unlearn" in New Bedford, but I needed to teach them what I expected. I did written reviews of all sales people and managers in New Bedford as in Boston. Needless to say, writing a performance review to share with LF was daunting!

LF and I had instituted changes based, in part, on our professional experience prior to coming to Foley Fish. I, especially, felt that we needed to go one step further to improve our sales approach. I engaged the Forum Corporation of Boston, a consulting company, to help us professionalize our sales efforts. We learned a lot.

The Forum instructor taught us that a sense of gain, i.e., a benefit and avoidance of loss were basic sales triggers. That early on in a sales call you need to articulate to the customer what is in it for him. How does he win by buying fish from Foley's? The sales teams from each plant came up with a number of benefits: positive word of mouth leading to increased business; repeat business; more compliments; no fishy odors in the restaurant or the supermarket; reduced shrink translating to higher profits; no returns. We all realized that we had been selling using features rather than benefits. We talked about "freshest," "best," "tastiest," but did not always translate that into a benefit for the customer.

The Forum instructor also emphasized the need to get better at handling objections. The objections we encountered usually were price, added transportation cost (as opposed to local wholesalers who dropped fish off "for free"), and needing to order a day ahead. A clear understanding of benefits would manage the first two objections. Adapting to day-ahead ordering was not difficult, just a change of habit. Furthermore, Foley's had systems in place to allow ordering and changes to orders late into the night before shipping.

Each Foley salesperson has his or her style. Each of us refined our approach to focus on benefits and to improve out handling of objectives. The combination of our extensive customer education programs combined with some Forum refinements brought major sales growth to both plants.

In 1986, when I took over Boston, their sales team included Nick Martin, Tom Colbert, Mike Doheny and Tom Kenney. In 1989 we added Mike Moloney. Mike had been head of sales at Turner Fisheries, a major Foley competitor, until Turner folded. Ironically, Mike was the nephew of Bill Moloney and son of Bill's brother Michael, both with histories at Foley Fish.

FF had opened the Chicago market, and Foley accounts there included Don Roth's Blackhawk and the Cape Cod Room at the Drake Hotel, both Chicago institutions. Nick Martin succeeded FF in Chicago and brought in the Morton's Steakhouse chain, Catch-35, units in the Lettuce Entertain You group, and many chef-owned high-end restaurants.

Nick opened up the Atlanta market for Foley's. He brought Foley fish to Chef Panos and the Buckeye Restaurant Group, who enjoyed Atlanta's biggest market share. Chefs who worked under Chef Panos took Foley's with them when they opened their own restaurants. An on-site seminar Nick did for the Renaissance-Atlanta led to Foley fish being used throughout the Renaissance chain. Under the auspices of the general manager, Mr. Commachio, and Executive Chef Reinbolt, the Renaissance opened the Foley Fish House restaurant in their flagship Times Square hotel. New business from the Buckeye Group alone exceeded the sales losses from the Chuck Muer group. Boston was back!

Nick also opened Arizona, bringing to Foley's-Boston accounts such as the Sanctuary Resort and the Eddie V's group. Mike Doheny had a more limited territory, handling the St. Louis, Kansas City, and Milwaukee areas. He managed the St. Louis Club, the Bristol Bar and Grill, The Ritz-St. Louis, Tony's, and the Old Wausau Country Club, in addition to the Milwaukee Club and River Lane. All were valued Foley accounts.

In addition to his territory, Mike Doheny, for a period of years, was the traffic manager for Foley's-Boston, fighting through the transportation thicket to get Foley fish delivered to far- flung locales with flavor and freshness intact. He had the unenviable position of having to deal with any upset account manager who had just been reamed by a customer whose shipment was late.

Renaissance Hotel promotional flyer for opening of the Foley
Fish House restaurant in flagship Times Square location

Tom Kenney managed accounts in Massachusetts, including Boston, as well as Ohio. He also managed the Culinary Institute of America in Hyde Park, NY, a longtime Foley customer. Robb and Madeleine Ahlquist, owners of restaurants, including The Sole Proprietor in Worcester, MA, bought their first Foley fish from FF. Tom managed their account until his retirement, and I am happy to say that The Sole Proprietor is still a Foley customer forty years later. In Boston, Tom managed a number of accounts, including the Sarkis Group and the Boston Harbor Hotel. It was not unusual for him to personally deliver a couple tins of fillets or a bag of shellfish if a chef had an emergency.

Tom Colbert, with his responsibility for the Anchor Desk, had his hands full but he did manage accounts in upstate New York and Connecticut. He was the face of Foley's at the Sherwood Inn, The Brewster Inn, and Lord Chumley's in New York, and famed Griswold Inn in Connecticut. Most of our customers became acquainted with Tom in his role as seminar coordinator.

When Mike Maloney joined Foley's, he was first assigned to manage and develop Michigan. FF had had significant success bringing Foley fish to Michigan diners. In addition to the famed Joe Muer's Seafood restaurant and the large Chuck Muer group of restaurants (the ones "highjacked" by Connelly), FF also brought Foley's to the Real Seafood group in Ann Arbor, the Detroit Athletic Club, the Machus Group, including the famous Sly Fox Restaurant, and Zingerman's Roadhouse. Some of these accounts are now being serviced by Foley's fourth generation owners. Mike Moloney added to these accounts. One of his most celebrated additions was the Golden Mushroom Restaurant operated by Certified Master Chef Milos Cihelka. Chef Milos not only served his customers exquisite meals, he was also instrumental in training younger chefs. These younger chefs became advocates of Foley's and used our fish in their own restaurants. Schoolcraft College's nationally recognized culinary program, another spawning ground for chefs, also came to us through Mike. Schoolcraft culinary faculty are all American Culinary Federation Certified Master Chefs or Certified Executive Chefs, and Foleys remains their seafood supplier to this day.

Mike Moloney also brought to us his Bermuda connections. Mike worked with Butterfield, a large food wholesaler in Bermuda who sold to all the major resort properties. Mike and Foley fish were introduced to Butterfield customers, many of whom then became Foley customers. Orders were taken in Boston and then shipped to Butterfield for distribution. Foley fish was served at the Elbow Beach Hotel, The Hamilton and South Hampton Princesses, the Coral Beach Club, and many others. We had one supermarket account there, Marketplace Supermarket in Hamilton. I remember being in my sport coat and helmet with paper flipchart strapped to the back of my scooter and putt-putting into town to do an onsite retail mini-seminar at Marketplace.

In 2001 as Mike Moloney neared retirement, he introduced Bill Gerencer, our buyer at the Portland Fish Exchange and resident fisheries expert, to the Michigan accounts. Mike was generous in offering Bill insights and suggestions so despite their very different sales styles, the transition went smoothly.

CHAPTER 72

UPSTREAM AGAIN

Despite the cold, many boats fish all winter long

From the mid-nineties on, fish shortages due to overfishing and the resultant stringent fisheries management restrictions began to push fish prices significantly higher. Restaurants could adjust menu prices and/or reduce portion size, but retailers had to sell on price per pound. When whole market cod is sold at auction for $3.00/lb., the fish cost off-the-knife for a skinless, boneless fillet is more than $8.00/lb. This is before processor markup to cover overhead. With markup and freight costs, this fillet gets to the retailer at about $10.00/lb. The retailer generally uses a percentage markup which will bring the fillet price close to $12.00/lb. in his fish case. While $3.00/lb. may seem like a reasonable price to pay a fisherman for risking his life, yield, overhead and markups price the cod out of many people's budgets. Many supermarkets needed to come up with cheaper alternatives, either lower quality fresh fish or "refreshed" frozen foreign fish.

We were fortunate to be able to sustain a considerable amount of retail business. The growth of the Roche Bros. chain certainly helped. We had excess capacity at the Foley's-New Bedford plant. Meanwhile, Boston was at capacity in spite of the higher prices. We realized that adding new supermarket business would be difficult until the fish stocks rebounded, restrictions eased and prices came down. LF and I decided that it made sense to transfer some Boston accounts to New Bedford. We opted to assign Florida restaurant accounts to the New Bedford sales team. I worked with the team to bring them up to speed on handling restaurant accounts. I also expected them to develop new restaurant accounts in areas not covered by Boston.

Fred Weckman, a marine biology major at the University of Rhode Island, and former offshore fisherman, had started with us as a summer intern. He knew his fish and was right at home calling on restaurants on the Newport, R.I. waterfront. Fred developed a solid book of business for us in Newport and Providence, R.I.

I had high expectations for Bill Doyle, who had been with us for almost twenty years. He knew the business inside out, and had handled a number of the major retail accounts that I had secured. In the end, Bill joined the ranks of Bill Moloney and Steve Connelly and became our generation's attempted "spoiler." After Laura and Peter had been onboard for four years, Bill gave notice that he was leaving Foley's to pursue a career outside the seafood industry. We wished him well and had a send-off lunch for him complete with cake. Very soon after we learned that Bill had obtained backing from a Foley customer to start his own fish company. He took some business with him but the Foley's-New Bedford team, under Laura and Peter's leadership, won back the business. They did it in the same way as prior Foley generations. They continued to consistently produce fish of a quality superior to any of their competitors.

Fortunately, Fred Weckman had worked closely with Foley customers, including Highland Park Markets, McGinnis Sisters, and Roche Bros. He also had excellent attention to detail and a sophisticated understanding of the computer system, which was very important when working with multi-store chains. Fred was also successful with in-store demos, getting Foley fish into the mouths of customers. His extensive fish knowledge enabled him to answer all the consumer's questions. Fred's work with the retail customer groups was extremely helpful to Laura and Peter, providing a seamless transition for major customer relationships.

CHAPTER 73

SUCCESSION

Laura Foley Ramsden holding son Charlie as FF, LF,
and MFF admire a salmon a few years before the
transfer of ownership to the 4th generation

The year was 2001. The seafood industry had changed more in the previous 25 years than in the 50 years that FF ran the business. We continued to turn out premium product, but LF and I could see that we did not have the energy to take on the internet, the continuing problems of fish supply and the corporatization of restaurants. If Foley Fish was to continue to be the premier seafood company, it was time for new, younger leadership.

    All three of our children had worked summers at Foley Fish, but only our daughter, Laura, had an interest in the fish business. Our older son

Michael had moved to Los Angeles right after college to pursue a career writing for the entertainment industry. Our younger son Mark was into art and music. Laura had worked in public relations after college and had a natural instinct for marketing. There was one problem, however: She was married to Peter Ramsden, and living in Darien, Connecticut with a toddler and a husband who was managing the New York office of Loomis Sayles, a large investment management firm. She was, however, keeping her hand in by making sales calls on Foley customers and creating marketing materials.

The alternatives to a fourth generation taking over at Foley's were not attractive. We could sell to a huge food supplier like Sysco, but it was unlikely that a company that sold napkins and frozen seafood would be able to adapt to the handling of a highly perishable product. Venture capital was out for similar reasons. A sale to a meat company or a larger seafood company was possible, but it meant that the work of three generations of Foleys to produce a premium quality product, and to educate restaurants and retailers how to preserve that quality would be lost. And perhaps most important, the deeply caring, loyal employees of the two Foley plants could lose their jobs.

While we didn't hold out a lot of hope that Laura would be able to become the fourth generation, her husband's employer's headquarters were in Boston. Perhaps Peter could transfer back to Boston? Linda and I decided there was only one way to find out if Foley Fish would have a fourth generation. Ask.

We called Laura and told her we were doing retirement planning and needed to know whether she had any interest in becoming the fourth-generation head fishmonger. We told her that we would like to be out of the company in approximately five years. She and Peter mulled over the ramifications of such a move, and then invited us to Darien for a meeting. We gathered up financial statements, sales reports, production reports, anything that we could think of that she and Peter, a certified financial analyst, might wish to study.

Each generation has purchased Foley Fish from the prior generation. It was not gifted. Therefore, it was not just Laura becoming a full-time manager that was at stake, but also a large financial commitment on their part. While there might have been a slight family discount, the sale would be based on fair market value.

When we met with Laura and Peter, we were thrilled to find out that Peter was willing to switch careers and become a co-head fishmonger! This was more than we could have hoped. Laura had no financial expertise and would have needed to hire a chief financial officer to fulfill that requirement. Peter, with his financial acumen and analytical abilities, would fill that role as co-owner-manager. We hoped that pride of ownership would make up a little bit for the salary concessions Peter would have to make.

The four of us worked out a timetable with a five-year transition period. If after working in the company for that period, they still desired to take it over, there would be a sale. Financing for the purchase would be obtained, and we would depart. No Monday morning quarterbacking and no long shadows.

According to the plan, the Ramsdens would relocate as soon as feasible and begin work at Foley Fish. Peter would rotate through the production areas of both plants: receiving, candling, packing, shipping etc. He would spend extensive time with the company's buyers to become familiar with all our sources. Fortuitously, Peter was a sport fisherman so he knew how a freshly caught fish looked and smelled. Eventually, he began traveling with me on sales trips to meet major customers. While there were probably many days that Peter felt highly overqualified for the work he was doing, I knew that he had to earn the respect of all the employees, just as his predecessors had done. Laura had worked on the production floor summers, and knew many of the longstanding employees in New Bedford. She was ready and able to work with our New Bedford sales staff to move into the internet age.

LF and I had an ongoing concern as to whether it was fair to offer the business to Laura and Peter at a time of so many challenges. We knew they were capable, but wanted an outside opinion on whether they were a team that could meet the current and future demands of the business. We hired Dr. Robert Smith of Clear Directions to come in and evaluate their likelihood of success.

We saw Laura as a natural leader. Her enthusiasm for the product and her high-energy personality made her the perfect embodiment of the fourth generation. We saw Peter, a Dartmouth College grad with an MBA from the University of Michigan, as the analyst, the planner, a highly knowledgeable executive with the ability to manage the many administrative, personnel, and financial challenges that take time away from doing the business of buying, processing, and selling fish.

Dr. Smith confirmed our opinion. He said they were a formidable team who exceeded the qualifications of many CEOs he'd interviewed. He said he had given them a "hard look," and found that that their abilities, temperaments, energy, and resilience would see them through future challenges. He also assured us that they were aware that success is not inevitable, and that there would be difficult times. He told us that accomplishments drive them, and that they were ready to put their stamp on the company.

Linda and I tried hard to make the new team aware of the less fun part of the business. Dealing with purchasing agents who think cheapest is best, the medical insurance sinkhole, the outrageous cost of workman's compensation insurance, the cost of government regulations, and union contract negotiations, to name a few. They were undeterred.

By the fourth year of the planned five-year transition, it was clear that Laura and Peter were running the company well and there was no reason for us to continue to draw executive salaries when those funds could be used to service the new team's debt. Linda and I retired January 1, 2005. Foley Fish had moved to the fourth generation!

After a period of time celebrating retirement by telling everyone I encountered, "I'm retired! Every day is Saturday!" I got the idea to write this book. It has been over a decade in the writing because I found that retirement can be a busy time. But once I realized my golf handicap would never be single digits, I began to write.

CHAPTER 74

ENTER THE FOURTH GENERATION

Peter Ramsden, co-owner with Laura Foley Ramsden,
harvesting Nantucket scallops on opening day

I have had the honor of typing chapters for Dad's book over the past
few months. Revisiting the history of the company was a gift that made
me reflect on the company today and how much we have gleaned from
the previous generations: from MF, FF, and MFF, and the many loyal
and talented people with whom they worked. Dad and I discussed the
succession plan and the transition era and decided it might make sense for
me to write these chapters from the perspective of the fourth generation.
Plus, Dad had funded my University of Michigan BA degree in English

and thought he would check on his investment to see if I had actually attended classes between football games.

Mom and Dad approached me about their desire to retire from the business in 1999. I was living in Darien, Connecticut with my husband Peter and our two children. Peter was in finance working as a portfolio manager, and commuting to Manhattan daily. I was telecommuting for Foley Fish, helping with marketing and sales. Peter had always wanted to do something entrepreneurial, and in fact, had won a business plan competition when he was getting his MBA at Michigan. In addition, my parents felt that running the two plants would be a lot for me while raising children, and didn't want their grandchildren to suffer from an overcommitted mother. Finally, my parents both felt that rather than selling to a larger broadliner firm, our ownership would be best for our employees, many of whom had worked for my parents for decades. It was very important to them that our team experienced a seamless transition.

We spent several weekends in Darien to discuss the future of Foley Fish. We treated it like a case study. Peter wanted to look under the engine to make sure it was a company with a sustainable future. We looked at the state of the fisheries, diving into the wealth of fishery management information Foley Fish had amassed so we could feel comfortable about the state of the resource. The key question: Would there be enough fish in the ocean to prepare and sell? It was a pivotal question for a company with two shore-side facilities. Who were our competitors? Did we have a truly unique product? Who was on the team and would they stay? Who were the customers? What kind of attrition might we expect? What were the costs of maintaining the plants, and what was the current condition of the facilities? If we took out a loan to purchase the business, could we service it?

In the end, we were satisfied with the answers to our questions. Another important factor was that running the business would give us the opportunity to raise our children in Rhode Island, close to their grandparents. This bonus was quite appealing. I might have believed that I would see more of my husband when he was no longer commuting to New York City, but that was wrong. Small business ownership would be much more demanding of his time. He brought a first-generation hunger to Foley Fish that would drive him to committing many extra hours to ensure that the company excelled.

Originally, the succession plan was for five years. We would move to Rhode Island, and Peter would work in each of the major positions in each plant for two years. The third year would be a sales rotation, and the fourth and fifth years would be in management. We would bring in an independent appraiser to value the business, and then find a bank that would make a loan. I would take a year to have our third child and launch the other two kids in a new community. My absence would allow Peter to establish himself at Foley Fish, thus minimizing the dreaded son-in-law uneasiness.

Peter traded his Brooks Brothers suits for Walmart khakis, flannel shirts, hair nets and rubber boots. He ran the cooler in New Bedford and then the cooler in Boston. He did the same in the freezer. He did a buying rotation in each plant. He drove trucks and pallet jacks. He served as the receiver in each plant, which enabled him to see every product purchased. After each rotation, he would write a detailed summary for my Dad, outlining areas he recommended for improvement. The company benefitted from having a young, hard-working MBA digging into inventory systems and operating practices. He made important recommendations that improved accuracy and efficiency. Most importantly, he established himself with the team in both plants. He was the first to arrive and the last to leave.

Peter also worked in sales in both plants and traveled to meet with customers. Dad introduced him to our "face to face" selling style where we meet in customers' kitchens and taste test products. It was a style that was comfortable to Pete, allowing him to focus on the attributes of the product rather than trying to be a showman.

After my year hiatus, I rejoined the company and continued my work in sales and management. We updated the logo, launched a website, and I wrote a cookbook. We had hundreds of recipes amassed over the years and the question of how to cook fish was still pervasive. We decided to compile a cookbook with recipes that would be consumer-friendly. We tested recipe after recipe, typically 12 per day, and ended up with a book of 240 recipes, one that could be sold by our retail customers or purchased online at Barnes & Noble. Mom is an excellent wordsmith and editor, and my Dad and the office team were excellent tasters. Together, we created a fun little book that represented our company values. We self-published and had to reprint three times.

After Peter had completed all of the rotations and the year of management, four years into the succession plan, history repeated itself and a sales manager defected. As with past generations, he took some business with him. Succession and transition were already well underway and we had a strong team. We were ready to take the helm. Mom and Dad were confident that we could handle this challenge and that we were ready to be owners. They retired a year early. We hired an independent firm to provide the appraisal. We interviewed several banks and only one, Bank RI would give us a loan without a personal guarantee. We will be ever grateful to Don McQueen at Bank RI for having faith in the next generation of Foley Fish owners.

Thanks to the strategic foresight of both Mom and Dad, and the strong relationship that the four of us forged, the managerial transition was seamless. The employees had faith in Peter, and most of them had known me since I started packing fish there at age 14. Many of the employees and I had grown up together. Our plant managers today are gentlemen I packed fish with in my teens. Importantly, Peter and I both had tremendous respect for the team. We knew we had big shoes (MFF's size 15) to fill at the top but also, that the company success depended on the execution by each member of the team. It was also very important to my Dad that he could step away completely. I think he recognized that we wouldn't be seen as the leaders of Foley Fish if people felt they could still "go to Mike." It was a gift to both of us that he was willing to walk away and give us space to lead, but was and is always available for counsel.

CHAPTER 75

THE NEXT GENERATION –
LESSONS FROM THE PAST

Stepping in as owners of a fourth-generation company has had many benefits. We were leading a company with a strong culture dedicated to quality, integrity, and hard work, and we had some incredible customers throughout the country who had worked with the generations that preceded us. We also had strong relationships with vendors who understood our standards. We wanted to take all the good, minimize the bad and continue to grow.

We were lucky that many lessons were learned by the generations before us, and we remained dedicated to those truths. My dad and my grandfather had maxims, adages and wise words adopted and adapted from others, but I heard from them from their lips. These truths guided us. Here are some of them:

You are only as strong as your weakest link...the goal is no weak links. When you enter an order, the specifications must be entered correctly. When you are processing a perishable product such as fish, you cannot have any interruption in the temperature chain. When you are processing an all-natural seafood product, you cannot let bad fish in the door because you cannot "fix" it with chemicals. When you pack fish to travel miles across the country, you cannot put mistakes in the tin. When the fish is traveling those miles, it must be kept cold and arrive in a timely fashion, or all that was done right prior is lost. Operationally, this was an important mantra that we worked to instill in our team, as well as our restaurant and supermarket customers, because the chain of care continues until the fish reaches the ultimate consumer.

Do not go out and sell, sell, sell. Go out and learn. This was important because there are plenty of slimy seafood sales people out there. We wanted to differentiate our sales team by having them think of themselves as account managers. As such, they would go out and learn about a customer's needs and challenges so they could make the best recommendations as far as the appropriate species, specs, etc. We also wanted them to learn where the constraints were — not enough storage time; too hard to order ahead of time; and food cost budgets — so that we could address constraints and win accounts.

You are only as good as your last order. We have ingrained in our culture that every order must be like a first order. In many instances, our customers are miles away from us and they have local distributors knocking on their door daily. Consequently, Foley Fish needs to be stellar every time. Consistency is rare in the seafood world, so achieving it acts as a differentiator and gives our customers a reason to order from us even when they have other choices.

Chains are big business opportunities but they also leave big holes. We have worked with retail and restaurant chains that look to provide consistency across all their locations by partnering with Foley Fish. It is good, steady business, that is, until it is not. When a food and beverage manager, or corporate chef, leaves and the new manager wants a new fish guy, or the chain gets bought by a larger corporation not committed to fresh, all-natural seafood, a large gap is created. It is so important to value all of your customers, large and small, single and multi- unit. All operations are significant to Foley Fish. Our best fit is the customer who cares about putting a great piece of fresh fish in front of their customers.

Build Loyalty to Price, they will leave you for price, build loyalty to goods and services, and you will win customers for a lifetime. My granddad used to rail against supermarkets advertising because he feared they made the customer feel that the reduced price reflected the real value and the everyday price was ripping them off. Foley Fish has never been about being the lowest price fish in the market, largely because we don't add chemicals that allow for soaked fish to be cheaper. Our costs are higher because we pay more to get the best fish and don't add chemicals to "enrich" it with water weight. We try to engage and educate customers with conversations about the fish itself — the characteristics of the species — how briny is the oyster, how sweet the all-natural scallop. We always want to represent value for our customers, but the slope is slippery in seafood when price becomes the number one objective. There is a cheaper product in each category, but with cheapness comes quality compromises. Many large-scale buyers aren't willing to acknowledge it, but anyone who has had a poor seafood experience recognizes that it is true. Sadly, the large buyers often stand in the way of US consumers getting a true all-natural seafood experience as evidenced by the refreshed, imported programs in many seafood cases across America.

CHAPTER 76

CHALLENGES AND OPPORTUNITIES FOR THE FOURTH GENERATION

Laura and Peter Ramsden, 4th generation
owners of Foley Fish Companies

Peter and I didn't enter Foley Fish with a whole list of things we would to do differently now that we were owners. We really felt that it was a well-run company, and that we should do our best not to ruin what the generations before us had built. We were acutely aware that less than four percent of family businesses last to the fourth generation so the former generations must have been doing things correctly to achieve that kind of longevity. We did have some decisions and unique challenges to face as owners in this new century.

One of the key decisions we made that impacted our ownership was not to hire a middle manager. Each generation prior to us had seen turmoil caused by a middle manager leaving the company and trying to start their own enterprise with our customers. We wanted to avoid this so we did not hire a layer of management between us and our customers or our team. This made running the two plants extremely time intensive as we were the go-to people for everything large and small. It also meant both employees and customers knew we were accessible. To this day, if a customer clicks on "contact us" at the Foley Fish website, it comes to Peter and me.

We also faced increased requirements for documenting our processing steps with regard to food safety. We were a Hazard Analysis and Critical Control Point (HACCP) certified plant, which was required by law. In order to maintain some customers, we had to commit to expensive, lengthy, food safety audits that were really designed for much larger companies. In the end, our participation in these audits made us a stronger company. We are a Safe Quality Food (SQF), level 2 certified company. Today, customers and vendors must sign in; we have hair nets, beard nets, glove protectors, mandatory training programs, and lots and lots of record keeping.

New challenges also included higher costs owing to workman's compensation insurance rates skyrocketing thanks to laws in Massachusetts, rising costs for health care insurance, rising fuel costs and exorbitant fuel surcharges that has made shipping our fish more expensive and thus less competitive in the market place. Pressure on margins during economic downturns coupled with higher costs created some very lean years.

Work force was a giant challenge for us as we faced the retirement of employees with major roles in sales and production. Fortunately, we had very experienced people willing to step up into roles of buying and production management in both plants. My grandfather didn't like bringing anyone from other fish companies because he feared their "bad habits" would come with them. The dedication to promotion from within remains today. On the sales side, we were able to replace retiring account managers with culinary experts, aquaculture buffs, and general, all-around fish heads who added their passion for great seafood to our team. Since our sales team leaders are account managers, not merely order takers, we need passionate folks who can speak about our fish with enthusiasm. Our teams are more diverse than ever, and we welcome that as it enhances our company. We have retired folks who worked for Foley Fish for 30, 40 even 50 years! It is always a privilege to say thank you to them for their service.

We have redoubled our efforts in fishery management, and I served three years on the New England Fishery Management Council, representing the state of Massachusetts. It provided a front row seat on rule-making in the fishery and definitely made me empathetic to the plight of the fishermen and the incredibly stringent regulations they face from the U.S. government.

Supply got trickier for our generation. The United States implemented a new fishery management system called "Catch Shares," which caused a tremendous upheaval in the fishing world. Allocations of quota put some lifelong fishermen out of business and created huge consolidations in the industry. We have had to work harder than ever to source the best quality fish as more and more quota gets gobbled up by foreign interests that freeze fish at sea and export the fish rather than bringing it to market. Fortunately, there are still some very good boats fishing and fishing stocks in New England are growing overall making delicious Northeast species such as haddock, redfish, and grey sole affordable and steadily available.

On the sales and marketing side, we faced a new 24/7 news cycle that filled air time by running scare tactics about the food chain. The news seemed to be on full attack whether it was the state of fish supply, the health of farmed fish, and the role of mercury in seafood — the media was quick with the soundbite and short on the facts. We added new sections at the Foley School of Fish to address concerns and allay fears. We conducted consumer seminars to educate our customers' customers.

Sustainability and traceability became big buzzwords during our tenure. Customers wanted to determine fish purchases by "fish lists" or "certifications" from well-funded environmental groups. We battled the perception that non-certified fish were non-sustainable. It merely meant the fishery didn't have hundreds of thousands of dollars to go through certification. Neither customers nor the public realized the fisheries had to "pay to play" (in some instances over $100,000) in order to be recognized as a certified fishery. We did become an MSC/ASC certified vendor to appease customers who required it, but cautioned them that these certifications say nothing about the quality of the fish in terms of days out of water or whether chemicals were added once the fish was processed. It was still important to partner with an all-natural processor to ensure quality end product. To address the smaller, New England fisheries that couldn't afford to go through a formal certification process but were still fully traceable, we created a Sea Trace program that would trace the New England fish and shellfish we sourced back to the boat, area and method of harvest.

We wrote this chapter prior to COVID 19 and as we look back on the "challenges" we faced in the prior 20 years, they seem small compared to the catastrophic implications of COVID 19.

Who Moved My Cheese? My mother had our entire team read this book during her tenure to instill in them the idea that a multigenerational company had to adjust and adapt with changing times. We understood that to mean the introduction of computers and monthly reports and performance reviews. Twenty years later, when confronted with COVID 19, a global pandemic, we realized we better find some new cheese because we had just lost 85% of our business overnight. We had to temporarily shut down our Boston plant and furlough our employees. It was and is an incredibly scary time as we navigate huge financial losses coupled with the fear of infection for our team.

Thankfully, we had participated in writing this book and knew that generations before us had to restart. We ruefully joked that the fourth generation had missed out on the starting-over phase. In a twist of fate, we had spent the summer prior listening to "How I Built This" podcasts about how companies like Lara Bar, Clif Bar and ChickaBoom Popcorn had been established because their creators were filling a need. The week that the world shut down, we received texts from friends requesting seafood for their families because all their kids were suddenly home from college and their jobs in cities, and they needed to feed them something healthy without a visit to the grocery store. Further, the radio stations kept broadcasting, and the Facebook feeds were filled with comments about all the "unhealthy" shelf-stable food that was being purchased for quarantine. We saw the need for a healthy protein that could be delivered to homes in frozen form so it would sustain them for an extended time period.

The Foley Protein Pack was born. We created Variety Packs of four different seafood items, individually wrapped and frozen in our -80° plate freezer. We talked to our daughters about it and they urged us to add a salmon pack, which we did. We went on to add swordfish, smoked salmon, cod, scallop, and lobster packs based on suggestions from friends, family and eventually customers. We asked in a COVID 19 local Facebook page whether people would welcome our product. We received a resounding yes. Fortunately, we had just launched a new website where we sold Foley apparel and our web designers helped us add a Seafood page. We launched the products on our page, announced in the COVID group and to our local friends and overnight received 100 orders.

We had instructed our production managers to keep our staffing at a minimum to reduce costs as much as possible while we serviced the small amount of business we still had. We couldn't add headaches by requesting manpower to wrap individual portions of fish in four-pound units. Peter and I put on our boots, hair nets, gloves and masks and packed the protein packs ourselves with the help of our production managers. We saw a friend who also ran a manufacturing plant who talked about "disrespecting your titles." We adopted the mantra and asked sales people from our closed Boston plant to come help us pack fish. Together, as a team, we launched the Foley Protein Pack program.

Distribution was initially only to local R.I. homes. Peter and I drove Foley vans and our daughters accompanied us and we dropped fish to homes throughout our community. People left us notes, snacks, even home-baked bread. We received emails, texts, and social media posts heralding our fish and thanking us for bringing it to their homes. We couldn't believe frozen fish would be so warmly received. We realized, however, that most frozen fish had chemical additives or was "leftover" fish. We were taking fresh fish right off the line, packing it, freezing it and in some instances delivering it with 24 hours. We had a differentiable product and people noticed.

We added online shipping and while Foley Fish wholesale can get fish to Singapore, Bermuda, Canada, Grand Cayman and throughout the USA, we stumbled with shipping small units as the USPS and UPS were totally overwhelmed with pandemic shipping. Even the mighty Amazon had issues. Fortunately, for the most part, consumers were forgiving when shipments were delayed and we did everything we could to replace, refund, and reship.

The Foley Protein Packs didn't make us profitable, but we were extremely proud that it was a top gross margin contributor during the COVID months. Further, because we received credit card payments daily, unlike institution business which typically has 14-30 day terms, the Protein Packs helped with cash flow. We are slowly crawling out of the pandemic as more cities re-open, but we remain committed to delivering Foley Fish to homes throughout America. We are heartened to know that people appreciate our seafood.

In the end, is it worth it? People ask us about the hours we put in and the headaches of running two manufacturing plants in Massachusetts, about being married and working together. I'd offer that the highs are extra high and the lows are hard to escape when you work with your spouse in a business formerly run by your parents. I'd also offer that running a business with an incredible legacy, an amazing, dedicated team and some very, very special customers is a pretty unique opportunity that we are lucky to have. We are doing our best to honor the legacy of the generations before us.

EPILOGUE

Writing this memoir required me to explore and ponder an archive of photographs, news articles, and family stories in an effort to create the useful fiction of walking around as a contemporary of my grandfather, Michael Foley (MF), and my father Francis Foley (FF), gaining the first-hand observations that I have drawn upon in writing the history of the family enterprise known as the Foley Fish Company, founded in Boston in 1906.

I never fully grasped my paternal grandfather. MF was of the school of whatever you say, say little. In writing this book I realized that I had underestimated MF's hidden shrewdness and calculated brinksmanship in retaining Bill Maloney until he was confident of FF's commitment and ability to eventually run Foley Fish. Only then did he relegate Bill Moloney to a secondary role below FF. I often compared FF to MF at the same age, and myself to them as well. The more I did, the more awed I was by MF's accomplishments against formidable odds He founded a company. He set the company's compass for quality. But all the while his manner was understated; he never boasted about his achievements. I regret not having more chats in later life with MF. I would have told him that I wish I had been more like him — kinder, more patient, more poised, and more gentlemanly. It's too late for that now, but I am trying to compensate by writing about his foundational accomplishments in this book.

FF was an enigma to many. He was a master of counter-intuitive thinking, thinking that was self-evident only to himself. His conclusions were often as jarring as they were startlingly prudent and farsighted. He was impossible to emulate because he was wired differently from anyone I've ever met. Fortunately, on my second return to Foley Fish, FF gave me room to be myself. He let me expand and modify his carefully scripted game plans, which proved to me that he esteemed my thinking. I almost excluded one chapter — "Mismatched Expectations" (Ch. 53), but I decided to retain it. I did so largely because his greatest impact on me was not in the fish business, but as a deeply devoted and loving husband during the time when my mother was hurting the most. He was my rock in life.

Writing about the various employees at Foley Fish, especially the more colorful ones, allowed me to realize that, while Foley Fish was a hard place to work, it was also at times a fun place. What characters! A few stand out: Ebullient Great (Bob) Abbott, a.k.a. the Mohammed Ali of the fish business; lock-jawed, inscrutable Frank Souza and his awful cigars; foul-mouthed Frankie Lynch, also known as the creator of the fictitious Mr. Mahoney (conjured up by Lynch as the scapegoat for a group of visiting nuns outraged by his obscenity-laden speech); the assertive and irreverent Russ Rohrbacher, the high school dropout who straightened out the Harvard grad who ran Foley Fish; and the Irish contingent headed by John Hurley, who in response to the accusation that he had a drinking problem, assured us that he absolutely did not have a drinking problem, saying, "I drink every day"; the then-rookie Bobby Boyd, frustrated by FF's dictatorial ways, telling FF that he would shove his broom up FF's arse once he won the lottery (yet at the end of his forty-year career, said, "I owe everything to FF. I would never work for anyone else"); and Frank Milley, answering MF's query about the age of any customer who had just died, by saying "He was your age"; and a co-worker during my college summer stint leaving me asleep on the stairs of Foley Fish with an empty pint bottle of scotch and a sign saying, "do not disturb." Writing about these individuals, and the other members of the Foley team over multiple generations, was an honor. They were team players, honest and passionate about the Foley Way. Their commitment underscored Foley Fish's success.

When beginning my book, I promised myself not to write a sanitized version of Foley Fish — rather just tell it like it was. Over the eleven-plus decades in business, there were many crises: WWI, The Depression, WWII, Bill Maloney's coup, Steve Connolly's hasty, unforeseen departure, and now, the unfolding pandemic of 2020. We always rallied, as we will in 2020. Some of the past notable rallying cries should not be forgotten. For example, FF's announcement, "We will win back the Foley accounts stolen by Bill Maloney within one year." And Russ Rohrbacher's speech at the launch of our New Bedford operation, "We have a winning formula that puts quality ahead of price. I will teach you the Foley Way—it works." Certainly my wife Linda's speech when introducing the new Foley software system to a doubting audience: "Good enough was never good enough before and it will never be going forward." These clarion calls exemplify the extraordinary resolve of the Foley teams, and best explain the longevity of Foley Fish over four generations.

MF said correctly that good fish and good people go together. The friendship we gained from the life-long partnership with our customers has made serving them an honor. Some customers in the 1950s asked FF if they could put the Foley Fish name on their menus as their fish purveyor. He declined, adding, "Your restaurant is the star, not us, your supplier. If you win, we win." Foley customers honored us with their business for over many years. Their loyalty is compliment enough.

I am blessed to have had Linda Johnson Foley, to whom I have dedicated this book, as my wife and co-owner. She bevelled my many rough edges, and cautioned me not to charge up the hill without a pail of water. When I get too uppity, Linda's Midwestern solidity and honesty has sustained me, kept me from flying, like Icarus, too fast, too high. "Take off your diapers," she has ordered me, "put on your big boy britches, and act like a grown-up."

Similarly, Linda and I are blessed to have Laura and Peter Ramsden running the fourth generation of Foley Fish. Laura and Peter have expanded products, services, marketing, and breadth of service internationally, while staying committed to our home base and locally caught fish. Marketing efforts based on education have continued to be successfully implemented. The Ramsdens have made Linda and me, and MF and FF, very proud.

Swimming Upstream was not only an apt title for the Foley Fish memoir, but also for my life. In my early years I struggled at Walnut Park, LaSalle Military, Brown and Nichols, and Harvard. So, it is especially pleasing that the ten-plus years of writing this memoir has given me a sense of fullness late in my life. I wouldn't change a thing.

ACKNOWLEDGEMENTS

Writing this book was a new and daunting experience. Fortunately, I had much assistance. I hope that with the help of those cited I have written an unburnished memoir that is faithful and comprehensive. The thumbprints are many but any errors remain mine.

It is my good fortune to have had the following people who were generous with their time and expertise: Uncle Andrew Foley, FF's youngest brother, is the intellectual in the Foley family. Possessing a scholarly bent, he shared not only family history but many of his writings on Irish history, especially the Celtic clan mentality. This was helpful to my understanding of MF's and FF's patriarchal management styles. Andy was a mentor, a cheerleader who encouraged and guided me these past ten years of writing. The Foley story is more complete due to his continuous support.

My son Michael Foley, a successful television writer, guided me throughout. Always patient in the face of my stilted and often clumsy writing, he proved to me that he is the kindest man I know. His admonitions, gently rendered: "Crisp it up"; his probing questions — "What is your POV? (point of view)"; and his timely advice to make my memoir as readable as I could. In a poignant role reversal, my son became my tutor. With his help and persistence, I found my voice. A heartfelt thanks to Jenny, Ella, and Dylan who generously gave up family time so that Michael could work with me.

There is no end to my gratitude to Laura Ramsden, my daughter, and her husband and co-owner Peter Ramsden, without whom there could be no fourth generation. Also, I owe much appreciation to Laura who patiently typed and retyped early drafts of the book. Laura also wrote the last three chapters of the book while, somehow, still steering, with husband Peter, the Foley Fish Company through difficult times, including the 2020 pandemic. Special mention and thanks to granddaughters Haley, a senior at Dartmouth, and Liza, an honors freshman at the University of Michigan, for bravely deciphering my scribblings and typing first drafts for me.

J. Michael Lennon, Emeritus Professor English, Wilkes University, a dear friend over these past fifty years since our Officer Candidate School teaching days in Newport, Rhode Island, a skilled editor and the acclaimed writer of the definitive biography, *Norman Mailer: A Double Life*, was my valued editor. His Midas touch made everything he touched so much better than I could ever do on my own. He exhaustively and meticulously fact-checked every sentence on every page, often rewriting my words (but in a much more impactful way), while deleting confusing repetitions. Ever the teacher, he stopped me from using the ever-present "conditional would," something even the nuns couldn't do. And thanks to his wife, Donna, who worked tirelessly typing multiple drafts and entering my inscrutable edits to get a clean copy for publication.

A special thanks to my son, Mark Foley, who spent many nights probing me about my family history and encouraged me to share my book ideas as we walked Rufus together in Wings Neck, Cape Cod, and who spent endless hours preparing photos for this book.

A special thanks to Linda Johnson Foley, my dedicatee. While always willing to answer questions or offer opinions when sought, Linda probably saved our marriage by insisting on me writing this book by myself (fifty-three years of marriage and counting). I greatly appreciate her prodigious editing efforts at the end, and for filling in gaps in my recollections.

Shout-outs to my sister Patricia DiSilvio, whose husband the late Allessandro DiSilvio was part of the Foley Fish team for many years and whose frequent visits to FF brightened FF's final years.

To others for their valued inputs: Genevieve Martin (V.V.) for the ancestral information on the Martin side of my family; Tom Colbert, the company historian and loving caretaker for MF in his last years; Bobby Boyd, a source of wonderful anecdotes that needed to be preserved; Bill Barry, my cousin, who took time to write me a letter about his time growing up at 56 Windsor Road during WW II when his father was overseas; Great Uncle John Foley of Tipperary, the historian of the Foley clan; Fran Rabuck and Maria Demelo, office managers at Foley Fish

Company, who provided important financial information; the Boston Public Library archives that allowed me to excavate historical data relative to the New England Fisheries and on Boston during the early 19th century; Bill Gerencer, Foley's in-house guru on fisheries management issues; and Mickey DeFanti, managing partner of Hinckley, Allen of Providence and Boston, a special friend who provided insightful analysis of FF, saying, "He was a person of low ego who was confounding at times to you, his associates, his customers and competitors because his counterintuitive thinking was so subtle, so simple as to be overlooked and underestimated by others with much larger egos"; friend Barry Treadwell, formerly of the Milton Can Company, who reminded me that in the 1960s other fish purveyors switched to cheaper, lighter plastic fish containers, while Foley's stayed with more costly tins because they were better at conducting cold; Chuck Reed, Professor at the Brandeis Graduate School of Business, who explained the entrepreneurial drive needed in each generation for a company like Foley Fish to survive four generations.

I wish I could recognize all the wonderful people who worked for LF and me during our tenure. Our New Bedford floor workers started even greener than I, but grew into their jobs and set new Foley Fish performance standards. Our unsung office staff, who dealt with payables, receivables, medical insurance, OSHA, HAACP, human resources and more, was and is outstanding. My thanks to Dotty Fernandes, who kept me organized, typed my letters into the computer (I was a Neanderthal), compiled seminar books, and so much more. You took care of me and always with a smile. Thanks to Lucy Meneses whose intelligence, tenacity, and willingness to take on additional responsibility helped Linda keep her sanity. And, thanks to Maria DeMelo, whose cheerful flexibility as she works in whatever plant needs her, is invaluable. To Joanne Silva and Edna Olivera who quietly and cheerfully go about their business. And to Ken Carlson, retired Navy Commander, who made up for my lack of technical expertise and kept the plant equipment humming.

Finally, thank you to AuthorHouse who brought this book into the world. To my book, *Swimming Upstream*, that gave me the gift of not having to say "I wish I had."

Printed in the United States
By Bookmasters